Public
Information
Campaigns &
Opinion
Research

# Public Information Campaigns & Opinion Research

## A Handbook for the Student & Practitioner

Edited by
Hans-Dieter Klingemann
Andrea Römmele

SAGE Publications
London • Thousand Oaks • New Delhi

First published 2002

SAGE Publications Ltd
6 Bonhill Street
London EC2A 4PU

SAGE Publications Inc.
2455 Teller Road
Thousand Oaks, California 91320

SAGE Publications India Pvt Ltd
32, M-Block Market
Greater Kailash - 1
New Delhi 110 048

**British Library Cataloguing in Publication data**

A catalogue record for this book is available from the British Library

ISBN 0 7619 6431 2

**Library of Congress Control Number 2001 132947**

Typeset by SIVA Math Setters, Chennai, India
Printed in Great Britain by Athenaeum Press, Gateshead

# Contents

# List of Contributors

BARBARA BAERNS
Free University Berlin, Institut für
Publizistik- und Kommunikationswissenschaft,
Malteserstraße 74-100, 12249 Berlin, Germany

MICHELE CORRADO
MORI, Social Research Institute,
32 Old Queen Street,
London SW1H 9HP, UK

THOMAS DÖBLER
University of Hohenheim, Institut für
Sozialwissenschaften, 70593 Stuttgart, Germany

RONALD HOLZHACKER
University of Twente,
Department of Political Science,
PO Box 217, Enschede,
The Netherlands, 7500 AE

HANS-DIETER KLINGEMANN
Berlin Science Centre,
Reichpietschufer 50, 10875 Berlin, Germany

LEON OSTERGAARD
Director General, Madvigs Alli
15,1, 1829 Frederiksberg C,
Denmark

ROLF PFLEIDERER
Infratest Burke Kommunikationsforschung,
Landsberger Straße 338, 80687 Munich, Germany

CHRISTINE PÜTZ
MZES at the University of Mannheim,
68131 Mannheim, Germany

JULIANA RAUPP
Free University Berlin, Institut für
Publizistik- und Kommunikationswissenschaft,
Malteserstraße 74-100, 12249 Berlin, Germany

SIMON RAYNER
National Farmers Union, 22 Long Acre,
London WC2E 9LY, UK

KARLHEINZ REIF
European Commission,
EAC (VM18 - 4/11),
B-1049 Brüssel,
Belgium

MALCOLM RIGG
Director of Research,
Central Office of Information, Hercules Road,
London SE1 7DU, UK

ANDREA RÖMMELE
MZES at the University of Mannheim,
68131 Mannheim, Germany

MICHAEL SCHENK
University of Hohenheim,
Institut für Sozialwissenschaften, 70593 Stuttgart, Germany

KLAUS SCHÖNBACH
Amsterdam School of Communications Research,
Oude Hoogstraat 24, 1012 CE
Amsterdam, Netherlands

KATRIN VOLTMER
University of Leeds, Institute of Communications
Studies, Roger Stevens Building,
Leeds LS2 9JT, UK

# List of Figures

# List of Tables

# Foreword

As for any other institution of public governance, the European Commission needs to disseminate information about its policies among the public at large as well as among specific audiences. It has its own Office for Publications. And of course it pays much attention to the mass media. With some one thousand journalists accredited at the European Commission, the Brussels press corps is the second largest in the world, only the press corps in Washington DC is bigger. In addition, the Commission has established several networks of 'information relays' in all member states of the European Union: 'Euro info-points' which are to be found in public libraries, 'European Documentation Centres' in numerous universities, 'European (business) Information Centres' (for small and medium size companies), mostly stationed within Chambers of Commerce, 'carrefours ruraux' (rural meeting points) and 'urban forums'. A lawyer specializing in European law is available for citizens' advice in the Commission's Representation in each of the member states. A network of specialist speakers exists for matters of the Single European Market. Last but not least, more and more information from the Commission and other institutions of the European Union is available on the web through the 'Europa server' (http://europe.eu.int).

In addition to these means of informing citizens – and often enough involving them – the Commission quite frequently launches specific campaigns (or 'information actions' as they are called nowadays, in an attempt to eschew the term 'campaign', for fear of its being associated with 'propaganda').

The subject matter of these campaigns varies considerably. Recent examples range from 'the Euro' to 'the European Year for Safety, Hygiene and Health Protection at Work'. Their strategy and their approach also vary.

Some are organized by the Commission Directorate General for Information and Communication (or, since the dissolution of this in 1999, by the Press and Communication service), some directly by the information unit of the Directorate General concerned. The Commission carries out some in co-operation with the European Parliament, others on its own. Some are organized in co-operation with the member state governments and public administration, others not. For some campaigns, specialized public relations companies are in charge of planning, implementation and evaluation; for others this is not the case or to a lesser degree. Finally, for some such campaigns, the responsible officials enlist the support of the Commission's own survey research (Eurobarometer) unit in the planning and/or implementation and/or evaluation phase.

Some time ago, the Eurobarometer unit considered it useful to compile (1) a set of examples of how the Eurobarometer survey instruments had been used for planning or implementing or evaluating campaigns that the Commission had launched in the past, as well as (2) a collection of practice-oriented contributions by specialists from universities and private survey research or public relations companies that would help officials in charge of launching a campaign or 'information action' to take an informed decision as to whether to include survey research in their operation or not.

The Survey Research Unit invited ZEUS, the University of Mannheim based 'Zentrum für Europäische Umfrageanalysen und Studien' to host the project, produce the compilation of past Eurobarometer usage for Commission campaigns and ask a well-known expert, Professor Klingemann of the Berlin Science Centre, to organize the contributions from specialists. Professor Klingemann accepted and won the support of Dr Andrea Römmele to carry the project through with him.

When the result was presented to the Commission, Professor Klingemann asked whether the collection of articles – after some further editing – could not be made available to students and practitioners in the field of information and communication campaigning, in the form of a book. The Commission saw no reason why not. The book now being ready, I am all the more convinced that this was a good option.

Karlheinz Reif
Eurobarometer
European Commission

# Campaigns and Surveys: An Introduction

*Hans-Dieter Klingemann and Andrea Römmele*

In recent years campaigns have attracted not only academic attention but also the interest of the public in general. Several reasons might be responsible for this development: simply the growing number of campaigns conducted, the professionalization with which campaigns are carried out, and the high quality of campaigns can be mentioned. But also the process of societal modernization brings a growing need for campaigns since citizens have a greater desire to be informed about the actions of government and to participate in various aspects. This was not always the case.

In the 1940s and 1950s, confidence in the effectiveness of campaigns was rather limited, partly due to the first systematic empirical study of media effects in political campaigns. In their work Lazarsfeld et al. (1944) came to the conclusion that the importance ascribed to the media by propaganda theories is greatly exaggerated. They developed the concept of opinion leaders and the two-step flow of communication. The key point in this model is that information from the mass media to the population is mediated through personal opinion leaders who interpret the received information in terms of their own social and cultural contexts. Thus, mass media have much less influence and opinion leaders much more influence than originally assumed by propaganda theorists. Since the mass media are an important vehicle for communication and information campaigns, it is not surprising to rediscover this paradigm in the literature on campaigns in those days. This view is probably best reflected in the title of an article: 'Some reasons why information campaigns fail' (Hyman and Sheatsley, 1947).

In the 1960s and 1970s, however, this view slowly faded. 'Some reasons why information campaigns succeed' (Mendelson, 1973) was the title of a widely recognized article. Various developments were responsible for this shift in opinion. First, some campaigns had proven very successful, such as the campaign for energy conservation in many countries around the world, arising from the oil crisis in the early 1970s. Also very successful campaigns were launched against cancer, with the American Cancer Society being one of the most active supporters. Starting in the 1980s, worldwide campaigns were launched to make people aware of the AIDs virus and of the precautions to be taken. A second factor changed the pessimistic view of campaign effects: the previously accepted laws of how media work – with selectivity and minimal effects – were seriously shaken by the legendary Kennedy–Nixon debates in the 1960 presidential campaign. Kennedy, who at the beginning of the campaign was still largely unknown, attributed his unexpected and extremely close victory to his television appearances: 'It was TV more than anything else that turned the tide' (White, 1961: 294). Thus the rise of television has led to a fundamental overhaul of the hypothesis of the media's minimal influence (Lang and Lang, 1953; Blumer and McQuail, 1968). Noelle-Neumann's studies in the 1970s also demonstrate how television in particular influences the public. Noelle-Neumann refers to television as an 'elephant in disguise' and discusses this new development in a widely read article 'Return to the concept of powerful media' (Noelle-Neumann, 1973).

While the growth of electronic media, especially TV, was remarkable in the 1960s and 1970s, the recent growth in new information and communication technologies (ICTs) can be seen as revolutionary. Nowadays, campaigners have an arsenal of different communication opportunities at hand, which allow for 'broad-casting', i.e. addressing a wide audience, as well as 'narrow-casting', i.e. targeting specific messages to specific audiences. This strategic and targeted communication is part of the ongoing professionalization of campaigning, giving a greater role to technical experts in public relations, news management, advertising and market research.

This increase in information resources has been accompanied by an increase in citizens' education. Educational opportunities expanded rapidly after World War II in all western democracies. As a result, citizens have higher cognitive competence, such as increased ability to process complex information and greater understanding of their own scope for action (Dalton, 1988). Consequently, citizens increasingly use and extend their action repertoire to express their political priorities. In order to pursue their own goals people are willing to engage in collective action, often acting as an opposition outside the established institutions of public decision making. Thus, citizens' support and compliance can no longer be taken for granted. It is therefore hardly surprising that executive, legislative, and administrative elites have increased their efforts to communicate political goals and political decisions to the public. Many aspects (i.e. environmental problems, integration of minorities) cannot be solved by elite decisions only, but require popular support. An open flow of information gives public decision making transparency and legitimacy. The increased need for information and communication as well as the actual increase in campaigns can be regarded as a general characteristic of political modernization. Nowadays, communication between leaders and led is a vital precondition for coping with the complexity of modern society and adapting to new circumstances. These two consequences of the modernization process have been of particular importance for our undertaking and can serve as a point of departure for this handbook.

The literature distinguishes between two different campaign types: the information campaign and the communication campaign. The first is unidirectional (sender to receiver), while the second is interactive (sender–receiver–sender). Information campaigns are organized by political clients to convince citizens of the legitimacy of the 'rules of the game' or the effectiveness of their policy decisions. Communication campaigns initiate a dialogue, emphasize interaction, and open up a longer-term perspective.

In general, modern information and communication campaigns are built upon a dual strategy. On the one hand, they are characterized by media orientation. Content and timing are adjusted to the logic of the media system in order to achieve the highest possible media resonance. On the other hand, campaigns show a clear audience orientation. They aim at attracting attention, at gaining trust from relevant subgroups and at mobilizing specific target groups. Under the conditions of a highly differentiated media system, organizations have to work harder to gain attention. On the other hand, due to the flood of information, organizations have greater difficulties in making themselves heard. Issues compete against each other for the limited attention of the audience and the mass media. Intelligent campaign planning is necessary in order to gain sufficient attention from the media as well as from the public in light of the ever-growing flood of information.

We believe that the success (or failure) of a campaign largely depends on planning, implementing and evaluating the campaign with all the scientific tools available. The modern social sciences have developed methods and research techniques to help political elites find more-effective means of political communication and of determining citizen preferences. In doing so, survey research plays a crucial and important role. It is our aim to demonstrate why and how survey data can provide necessary information for planning, implementing and screening campaigns. How can survey research be useful during the different steps of a campaign? How can survey research contribute to optimization of these campaigns? These are the two principal questions that the handbook addresses. We ask what role survey research plays

- in the campaign planning phase, that is, in developing and structuring a campaign;
- in the campaign implementation phase, that is, in deciding what to do when and how; and
- in the campaign assessment phase, that is, in determining whether the goals of the campaign have been reached.

The book tries to address several audiences: first, it aims to give students of communication and of political science a general understanding of and introduction to the field of communication campaigns. It also aims to help those who teach and do research in this area to gain new insights into how campaigns can be conducted. At the same time, it also addresses the campaign practitioner. This is reflected in the general approach of the book: it is our goal and the goal of our contributors to relate the existing theory in the field of campaign communication to the practical and, by doing so, to overcome some of the barriers concerning 'theory' often experienced by students and practitioners.

Following the structure of a campaign, the book is divided into four parts. First we present different theoretical approaches relevant for conducting campaigns. In the second and third parts we focus on the implementation of campaigns, national (part II) as well as international campaigns (Part III). The final part concentrates on campaign evaluation. Katrin Voltmer and Andrea Römmele open up part I by discussing and presenting the most relevant communication theories and demonstrating how they can be applied to campaigns. After introducing the different elements of communication models (sender, receiver, message, channel), the authors introduce the two models most often related to in communication theory: the transmission model and the interaction model. Although they make very clear that the preference given to one model over the other depends on the particular problem to which the model is applied, public communication campaigns mostly fit the transmission model. In a second step, Voltmer and Römmele focus on the construction of the message being transmitted in campaigns. It is not only the selection of the issue that plays a crucial role but also putting it into the right 'context'. By relating their discussion to important work in the field of social cognition and psychology, Voltmer and Römmele provide useful criteria for planning and implementing a campaign. Barbara Baerns and Juliana Raupp present a four-step decision-making model incorporating the different steps of public relations campaigning. By reconstructing and re-evaluating 173 public relations campaigns nominated between 1970 and 1995 for the *Goldene Brücke* (a prize awarded by the German Public Relations Association), the authors are able to determine whether practitioners launching these campaigns really adhere to the outlined decision-model. The authors also investigate to what extent and how models of effect have been used as a basis, either explicitly or implicitly. The goal is to determine whether over the 25-year-period evidence exists to support the assumption of improved quality made in the scholarly literature.

The third and final contribution in this part deals with communication channels. Michael Schenk and Thomas Döbler focus on the role of direct interpersonal contact in a campaign, an aspect often neglected in contemporary campaign designs and studies. Whereas the mass media can reach a wider audience, the effect of the mass media is often overestimated. Research has shown that interpersonal communication through personal opinion leaders often proves more effective than media messages. The authors take up the opinion-leader model developed by Lazarsfeld et al. This is a robust theory that has influenced the communication field for over 50 years. Recognizing that individuals receive information from each other within a communication environment as well as from mass media, the model structures the process by which messages move through mass media and interpersonal channels from source to receiver. The challenge for the communication planner is to take advantage of this structure. This involves the fundamental step of identifying and enlisting the support of opinion leaders. Hence, the model's usefulness hinges on the ability to identify the opinion leader. The piece by Michael Schenk and Thomas Döbler makes an extremely valuable contribution in this regard by showing a new way of identifying opinion leaders. While the classic opinion-leader concept referred to influence exerted in homogeneous small groups, the concept of personality strength developed by Schenk and Döbler allows a change of the theoretical view from the small group to social networks containing diverse and heterogeneous social relationships. The personality strength concept seems broader and especially suitable for many campaign studies in identifying influential individuals via survey research who exert multiplying and supporting influences in the social environment.

The second and third part of the handbook concentrate on the planning and implementation phases of a campaign. Both theoretical *and* organizational aspects must be taken into consideration at this stage. In the second part, the role of survey research in the planning and implementation phase of a *national* campaign is analysed. Campaign practitioners present practical insights and experiences using illustrative examples. Our first example presents a campaign funded by the UK Government Home Office designed to raise awareness of the risks of fire at home and the value of installing smoke alarms. Malcolm Rigg shows the use of various qualitative and quantitative methods in the planning and implementation phase of the campaign. Simon Rayner presents valuable insights from the perspective of a campaign manager at the National Farmers Union. The first case study Rayner presents aims at raising the profile of the positive aspects of British agriculture and strengthening public trust in farming; the second campaign is aimed at preventing rural crime. He clearly shows how survey research is used at various stages of a campaign, the daily difficulties he has to deal with as a campaign manager, and helpful insights into how to handle and overcome them. Both of these contributions show that qualitative research is most powerful in the development stage of a campaign, when its primary role is aiding understanding of the audience and in forming the development of the communications strategy. In addition, it can play a crucial role in checking communications in draft or final form in order to test whether the approach is succeeding in conveying the messages which the communicator intends to convey. In a final contribution in this part, Ronald Holzhacker focuses on a very specific kind of campaign, namely an election campaign. The use of survey research is demonstrated in the Minnesota race for governor in 1998. Interviews with all campaign managers and campaign strategists give informative and unique insights into how campaign strategists use survey research to measure public opinion at different stages of a campaign and how it is put to strategic use.

After these practical insights and the use of survey research in *national* campaigns, we focus on *international* campaigns in the third part of the handbook. Three contributions tackle this problem from different angles. The contribution by Hans-Dieter Klingemann and Andrea Römmele focuses on the European multi-level system and on the question of how European citizens gain information about European politics. Since citizens display serious information deficits regarding the EU, opinion leaders play a central role in this regard and are a crucial factor in campaigns conducted by the

European Commission. These European opinion leaders – personalities as well as institutions – are identified via survey research. The empirical analysis brings to light those sources which are trusted the most when it comes to finding reliable information about European issues. The contribution by Christine Pütz also sticks to campaigns run by the European Commission and brings in yet another interesting aspect, namely the use of the Eurobarometer survey, a particular survey instrument of the European Commission. Pütz discusses the specific characteristics of international campaigns run by the European Union by presenting two aspects: first, she shows how the Eurobarometer survey is used in the different phases of campaigns. Through a series of qualitative interviews with campaign managers of the European Commission she also presents information on the practitioners' attitude towards survey research. Michele Corrado leads us through the process of planning, implementing and evaluating *international* campaigns run by international organizations, namely Greenpeace International and WWF International (World Wide Fund for Nature). Corrado gives the reader an invaluable insight into the role a survey institute (in this case MORI) plays in this enterprise. In contrast to national campaigns, international campaigns face the difficult and challenging task of having to convey a consistent message across countries while taking into account each country's specific characteristics and cultural nuances. For this reason, both international organizations asked MORI, a leading survey institute, for positioning research informing Greenpeace and the WWF about how they are perceived and how an issue is perceived (in this case the environment). The results were used to help WWF and Greenpeace tailor their environmental advertising messages to different countries and cultures. Corrado clearly demonstrates the key role survey research plays in this process which provides international organizations with a better understanding of its potential supporters around the globe and how they may be reached through campaigning.

The final section of the book focuses on the evaluation phase of a campaign. The overall outcome of a campaign is often summarized as 'positive' or 'negative'. However, in order to really learn something from the last campaign, which can be applied to the next one, the question of evaluation has to be better refined. Have the people been reached who should have been reached? Was the timing right? Have the initial goals been reached? How can a campaign be assessed and how can survey research be useful in that regard? Three contributions tackle this problem, again with different emphases and approaches.

Leon Ostergaard argues for an overall campaign assessment, an evaluation of the campaign at its different levels. This is only possible, Ostergaard points out, if the campaign is a result of a bottom-up strategy. A top-down strategy normally misses a clear campaign concept which is a necessary condition for proper campaign evaluation. Ostergaard presents a detailed bottom-up campaign strategy where campaign assessment is not only possible, but probable. He systematically discusses the importance of assessment at the various levels of a campaign. After careful evaluation on all campaign levels, overall conclusions can be drawn. He also reminds practitioners that it is never possible to measure the *success* of a campaign: one can only draw conclusions when a campaign has failed, but only through these failures can one learn and improve future campaigns. Klaus Schönbach makes the practitioner aware of the problem of causality. Besides having a clear notion of the campaign's long-term and short-term objectives, practitioners have to be aware of the causality problem and, closely related to it, the amount of impact a campaign has had. Can the desired effects really be attributed to the campaign or would they have occcurred anyway? Schönbach demonstrates how this causality-puzzle can be solved with survey research. He lays out the different steps to be taken. He also points to other techniques useful in measuring the success of a campaign (controlled experiments, offical statistics, etc.). Finally, Rolf Pfleiderer shows how market research techniques can be used to evaluate information and communication campaigns. Since almost all campaigns are transmitted via some medium, it is important to measure the effect of advertising. Pfleiderer introduces marketing research techniques that in fact were not developed for information and communication campaigns but rather for commercial advertising for consumer goods and services. However, Pfleiderer convincingly demonstrates how these techniques can be put to good use in order to test and measure advertising effects in information and communication campaigns. He also gives helpful suggestions on how to choose a marketing research institute.

As a conclusion, Hans-Dieter Klingemann and Andrea Römmele summarize the major findings of the handbook in a checklist which can serve the campaign practitioner as a guideline; it also serves the scholar and student as a summary focusing on the use of survey research in the different phases of an information and communication campaign.

## REFERENCES

Blumer, J. and McQuail, D. (1968) *Television in Politics: Its Use and Influence.* London: Faber.

Dalton, R.J. (1988) *Citizens' Politics in Western Democracies: Public Opinion and Political Parties in the United States, Great Britain, West Germany and France.* London: Chatham House.

Hyman, H. and Sheatsley, P. (1947) 'Some reasons why information campaigns fail', *Public Opinion Quarterly*, 11: 412–23.

Lang, K. and Lang, G.E. (1953) 'The unique perspective of television and its effect: a pilot study', *American Sociological Review*, 18: 3–12.

Lazarsfeld, P., Berelson, B. and Gaudet, H. (1944) *The People's Choice.* New York: Columbia University Press.

Mendelson, H. (1973) 'Some reasons why information campaigns can succeed', *Public Opinion Quarterly*, 37: 50–61.

Noelle-Neumann, E. (1973) 'Return to the concept of powerful media', *Studies of Broadcasting*, 9: 67–112.

White, T.H. (1961) *The Making of the President.* New York: Harper.

# Part I COMMUNICATING THE MESSAGE: THEORETICAL APPROACHES

---

# 1 Information and Communication Campaigns: Linking Theory to Practice

*Katrin Voltmer and Andrea Römmele*

## INTRODUCTION

The characterization of modern societies as 'information societies' has become commonplace when recent technological developments and the future of our social environment are discussed. In general, all societies are constituted by communication, as all social processes are performed by the exchange of information. But more than ever before, the control of information has now become the central determinant of political power and social structure (Bell, 1973; Salvaggio, 1989). Success and failure of individual and collective actors alike depend increasingly on their ability to accumulate and distribute information. Because of the growing complexity of modern societies, public communication cannot be left to the spontaneous intuition of do-it-yourself campaigners. Rather, it needs systematic planning in order to reach its goals. According to the rule that 'there is nothing more practical than a good theory' we believe that a theoretical understanding of the communication process can provide the practitioner with useful criteria for planning and designing campaigns.

In this chapter we present an overview of major concepts of communication theory and their application to public communication campaigns. The focus will be on the 'input' processes of communication, i.e. how messages are conveyed to the recipient and how the content of messages is constructed. 'Output' processes, i.e. how messages are perceived by the recipient and to what extent they can influence attitudes and behaviour, will be discussed in other chapters (see chapters 10 and 11). As a first step, we present the different elements of the communication process, focusing primarily on the message and the channel. Thereafter we introduce two different theories of how these elements can be linked with each other. The possible use of survey research will be touched upon in a final step.

## ELEMENTS OF COMMUNICATION

According to the notion of sharing, the communication process links four basic elements: the sender, the receiver, the message, and the channel. Sender and receiver refer to different roles the participants take in the communication process; message and channel refer to what is transmitted and how.

The *sender* is the source of a message and initiates and controls the flow of information. Since communication is a social act, the sender enters the communication process with a certain intention which may range from the cognitive sharing of information to persuasive attempts to change the attitudes or behaviour of the receiver. In the context of communication campaigns the sender is usually a collective actor, such as a party, a government, or an NGO. In this case, the intention of the campaign itself is the result of a complex communication process among the members of the organization. The more the definition of the goal is based on broad intra-organizational support, the more the public campaign can be expected to be successful in the end.

The *receiver* is the destination of the message, i.e. to whom the information is directed. Just as planning public communication involves a clear definition of the sender's intention, it also requires the specification of the receiver. Usually, the receivers at whom a campaign is aimed are collectives, such as 'the public'. However, the public is too heterogeneous an entity to be meaningfully addressed. Groups that share particular problems, interests or cultural experiences can be more explicitly addressed than diffuse aggregates. Due to the higher social cohesion of groups, messages can be expected to spread further by subsequent intra-group communication, thus enhancing the effectiveness of the campaign (Katz and Lazarsfeld, 1955; Rogers, 1962).

Often the receiver who is explicitly addressed is not the one the campaign is aiming at. In this case the intended and the actual receiver differ. The strategy is to use the actual addressee (for example parents, car drivers, or people who are potential victims of environmental conditions) as a resource of public mobilization to put pressure on decision-makers, most often the government, but also firms or organizations. In contrast to most communication models (Windahl et al., 1992: 12–16), it is necessary therefore in this case to distinguish between 'target population' and 'receiver group', indicating receivers who are intended to be influenced by a message and those who actually receive the message. However, 'detour communication' bears particular risks because the flow of information and re-interpretation of the message on the way to its eventual target are difficult to control.

The *message* refers to what is transmitted in the communication process. Communication theory distinguishes between two dimensions of the message, namely signals and meaning. Signals can be understood as the surface aspect of the message. They may consist of spoken words, images, music, or gestures. Meaning is certainly the least precise part of the message. It denotes the content aspect of messages and carries the purpose or intention of what is communicated. The ambiguity of language makes it difficult to control the meaning of messages, but it can also creatively be used to extend possible interpretation in order to reach wider audiences.

Besides the specification of the message by the sender, communication as shared meaning requires careful consideration of the predispositions of the receiver. As research on interpersonal and mass communication has found, the meaning intended by the sender does not necessarily equal the meaning eventually understood by the receiver. Instead, perception of messages is highly selective according to the receiver's cognitions and values (Festinger, 1957). By connecting new messages with pre-existing knowledge and judgements the receiver constructs his/her own meaning out of what the message contains. This process of assigning and reconstructing meaning is called encoding and decoding (Fiske, 1982). Whether the actual message represents the intended meaning and whether it is understood by the receivers in the intended way are the crucial problems the campaigner has to deal with. It depends on whether the message was put in the right envelope and whether it is formulated in the right language.

## CONSTRUCTING THE MESSAGE

Every message is the result of two basic decisions on the part of the sender. First, from the universe of possible objects a particular topic has to be chosen to be the focus of attention and exchange in the actual process of communication. Second, by drawing on particular values the topic has to be linked to a preferred interpretation. Bennett (1981: 93–100) refers to these basic features of message construction as 'selection' and 'symbolic transformation'. Selection limits the range of aspects of the reality to be considered, while symbolic transformation excludes alternative perspectives of evaluation. Neither interpersonal communication nor public campaigns would be possible without the selective reduction of complexity; and without the evaluative definition of relevance, communication would be as meaningful as reading the telephone directory.

### Selection of Issues

The goal of every campaign is to gain publicity. Public debate draws the attention of individuals to particular problems. It also puts heavy pressure on political decision-makers to consider particular issues. However, the public agenda is a highly contested arena. Publicity likely comes close to a zero-sum game: access of a particular issue implies the exclusion of another one. Thus, each message competes with other messages for public attention. In addition, ordinary people are primarily engaged in coping with the problems of everyday life, leaving little attention for public affairs. The ability to promote issues by determining what is on the public agenda and what is excluded, and to attract the attention of the relevant population, has become an important power resource (Cobb and Elder, 1981; Kingdon, 1984). Some scholars of political science even speak of a paradigm shift, which Mansbach and Vasquez (1981) put into the concise formula: 'From the issue of power to the power of issues'. The control of the range of issues considered by the public and the effects of issue salience on public opinion are termed 'agenda-setting', which has become one of the most influential theories of mass communication research. The basic assumption is that the mass media may not be able to influence what people think, but they have an impact on what people are thinking about (McCombs and Shaw, 1972). Empirical findings corroborate that the importance people attribute to certain problems is influenced by the extent to which the media address these problems (Protess and McCombs, 1991; Dearing and Rogers, 1996).

At first glance these findings may appear to be trivial when a public campaign aims at changing attitudes or even behaviour. Why is agenda-setting such an important aspect of public communication? Research in social cognition has shown that the selection of topics limits the basis for judgement on the part of the receiver. In order to make up their minds, people do not use all the information they have stored in their memory. They do not even use the most relevant considerations. Instead, they use that information which is on the 'top of their head' (Fiske and Taylor, 1991). And usually those issues that dominate the public agenda are the most accessible information. Thus, as Iyengar (1990) points out, the accessibility bias resulting from agenda-setting processes has implications not only for the perception of salience, but also for the evaluation of issues. On the basis of several experimental studies Iyengar and Kinder (1987) proved the relationship between agenda-setting and opinion building in election campaigns. If people perceive, for example, unemployment to be the most important problem facing the country, they evaluate political parties or candidates mainly from the perspective of whether or not they will be able to solve this particular problem. Evaluation – and eventual vote decision – would take a different direction if, for example, foreign affairs dominated the public agenda.

### Attribution of Values

Having discussed the implications of issue selection, we will now turn to the second dimension of the construction of messages. According to Bennett (1981: 95) 'symbolic transformation' comprises 'categorization operations, persuasion techniques, and cueing practices'. In other words, the second step of planning communication is to decide on the evaluative or normative significance of an issue. The objective of a campaign can be simply declared: Vote for XY! Stop smoking! Donate for the poor! However, it is not the pure argument that convinces individuals. Rather, the response to a message is considerably directed by the evaluative context in which it is set. The reason is that most problems are multifaceted and yield different conclusions depending on the perspective from which they are viewed. The process of controlling the value preferences on which the audience will base its judgement is called 'framing'. Various studies have demonstrated the effect of alternative frames.

As the social psychologists Kahneman and Tversky (1983) show, people make biased decisions depending on how the anticipated outcomes are described. In an experiment two groups of subjects were confronted with an identical problem, namely a hypothetical government health programme to combat the outbreak of an unusual disease. The expected outcome was alternatively framed either in terms of expected mortality or in terms of survival. The results indicate that people favour the solution that is depicted as gain and reject the alternative that puts risks to the forefront (see chapter 4 in this volume). Nelson et al. (1997) examined the effect of different ideological frames. They manipulated news stories about a demonstration of the Ku Klux Klan and asked people whether or not this demonstration should be prohibited. People who watched the version which framed the conflict as a free speech issue were significantly more permissive than those who were exposed to the alternative story which emphasized aspects of public order.

Besides these examples which demonstrate the implications of content-related framing, Iyengar (1991) studied the effect of different forms of presentation. News stories were manipulated according to whether public issues were presented in either an episodic or a thematic frame. Episodic coverage focuses on concrete cases or events, e.g. the situation of a homeless person, an unemployed worker or a victim of racial discrimination. Thematic coverage provides primarily background analyses, which places the problem in a more general perspective, e.g. changes of the economy, budget cuts in social welfare or government programmes in affirmative action. These news frames were tested as to their effects on how people attribute responsibility. Attribution of responsibility was differentiated into causal and treatment responsibility, referring to perceptions of who has caused a certain problem and who is responsible for solving it. The results of this study show that the presentation formats determine the viewers' attribution of responsibility. Episodic frames, which dominate media coverage, lead people to interpret problems as caused by individual failure, whereas thematic frames direct the attribution of responsibility to government action.

### Issue Types

Issues can be characterized more precisely by looking at their structural and content-related characteristics. Butler and Stokes (1974) draw the distinction between valence issues and position issues. Valence issues address common values where there is a broad societal consent, such as peace or saving the environment. Hence, valence issues do not demonstrate alternative viewpoints but present issues with conditions or goals or symbols of which almost everyone approves. Position issues, on the contrary, 'are defined in terms of alternative forms of government action' (1974: 277). Position issues show two contrary positions on one dimension, e.g. pro or anti abortion, pro or anti military intervention, etc. Although campaigners know which issue they have on their agenda and know the goal they want to achieve, these distinctions made in electoral campaigns and electoral research might give some insight into how an issue can be presented to the audience it is aimed at. We see here that elements of comparison and juxtaposing can be a tool to construct the message.

Salience is yet another central structural element of issues. Through selection and visual or acoustic emphasis the media produce a hierarchy of relevance among the issues on the public agenda. Drawing on the concept of 'accessibility bias' in the process of information processing, Iyengar and Kinder (1987) have demonstrated that issues with high salience dominating the actual agenda were more easily activated by recipients. The same line of argument can be used for position issues: issues dominating the public agenda are activated more often and are enriched with additional supporting arguments.

An issue can also be classified according to its direction. From electoral research we learn to distinguish between retrospective and prospective issues. In his seminal work, Fiorina (1981) sketches out a theory of retrospective voting. Citizens take past performance as a prima facie indicator of the government's judgement and competence. Good performance in the past reinforces the presumption that the administration is competent to govern. By contrast, prospective voting presumes a policy orientation in the electorate and therefore demands more of the citizen than does retrospective voting.

Closely related to the concept of issues is that of images. Some of the early definitions of image stem from Boulding's (1956) description of image as subjective knowledge – what an individual believes to be true. In Boulding's view, images are controlling mechanisms that govern behaviours. Popkin (1991), focusing on political campaigns, argues that campaigns do in fact present issues but are mainly about choosing a leader who can best deal with these issues. Assuming that Popkin is correct, candidate images may have critical importance for voting analyses in that they reflect how voters make their selection decisions with regard to which candidate can provide the best means of dealing with what they perceive are the most important issues. These findings suggest that issues are partly presented through images. It is important to note, however, that image is more than a visual picture we might have of a candidate or a well-known person hired for a public campaign. As Barths points out, in mass communication 'the linguistic message is indeed present in every image: as title, caption and accompanying press article'.

## CHANNELS OF COMMUNICATION: A CLOSER LOOK

The *channel*, the fourth element of the communication process, is the medium by which the message is conveyed to the receiver. The physical means of transmitting the signals from the sender to the receiver, for example the paper on which the message is written, telephone, or in case of direct contact the air which transmits the acoustic waves, are usually regarded as the channel. Early communication theories understood the channels of communication mainly as neutral devices. However, this view has been challenged by numerous scholars, most prominently by McLuhan, who expressed his position in the famous statement 'The medium is the message' (McLuhan, 1964). He argues that new communication technologies not only change the amount of communication that takes place in a society, but also affect its content. The reason is that the form of presentation determines the kind of meaning that can be conveyed as well as the degree of ambiguity. The difference between visual images and written text points to the specific potential of communication channels. The Internet, which has rapidly spread since the early 1990s, is a recent example of how new technologies are changing both the process and the content of public communication.

In the following we will first take a closer look at the mass media as channels of public communication and how they alter the dynamics of public communication. In a second step we will focus on the use of new information and communication possibilities such as direct mailing, telemarketing, and the Internet.

## Mass Media

In public communication it is the mass media that most often serve as channels conveying the message from the sender to the receiver since only through the mass media can a broad audience be reached. The mass media enable citizens to gain more knowledge on matters beyond their own experience by making information accessible which an individual could otherwise not obtain. However, the notion of a neutral device cannot be applied to the media. On the contrary, press and broadcasting have to be considered as actors in their own right who enter the communication process as a third participant in addition to sender and receiver. The mass media function according to their own set of rules, whose aims may or may not match those of the campaigners. The literature distinguishes between free and paid media. Paid media are advertisements freely designed by the sender (newspaper advertisements, TV commercials). The sender has complete control over the message being sent. The free media, on the other hand, describe news reports without direct control by the sender. Therefore, the significance of active news management through the sender is essential for influencing the framing of mass media reporting.

Undeniably, the media are the central actors in public communication. However, the absolute gatekeeping power of the media as presumed by Westley and MacLean (1957) is certainly arguable. In fact, this view has contributed to the myth of political success or failure, especially in election campaigns, being ultimately determined by the media.

The first systematic empirical study of media effects on the vote, however, significantly relativized the influence of the mass media. Lazarsfeld et al. (1944) came to the conclusion that the importance especially ascribed to the media by propaganda theories is greatly exaggerated. In their pathbreaking work, Lazarsfeld et al., showed the interplay between mass media and personal communication and developed the concept of opinion leaders. The central argument in this model is that the flow of information from the mass media to the general population is mediated through personal opinion leaders. These opinion leaders interpret the information they receive via the mass media in terms of their own social and cultural context (see chapter 3 in this volume). Empirical research has demonstrated the importance of opinion leaders.

### Targeted Information

However, there are many ways for communicators to circumvent the media and address the public, or certain groups, directly. Technological development recently made new forms of communication possible. With computerized mailings and phonebank-based telemarketing, subgroups of society can be directly contacted. All three channels not only enable the sender to control the content of the information and target it to identified subgroups of society but also give the receiver a possibility to reply. Whereas telemarketing and direct mailing were also extensively used in the 1980s, it was not before the late 1990s that the Internet moved from margin to mainstream in Europe, reaching more people than many traditional media outlets. By the late 1990s, about a fifth of all Europeans and half of all Americans and Scandinavians were online. Getting news is one of the most popular uses of the Internet. These new forms of communication have several advantages for both sender and receiver. As mentioned before, the sender has complete control and can tailor the content of the message to the target audience. For the receiver, it also bears significant advantages: citizens appear to prefer information which presents facts in an interpretive context and thus assists with orientation. In short, citizens seek an 'information shortcut'. However, in the mass media, information and orientation will always be in conflict, not least since they are essentially providers of information and more effective in doing so than other actors in the political system. Direct communication is free from such conflict. The sender (government, NGOs, etc.) can provide structured information, that is, present their preferred view of reality to citizens.

## PUTTING THE ELEMENTS TOGETHER: TWO MODELS OF THE COMMUNICATION PROCESS

After discussing the elements of communication we ask how sender and receiver, message and channel are related to each other. As mentioned above, theoretical models identify not only the relevant elements of a phenomenon, but also the relationship between them. Models are theoretical tools to conceptualize the complex process of communication by identifying its elements and how these elements are related to each other (McQuail and Windahl, 1981). The purpose of conceptualizing the relational aspects of communication is to understand the dynamics of message transmission in different communication settings.

Communication theory provides us with basically two accounts of conceptualizing communication processes (Severin and Tankard, 1979; Windahl et al., 1992), namely the transmission model and the interaction model. Neither should be regarded as generally preferable. Rather, each of the models captures different contextual settings in which communication takes place.

The *transmission model* conceptualizes communication as a unilinear and directed process. This perception implies that the flow of information invariably runs from the sender to the receiver. There is no alternate role-taking between the two participants of the communication process, as the sender always takes the active part while the receiver remains passive. Further, the transmission model stresses the intended influence the sender seeks to exert over the receiver. The underlying assumption is that all communication is essentially persuasion. Thus, the flow of information is viewed as a cause-and-effect relationship between sender and message on the one hand, and receiver and his or her response on the other hand.

The basic structure of the transmission model has been extended by adding feedback processes from the receiver back to the sender, indicating that the audience's response may alter the communicator's subsequent behaviour. While direct communication enables the participants to observe spontaneous reactions, such as facial expression or verbal comments, feedback becomes a crucial problem in the context of indirect communication where sending and receiving the message is disconnected in time and space. Hence, planning public communication includes planning possibilities for feedback. In fact, the capability of the communicator to respond to audience reactions is an important precondition for effective communication. In this book surveys are discussed as a valuable source of feedback from which campaigners can learn about the preferences of the public and possible effects of the campaign.

The transmission model has been widely criticized for its restricted and instrumental view of communication. The alternative conceptualization of the communication process, which has been developed recently with reference to critical theory (Habermas, 1984, 1987) is the *interaction model*. It takes the etymological root of the word communication more seriously by focusing on the notion of 'sharing of meaning', rather than 'transmission of messages'. The emphasis of the interaction model is on mutuality, as it makes no clear distinction between sender and receiver. Instead, both parts equally contribute their views to a shared universe of knowledge and interpretations. According to the interactive approach, most communication takes place in order to maintain social relationships, while persuasion and the attempt to change the communication partner's attitudes or behaviour are regarded as a special form of communication.

In our view, preference for one of the two approaches is not just an academic question, but depends on the particular problem the model is to be applied to. For the most part, public communication campaigns can be described more adequately by means of the transmission than the interaction model because planned communication is by nature intentional and bears only limited possibilities of exchange. However, the interaction model should not simply be rejected as a guide for designing campaigns. In particular, when decisions of far-reaching consequences are to be met, e.g. about environmentally problematic issues, the active participation of the affected community can contribute to a solution that is based on a broader consensus than an imposed decision 'from above' (Burkart and Probst, 1991).

## SURVEY RESEARCH

After reviewing the elements of the communication process and major concepts we now would like to shed some light on how survey research can be helpful in the different steps of a campaign. Let us follow the path the communication process normally takes.

*Sender.* How well is the sender known among the target audience? What standing does the sender have? Is the sender regarded as trustworthy and highly respected or are people sceptical or critical? Answers to these questions are highly relevant for the construction of the message and, consequently, for the success of the campaign. A survey among the target audience testing attitudes towards, knowledge about, and general performance of the sender can provide answers to these questions.

*Receiver.* Survey research can also give invaluable insight about the receiver to whom the message is targeted. Ideally, the sender should have to hand as much information about the target audience as possible. This knowledge enables precise tailoring of the message, in terms of content and framing.

*Message.* With the knowledge about the target audience, and the reception of the sender by the target audience at hand, the message can be constructed. According to the knowledge gained via survey research the campaigners need to decide whether the message should have more of a prospective character or whether retrospective elements would work better. Should the message be constructed by juxtaposing two positions? One way of testing the message is via focus groups.

*Channel.* Survey research can also be helpful when it comes to deciding which channel to use. If a wide audience is to be addressed, the mass media are probably the best channel. But the campaigners need to know which channel is watched the most, which newspaper is read the most by their target audience, and so on, in order to reach a maximum of people. Survey research may also be very helpful in identifying opinion leaders who spread the message in their social networks.

## REFERENCES

Bell, Daniel (1973) *The Coming of Post-industrial Society*. New York: Basic Books.
Bennett, W. Lance (1981) 'Perception and cognition. An information-processing framework for politics', in Samuel L. Long (ed.), *The Handbook of Political Behavior*, Vol. I. New York, London: Plenum. pp. 69–193.

Boulding, K.E. (1956) *The Image: Knowledge in Life and Society*. Ann Arbor: University of Michigan Press.

Burkart, Roland and Probst, Sabine (1991) 'Verständigungsorientierte Öffentlichkeitsarbeit: eine kommunikationstheoretisch begründete Perspektive', *Publizistik*, 36: 56–76.

Butler, David and Stokes, Donald (1974) *Political Change in Britain. The Evolution of Electoral Choice*, 2nd edn. London: Macmillan.

Cobb, Roger W. and Elder, Charles D. (1981) 'Communication and public policy', in Dan D. Nimmo and Keith R. Sanders (eds), *Handbook of Political Communication*. Beverly Hills, CA: Sage. pp. 391–416.

Dearing, James W. and Rogers, Everett M. (1996) *Agenda-Setting*. London: Sage.

Festinger, Leon A. (1957) *A Theory of Cognitive Dissonance*. New York: Row Peterson.

Fiorina, Morris P. (1981) *Retrospective Voting in American National Elections*. New Haven, CT: Yale University Press.

Fiske, John (1982) *Introduction to Communication Studies*. London, New York: Methuen.

Fiske, Susan T. and Taylor, Shelley (1991) *Social Cognition*, 2nd edn. New York: McGraw-Hill.

Habermas, Jürgen (1984, 1987) *The Theory of Communicative Action*, Vols 1 and 2. Boston: Beacon Press.

Iyengar, Shanto (1990) 'The accessibility bias in politics: television news and public opinion', *International Journal of Public Opinion Research*, 2: 1–15.

Iyengar, Shanto (1991) *Is Anyone Responsible? How Television Frames Political Issues*. Chicago, London: The University of Chicago Press.

Iyengar, Shanto and Kinder, Donald R. (1987) *News that Matters. Television and American Opinion*. Chicago, London: The University of Chicago Press.

Kahneman, Daniel and Tversky, Amos (1983) 'Choices, values, and frames', *American Psychologist*, 39: 341–50.

Katz, Elihu and Lazarsfeld, Paul W. (1955) *Personal Influence: The Part Played by People in the Flow of Mass Communications*. New York: The Free Press.

Kingdon, John W. (1984) *Agendas, Alternatives, and Public Policies*. Boston, Toronto: Little, Brown.

Lazarsfeld, Paul F., Berelson, Bernard and Gaudet, Hazel (1944) *The People's Choice. How the Voter Makes up His Mind in a Presidential Campaign*. New York: Columbia University Press.

Mansbach, Richard W. and Vasquez, John A. (1981) *In Search of Theory. A New Paradigm for Global Politics*. New York: Columbia University Press.

McCombs, Maxwell E. and Shaw, Donald L. (1972) 'The agenda-setting function of mass media', *Public Opinion Quarterly*, 36: 176–87.

McLuhan, Marshall (1964) *Understanding Media*. London: Routledge and Kegan Paul.

McQuail, Denis and Windahl, Sven (1981) *Communication Models for the Study of Mass Communications*. London, New York: Longman.

Nelson, Thomas E., Clawson, Rosalee A. and Oxley, Zoe M. (1997) 'Media framing of a civil liberties conflict and its effect on tolerance', *American Political Science Review*, 91: 567–98.

Popkin, Samuel L. (1991) *The Reasoning Voter: Communication in Presidential Campaigns*. Chicago, London: University of Chicago Press.

Protess, David L. and McCombs, Maxwell (eds) (1991) *Agenda Setting. Readings on Media, Public Opinion, and Policymaking*. Hillsdale, NJ: Erlbaum.

Rogers, Everett M. (1962) *The Diffusion of Innovations*. New York: Free Press.

Salvaggio, Jerry L. (ed.) (1989) *The Information Society. Economic, Social, and Structural Issues*. Hillsdale, NJ: Erlbaum.

Severin, Werner J. and Tankard, James W. (eds) (1979) *Communication Theories. Origins, Methods, Uses*. New York: Hastings House.

Westley, Bruce H. and MacLean, Malcolm S. (1957) 'A conceptual model for communications research', *Journalism Quarterly*, 34: 31–8.

Windahl, Sven and Signitzer, Benno (with Jean T. Olson) (1992) *Using Communication Theory. An Introduction to Planned Communication*. London: Sage.

# 2

# Modelling and Evaluating Public Relations Campaigns

*Barbara Baerns and Juliana Raupp*

## DECISION-MAKING IN PUBLIC RELATIONS: SEARCHING FOR SCIENTIFIC APPROACHES AND DEVELOPMENTS IN CONCEPTUALIZATION, STRATEGY, AND EVALUATION

Public relations is regarded as the management of communication processes between organizations and their publics (DPRG, 1996: 1; DPRG and GPRA, 1990: passim). Thus, public relations is a process, not a bundle of measures. This process is managed, i.e. planned, controlled, evaluated, and therefore strategically arranged. Consequently, public relations practitioners who explain their work to the public have long presented a relatively simple decision-making model ranging from situation analysis to the measuring of results, to help people plan, check, evaluate and thus manage. *If* public relations strategy models feature (1) investigation of the starting position or *situation analysis*, (2) *conceptualization* (such as setting goals and objectives, recognition and selection of publics, development of the central idea(s), selection of media, calculation of time and costs), (3) *implementation*, and (4) *evaluation* of results as major stages in communications planning, then the methods and results of empirical communications research in particular should be examined and reviewed in order to determine systematically whether they are useful decision-making aids when seeking links between *particular* goals, *particular* instruments, and *particular* effects.

The study in question reconstructs and re-evaluates 173 of a total of 209 German public relations campaigns nominated between 1970 and 1995 for the *Goldene Brücke* (Golden Bridge), a prize awarded since 1970 by the German Public Relations-Gesellschaft e.V., DPRG Berufsverband Öffentlichkeitsarbeit (German Public Relations Association) for outstanding work in the field of public relations.[1] These campaigns will be examined to determine whether public relations practitioners really do adhere to the decision-making model outlined. The findings will, moreover, enable us to ask, first, to what extent and in what manner scientific methods have been applied: in particular, it must be proved whether survey research ranks very high in these contexts. Second, we asked to what extent and in what manner models of effect have been used as a basis, either explicitly or implicitly. The object is to determine whether over the 25-year period there is evidence to support the assumption, made in the scholarly literature, of improved quality, increased efficiency and effectiveness, proven achievement, and greater transparency.

Anglo-American research seems to support such assumptions. In 1990 the American communications researcher James H. Bissland studied the winners of the Silver Anvil Award, a prize conferred annually by the Public Relations Society of America (PRSA), from the viewpoint of the methods of evaluation applied. He compared the 60 winners from 1980/81 with the 72 from 1988/89 and found a clear increase in the methods of evaluation applied. Even more obvious was the change in the language of the entries: whereas in 1980 only one winner mentioned the word 'evaluation', it appeared in 60 cases in 1988/89. 'If nothing else, Silver Anvil winners (and their judges) changed their vocabulary' (Bissland, 1990: 31).

The Australian communications researcher Gael F. Walker focused on the use of research methods in the conceptualization and evaluation phases, analysing 177 entries for the Golden Target Award of the Public Relations Institute of Australia (PRIA) for 1991 and 1992 in terms of content. Next, she interviewed twenty award winners to investigate their attitudes toward scientific methods in public relations. Walker maintains that sophisticated campaigns especially depend on scientific methods and adopts Grunig's typology in arguing that 'this dependence on research increases as public relations is conceptualized along a scale of complexity and perhaps legitimacy from press agentry, journalistic persuasive campaigns, and two-way asymmetrical public influence strategies to the two-way symmetrical communication advocated by Grunig et al. (1984)' (Walker, 1994: 141). Walker inductively developed 15 possible methods for situation analysis and seven possible evaluative methods.[2] For situation analysis, surveys seemed to be the method employed most often, to which she added that the material did not make it entirely clear whether formal scientific or informal methods had been used. In the interviews, in any case, the award winners unanimously emphasized the need for scientific research methods. Practical constraints, however, often made this impossible: 'The ideal situation cited was that public relations could be measured, but all stressed the difficulties of funding and time to allow for such *nonessentials*' (150).[3] Upon interpreting her results Walker reached the conclusion that many informal methods used in actual practice were not identified as such: 'Practitioners constantly talked about 'real research' as if their own informal processes were not regarded as research at all' (156). Referring to Brody and Stone (1989), she pleaded for the disclosure of any and all methods in order to enhance, through verification, the appreciation of public relations.

In contrast to Bissland (1990) and Walker (1994), we have considered not only situation analysis and final evaluation as a characteristic of quality, but also the overall decision-making process, a prerequisite for systematic public relations work. Our results can be categorized under the following headings: (1) practitioners' descriptions of conceptualization and strategy; (2) methods and results of the measurement of effects; and (3) discussion of developments.

TABLE 2.1  *Overview of cases submitted and analysed*

| Year | Submitted cases | Analysed cases | Winners (analysed winners) |
|------|-----------------|----------------|----------------------------|
| 1970 | 26 | 17 | 3 (2) |
| 1972 | 5 | 3 | 1 (0) |
| 1974 | 26 | 16 | 3 (3) |
| 1976 | 18 | 12 | 3 (3) |
| 1978 | 6 | 3 | 2 (2) |
| 1980 | 9 | 4 | 2 (1) |
| 1985 | 11 | 10 | 3 (3) |
| 1988 | 16 | 16 | 2 (1) |
| 1990 | 14 | 14 | 3 (3) |
| 1992 | 22 | 22 | 4 (4) |
| 1993 | 15 | 15 | 4 (5) |
| 1994 | 41 | 41 | 6 (6) |
| **Total** | **209** | **173** | **36 (33)** |

TABLE 2.2  *Distribution of applicants by year*

| Year | Agency | In-house public relations | Joint application |
|------|--------|---------------------------|-------------------|
| 1970 | 2 | 14 | 1 |
| 1972 |   | 3 |   |
| 1974 |   | 16 | 1 |
| 1976 | 3 | 9 |   |
| 1978 |   | 2 | 1 |
| 1980 | 2 | 2 |   |
| 1985 | 6 | 3 | 1 |
| 1988 | 11 | 4 | 1 |
| 1990 | 7 | 7 |   |
| 1992 | 12 | 10 |   |
| 1993 | 9 | 5 | 1 |
| 1994 | 29 | 12 |   |
| **Total** | **81** | **86** | **6** |

## PRACTITIONERS' DESCRIPTIONS OF CONCEPTUALIZATION AND STRATEGY

The 173 cases analysed represent 83 per cent of the assessed entries for the *Goldene Brücke* and are at the same time a non-representative cross-section of the professional practice of public relations in Germany (see Table 2.1). Within this framework 33 out of 37 award winners were included. Half of the re-evaluated applications (86 cases) came from the public relations departments of larger organizations, including companies and public institutions; 81 cases (47 per cent) originated in agencies (see Table 2.2). Six campaigns were jointly submitted by in-house public relations departments and agencies. Over the years agencies have substantially increased their participation in the *Goldene Brücke* competition, from only two applications in 1970 (12 per cent of the analysed cases for that year) to 29 applications in 1994 (71 per cent of the analysed cases for that year). The kind of public relations work studied covers a broad spectrum, from the large-scale international campaign for the UN summit in Rio de Janeiro to specific single

TABLE 2.3 *Explicit description of strategic steps*

|  | Yes | No | Don't know |
|---|---|---|---|
| Situation analysis | 119 | 46 | 8 |
| Conceptualization | 157 | 10 | 6 |
| Implementation | 115 | 51 | 7 |
| Evaluation | 93 | 75 | 5 |
| Four steps of decision-making | 50 | 116 | 7 |

TABLE 2.4 *Explicit description of strategic steps by applicants*

|  | Agency | In-house public relations | Joint application | Total |
|---|---|---|---|---|
| Situation analysis | 56 | 60 | 3 | 119 |
| Conceptualization | 74 | 78 | 5 | 157 |
| Implementation | 48 | 62 | 5 | 115 |
| Evaluation | 49 | 42 | 2 | 93 |
| Four steps of decision-making | 27 | 22 | 1 | 50 |

measures such as the preparation of a press conference. However, press and media work is relatively rare, at 10 per cent. Almost two-thirds of the applications (98 cases or 61 per cent) concern relatively long-term campaigns, while the remainder represent single measures. Ninety-nine projects (57 per cent) dealt with external relations, 17 (10 per cent) with internal relations, and 55 (32 per cent) consisted of total communications projects.

Following the wording of the authors' reports, 119 applications contain a 'situation analysis', 157 present a 'plan' or 'concept', focusing on any aspect of conceptualization, 115 mention an 'implementation', a 'translation into action' or a 'realization', and 93 claim that an 'evaluation' or 'assessment' took place. A review of the reports shows that in only 50 cases (29 per cent) are all four strategic steps dealt with and treated systematically (see Table 2.3). In this respect there are no significant differences between public relations agencies and the public relations departments of organizations (see Table 2.4). In 66 cases (38 per cent) there is no clear division between conceptualization and implementation. It can be assumed that in most cases the planned campaign was actually carried out, but practitioners obviously did not view this phase as distinct from the planning. This corresponds to the fact that problems connected with the realization and execution of what was planned were almost never discussed, whereas positive experiences were discussed in evaluations.

According to the guidelines for action emerging from public relations principles underlying this analytical step, the planning phase, which is a complex activity going beyond that already discussed, consists of several components. Planning strategies demand at least a concrete objective, a requirement met by 72 per cent of the campaigns and measures studied. Close inspection of the *particular goals* articulated gives rise to the following list of objectives ranked by frequency (in which multiple recoding was possible):

TABLE 2.5  *Distribution of types of objectives by year, mentioned by*
*public relations practitioners (multiple recoding possible)*

|   | 1970 | 1972 | 1974 | 1976 | 1978 | 1980 | 1985 | 1988 | 1990 | 1992 | 1993 | 1994 | Total |
|---|------|------|------|------|------|------|------|------|------|------|------|------|-------|
| 1 | 6    | 3    | 11   | 9    | 2    | 4    | 4    | 7    | 10   | 12   | 8    | 25   | 101   |
| 2 | 10   | 2    | 11   | 7    | 1    | 1    | 8    | 10   | 4    | 14   | 7    | 24   | 99    |
| 3 | 8    | 1    | 3    | 1    | 1    | 0    | 4    | 1    | 7    | 15   | 7    | 11   | 59    |
| 4 | 2    | 1    | 2    | 1    | 1    | 0    | 1    | 2    | 4    | 11   | 4    | 5    | 34    |

1 = 'Information'
2 = Improving or creating an 'image'
3 = 'Persuasion'
4 = 'Dialogue'

- Objective: 'to inform' (e.g. provide information about organizations, their achievements and products) was named in 58 per cent (101 cases) of the applications analysed.
- Objective: to improve or build an 'image' (e.g. enhance the 'image' of industries, organizations, products, or achievements) was named in 57 per cent (99 cases).
- Objective: 'to persuade' (e.g. in favour of products or of political, social, or economic institutions and viewpoints) was mentioned in 34 per cent (59 cases).
- Objective: 'dialogue' (e.g. in view of controversial questions or extant conflicts, or as a preventive measure) was named in 20 per cent (34 cases) (see Table 2.5).

All of these formulations appear throughout the entire period under study, including the objective 'dialogue', even though in public relations literature and in scholarly literature in general it is expressly treated as a new development (Bentele et al., 1996: 11).

Planning strategies also reflect the publics that the campaign or measure is supposed to reach. This step is made explicit in nearly half of the cases; in a third of the cases the intended public is left implicit, while 32 applications (19 per cent) give no indication whatsoever in this respect. Eighty per cent of all applications (138 cases) that name publics explicitly or implicitly differentiate either according to age or occupation, or according to the relationship with the organization (for example customer, client, supplier). Diffuse entities such as 'the entire public' or 'all people' are designated as a target audience by 42 per cent of the applications (72 cases); 35 per cent (61 cases) list opinion leaders such as journalists separately.

Besides defining objectives and publics, planning strategies concern themselves thoroughly with the selection of media. More than half of all the entries (98 cases or 57 per cent) give evidence of clear and well-founded decisions to use certain media and instruments and elaborate them in detail. One hundred and thirty cases make use of traditional media such as brochures, posters, and own publications; 80 cases employ press releases or press conferences as a means of public relations work – a finding that does not tally with the relatively infrequent mention of journalists as a public.

TABLE 2.6  Choice of media by year (multiple recoding possible)

| | 1970 | 1972 | 1974 | 1976 | 1978 | 1980 | 1985 | 1988 | 1990 | 1992 | 1993 | 1994 | Total |
|---|---|---|---|---|---|---|---|---|---|---|---|---|---|
| 1 | 14 | 0 | 12 | 9 | 3 | 3 | 6 | 8 | 12 | 19 | 9 | 35 | **130** |
| 2 | 5 | 0 | 12 | 8 | 1 | 2 | 5 | 4 | 7 | 13 | 11 | 17 | **85** |
| 3 | 12 | 2 | 2 | 8 | 1 | 1 | 6 | 5 | 9 | 7 | 10 | 17 | **79** |
| 4 | 3 | 0 | 3 | 4 | 0 | 1 | 5 | 1 | 6 | 17 | 7 | 17 | **64** |
| 5 | 4 | 2 | 3 | 6 | 0 | 1 | 5 | 5 | 4 | 6 | 10 | 17 | **63** |

1 = Print media
2 = Audio-visual media
3 = Events
4 = Press releases and press conferences
5 = Other media

Audio-visual media such as audio cassettes, film, and video as well as electronic and the so-called new media are deployed in 64 cases. Events ranging from lectures, fairs, open houses, and exhibitions to competitions, car races, rafting, and cooking contests are named in nearly half the cases as a means of public relations work. The founding of associations and clubs also comes under the heading of public relations. As is to be expected, the use of audio-visual and electronic media has clearly risen in the last few years. Otherwise, there are no additional developments (see Table 2.6). It should be noted that half of the campaigns (89 entries or 51 per cent) were organized as multiple-stage processes, in which interpersonal communication, mostly as the first stage, played a special role in 58 cases. Upon questioning whether the choice of media harmonizes with the choice of a public, one finds a positive answer in just under two-thirds of the public relations projects studied.

Last but not least, the time schedule and budgeting can be considered basic aspects of planning strategies. Forty-one applicants (24 per cent) availed themselves of the former and 44 (25 per cent) of the latter. The mere mention of a budget was not taken into account here since it fulfilled neither the entry conditions of the *Goldene Brücke* nor the requirements of the literature from public relations practice in general. When the planning strategies are viewed retrospectively, it becomes evident that the great majority of the authors have named objectives, for example. However, the more precisely the conceptualization is broken down into particular components, the less often are the individual subordinate steps formulated. Judged on the basis of the public relations experts' own statements, only seven applications (four by public relations agencies, two by in-house public relations departments, and one joint application) meet *all* the requirements of systematic public relations work discussed so far (see Table 2.7). Thus there are no significant differences between the materials produced by public relations agencies and those produced by the public relations departments of organizations.

The findings so far can be more precisely categorized and considered in terms of their overall content. Among the best-known models of public relations work are the 'four models of public relations', which James E. Grunig

TABLE 2.7  *Explicit description of nine steps of decision-making*

|  | Yes | No | Don't know |
|---|---|---|---|
| Situation analysis | 119 | 46 | 8 |
| Conceptualization | 157 | 10 | 6 |
| – Objectives | 124 | 38 | 11 |
| – Publics | 82 | 88 | 3 |
| – Central Idea | 75 | 95 | 3 |
| – Selection of media | 98 | 72 | 3 |
| – Time schedule | 41 | 123 | 9 |
| – Budgeting | 44 | 123 | 6 |
| Implementation | 115 | 51 | 7 |
| Evaluation | 93 | 75 | 5 |
| Nine steps of decision-making | 7 | 162 | 4 |

and Todd Hunt formulated in connection with the development of public relations in the United States and first published in 1984 (Grunig et al., 1984: 22). According to this schema the following distinctions can be made:

1  *Press agentry* is one-way publicity for the purpose of persuasion.
2  *Public information* is one-way publicity for the purpose of spreading information truthfully.
3  *Asymmetrical communication* is two-way communication that is also designed to persuade, on the basis of scientific knowledge about the publics or target audiences.
4  *Symmetrical communication* is two-way communication that serves the purpose of mutual understanding.

Grunig's lesser-known *negotiations model*, derived from game theory, which has only recently replaced his concept of symmetrical communication, is also included here (Grunig et al., 1996: 219). Against this background it is apparent that the majority of the cases studied deals with one-way 'communication': 61 applications (35 per cent) followed the information model, and a slightly smaller number (54 applications or 31 per cent) followed the press-agentry model. Only 19 per cent (33 cases) were at all interested in feedback. Of those, 27 applications (16 per cent) can be categorized as asymmetrical communication, four (2 per cent) as symmetrical communication, and two (1 per cent) according to the negotiations model. As will be shown, these findings are congruent with the infrequent use of scientific methods, which are taken for granted, at least in Grunig's last three models (see Table 2.8).

## ANALYSIS OF METHODS AND RESULTS OF THE MEASUREMENT OF EFFECTS

Slightly over two-thirds of all the PR projects assumed, explicitly (18 per cent) or implicitly (51 per cent), that some kind of effect would be produced. But scientific methods were seldom used to evaluate these effects: as the analysis of the strategy has shown, only 37 applicants (21 per cent)

TABLE 2.8  *Application of scientific methods according to the models of Grunig/Hunt and Grunig/Grunig*

| Model | Scientific methods of situation analysis | Scientific methods of evaluation | Grunig's models applicable |
|---|---|---|---|
| Publicity | 7 | 8 | 54 |
| Public information | 15 | 17 | 61 |
| Two-way asymmetrical | 12 | 10 | 27 |
| Two-way symmetrical | 1 | 2 | 4 |
| Negotiations | 1 | 1 | 2 |
| Not applicable | 49 | 63 | 25 |

applied scientific methods; 92 applicants (53 per cent) relied on other methods, and in 44 cases (25 per cent) no evaluation took place or none was found in the material at hand. As a follow-up to a well-founded situation analysis, evaluation is an urgent necessity. Furthermore, knowledge from an evaluation can serve as the starting-point for the succeeding situation analysis, from which objectives are formulated. These objectives then require further evaluation. Ideally, systematic public relations work creates in this manner a dynamic, continually improvable process.

Survey research plays an important role in two respects. Practitioners can carry out or order their own survey according to the special interest of the particular phase of the campaign, thus gathering exactly the information they need for well-founded planning or evaluation. But already-available survey research findings can also provide useful information; practitioners can derive relevant insight from data stemming from other surveys, such as marketing surveys or opinion polls. On the other hand surveys, *if published*, will establish essential elements of a public relations campaign itself. Thus, a German pharmaceutical company contributed to socially useful knowledge by gathering representative qualitative data on youths' needs and sources of information about sexual behaviour. Later, a youth information service was created, including a kind of hot-line providing personal advice from experts, including medical doctors, on demand. Finally, between 1990 and 1994, 12,132 accumulated telephone calls and 2,000 letters were again analysed and classified by social scientists according to main topics and demands, in order to continue to improve the service (Case No. 178, Schuster, 1996: 152–63).

In our research we have taken into account the following means of conducting a scientific situation analysis and a scientific evaluation:

- Media coverage analysis, i.e. a content analysis of the desired media coverage on the basis of a previously formulated frame of reference.
- Special surveys commissioned for the public relations project in question.
- General public relations surveys which may be consulted for use in a special public relations project.
- Marketing surveys carried out for marketing purposes but still useful as a basis for public relations work.

- Available survey findings which, as data collections, are accessible for public relations work. (We even went so far as to accept collections of data of indeterminate origin as a scientific foundation.)
- Other scientific methods, such as experiments and interviews with experts.

By contrast, unsystematic discussions with colleagues and clients or superiors and employees, documentations of press clippings, radio and television recordings, and the unsystematic study of literature should be regarded as unscientific.

Twenty-five applications in which a scientific evaluation took place (14 per cent) commissioned surveys in order to measure their success. Seven applicants (4 per cent) conducted an analysis of the media response, and five applicants (3 per cent) made use of other scientific methods in their evaluation of public relations work.

The following unscientific methods of evaluation were much more widely employed:

- 'Media analysis' (ranging from the simple collection of articles to the counting of the clippings along with a statement of the estimated range and circulation) was named in 50 per cent of all applications.
- Searching for 'definite' results (such as sales figures, a higher hotel bed occupancy, or a greater use of services) was named in 45 per cent of applications.
- Praise and recognition (extending from 'positive feedback from top management', 'our agency got a follow-up contract', and 'a lot of calls confirmed that we had done good work' to 'enthusiastic onlookers lined the streets') was named in 41 per cent of applications.

Within the framework of the situation analysis a total of 43 applicants (25 per cent) applied scientific methods, with the use of data collections the most frequent (16 cases); 14 applicants undertook their own surveys; three drew on marketing surveys, and two on general surveys about public relations work.

Fifty-seven per cent of the applications (98 cases) applied unscientific methods, often merely describing the situation at the outset: 'Today is 15 October 1966. Starting on 15 August 1967, the opening day of the Berlin Radio and Television Exhibition, German television in the Federal Republic intends to broadcast colour programmes ... The broadcasters are the ZDF and ARD, public bodies. How can we secure a large part of their broadcasting monopoly for our studios and production firm?' (Case No. 4). The remainder, as already noted above, did without a situation analysis. The considerable discrepancies between the claims of practitioners' self-description and everyday action and the search for reasonable explanations has already led us to examine the whole context of decision-making in public relations work using qualitative methods and problem-oriented interviews (in particular Baerns, 1995: 9–29). On the one hand, the new findings confirm what has been brought to light so far. On the other, they point directly to the key question, which had not been discussed for a long time: how can *success* in public relations be defined?

It seems that this is a question few practitioners think about. What was articulated in depth interviews was contradictory: success was acceptance, positive resonance toward the company, toward the product, toward one's own work. Success meant large numbers of visitors, high viewing figures, meant 'getting into a working relationship'. Success was 'the success in initiating communication activities'. 'Success in public relations is defined by the possibility of controls' – which, however, supposedly do not exist. In one interview we found the following statement: 'to ensure our continued existence here we have always limited ourselves to seeing success as what you can read in the newspaper'. In another, the interviewee said: '[success] is the client's satisfaction. If he is satisfied, nothing more is necessary. If he is unsatisfied, even the best evaluation is useless'. This argument came up repeatedly in one form or another.

Serious public relations requires its own specific concept of success, not one derived from the satisfaction of the client, from a marketing mix, or from some other source. The following expectations of success, for example, can be contemplated based on knowledge of communications science. Reasonable strategic steps would be oriented on (previously formulated) expectations (or objectives). This approach would make meaningful evaluation of actual achievements possible:

- Expectations of success following the sequential logic of *agenda-setting* regarding awareness of … knowledge about …, attitude to …, behaviour: the Federal Centre for Health Education made use of this and sensibly took into account that the reports of the popular media are at best able to produce the cognitive effect of 'awareness of something', whereas all more highly-valued or further-reaching effects must be attempted by other means (*Goldene Brücke* award winner 1992: 'AIDS: A Challenge to Public Relations', Baerns, 1995: 97–113).
- Expectation of success following the *uses-and-gratifications approach* regarding usefulness for a public and the fulfilment of existing needs and expectations: on this basis we ourselves evaluated a public relations project that was adapted for various European countries and could have conveyed information, if this information had been desired. Here we showed the firm whether and to what extent the public expected, valued, used, and wished to have information from this source (Baerns and Luedke, 1996, passim).
- Expectation of success regarding a *communicative relationship*: the Energie-Versorgung Schwaben AG, an energy supply company, employed this approach. At first it was 'purely a technical matter' of establishing contacts, i.e. of bringing 'those outside' and 'those inside' together, in order to develop and structure goal-orientated interpersonal communication (Baerns, 1995: 85–95).

- Expectation of success regarding *mutual understanding*: the ideal of communications management, the process of creating understanding, aims at leading equal partners either to mutual agreement or to common identification of controversial points, i.e. rational disagreement, within a framework of shared knowledge, understanding, and trust. The government planners of a hazardous waste disposal site in Lower Austria employed this approach – and the project remained unfinished (Baerns, 1995: 71–84).
- Expectations of success regarding *credibility through openness and transparency*: when they go beyond their declarations of commitment, practitioners of public relations make their activities transparent and understandable in the truest sense of the word. This thought has long found expression in the ethical guidelines of the profession as expressed in the European Code of Professional Conduct in Public Relations, the 'Code of Lisbon', Clause 4: 'Public relations activities must be carried out openly; they must be readily identifiable, bear a clear indication of their origin, and must not tend to mislead third parties' (Baerns, 1991: 200–2).

  However, we are not concerned (only) with professional ethics here. The idea of revealing methods, whether a means of argumentation or a guarantee of quality, or even a principle and means of social control in modern societies, should hardly be new to *public* relations practitioners. It (still) meant little to the ones we interviewed.

By re-evaluating the cases submitted for the *Goldene Brücke* over a period of 25 years which can be reconstructed, we can determine which models have been relevant in actual practice up to now. First comes the *agenda-setting hypothesis*, which is assumed explicitly or implicitly in 28 per cent of the cases (48 applications). Establishing *communication via relations* is the intended effect of public relations work in 21 entries (12 per cent). The *uses-and-gratifications approach* is followed in five entries. *Credibility by transparency* is attempted four times, and *mutual understanding* twice. In contrast, a simple *stimulus–response* model, unacceptable from a scientific point of view, underlies 20 applications. In 25 cases mutually exclusive objectives and models serve as the principle, as can be deduced from this quotation from case No. 146: 'This initiative will establish and maintain contact with new publics. It is intended to offer people of all ages an opportunity to make an ecological and social commitment. It is expected that this initiative will lead to the creation of new jobs. The initiative is intended to generate a financial return', etc. In addition the client was supposed to become better known 'in public'. In principle, 13 further cases can be assigned to this group of applications which start out from more or less plausible but scientifically unsubstantiated everyday experiences.

Thirty-four per cent (27 cases) of those applications demonstrating a meaningful model of communications science applied scientific methods in their situation analysis. Of the 58 cases lacking such a model, 22 per cent

TABLE 2.9 *Application of scientific methods using models from communications science*

| Model | Scientific methods of situation analysis | Scientific methods of evaluation | Communication science models applicable |
|---|---|---|---|
| Agenda setting | 17 | 14 | 48 |
| Uses-and-gratifications approach | 3 | 3 | 5 |
| Establish communication relations | 4 | 6 | 21 |
| Mutual understanding | | | 2 |
| Credibility by transparency | 3 | 2 | 4 |
| Stimulus–response | 4 | 5 | 20 |
| Several mutually exclusive models | 6 | 5 | 25 |
| Other models | 3 | 2 | 13 |
| Not applicable | 56 | 65 | 35 |

(13 cases) used scientific methods in their situation analysis. Here we find a significant correlation: 31 per cent of those cases (25 applications) to which a reasonable model of effect derived from communications science can be ascribed make use of scientific methods of evaluation. By contrast, 20 per cent (12 applications) of the group of scientifically evaluated applications display no reasonable model of effect. Again we discover a significant correlation (see Table 2.9).

## DISCUSSION OF DEVELOPMENTS

One hundred and seventy-three case studies of public relations work, all applications for the *Goldene Brücke*, were subjected to re-evaluation with a view to qualitative progress. Given its comprehensiveness, this source material covering 25 years of professional practice provides an especially valuable fund of information. It should, however, be noted that the interpretation of the data analysed refers to a cross-section of public relations work which, at least in terms of its self-perception, should be regarded as especially professional. For this reason the findings cannot be considered representative of public relations practice in general.

Broader changes over the years can be noted: for example, a general rise in the number of applications, pointing to the growing popularity of the *Goldene Brücke* and thus to the increasingly widespread recognition of the professional association, the DPRG. The latter can be regarded as a step toward greater professionalization of public relations. As could be expected, the use of electronic media has also increased, showing that the industry has remained abreast of new technologies. Although a modernization of the instruments can be observed (also reflected in the ever more elaborate applications submitted), the question remains: has quality improved, irrespective of the variety of the instruments used?

As has become apparent, systematic ways of working are closely related to the application of scientific methods and criteria in public relations.

Survey research is the scientific method used most frequently. Concerning situation analysis, practitioners rely on available data from existing surveys nearly as often as they carry out their own research (41 to 43 cases). In evaluating campaigns, own research outweighs the use of existing data (37 to 25 cases). This indicates that evaluation in particular requires carrying out special public relations survey research. Application of scientific methods and criteria in public relations stand out as qualitative criteria, independent of the judgements of the *Goldene Brücke* jury. As a result, we have developed two indices of quality, which we applied to each year in order to obtain information about the qualitative progress over the entire period under study. The first index consisted of adding up all characteristics indicating the existence of the strategic steps (including the subordinate phases of the conceptualization): situation analysis, setting objectives, defining publics, developing a central idea, selecting media, calculating time and costs, describing the implementation of the project, and describing the evaluation. These variables were counted according to their presence in the application: explicit presence was assigned a value of 2, implicit a value of 1, and absence of the variable a value of 0. The sum of these values provided information about the characteristics of the variables relevant for us. The highest possible value was 18, meaning that all the aspects named are explicit. Seven of the cases submitted, or only 4 per cent, achieved this number. At the other end of the scale, one application received a score of 0, with none of the criteria even implicitly fulfilled. A correlation calculation showed that only a weak correlation exists between the quality of the applications, measured in terms of the strategic procedures, and the year in which the application was submitted.[4] A further index in relation to the year of application was set up with reference to the application of scientific methods and the orientation on a model. No statistically significant correlation was found here.[5]

A study is valid to the extent that the object of research is that which is in fact measured. If measuring the same facts with different instruments leads to similar results, then the validity of the method has been confirmed. For the purposes of our study the juries' evaluations served as a standard (so-called concurrent criterion) for the validity: it can be assumed that a relatively large number of award winners achieved a high number of points on the quality index. This assumption is confirmed by the fact that 64 per cent of the award winners scored in the range 13 to 18 on our quality index, whereas those receiving between 0 and 6 points made up only 4 per cent of winners.[6]

Thus we may conclude that, over the past 25 years, German public relations has maintained a certain level of quality – but not much more than that.

## NOTES

1  The *Goldene Brücke* is a prize awarded by the DPRG, the German Public Relations Association, in the field of public relations. 'Its purpose is to provide recognition of solutions to a task and a problem that can be regarded as outstanding and exemplary with regard to the conceptualization, preparation, and

execution and in view of the means available and the costs involved. It may concern measures for a single task, actions for a certain purpose or for a certain period of time, or long- or short-term problems' (DPRG, 1970). This first announcement was made in 1970 and has been followed by 12 others. Initially restricted to the members of the professional association, the competition was opened to all interested parties in 1978. From 1970 until 1980, the *Goldene Brücke* was awarded every two years; from 1981 until 1994, it was awarded at irregular intervals (in 1990, 1992, 1993, and 1994). In 1994 the text, until then only slightly altered, was thoroughly updated: 'The purpose of the competition is to recognize and make known excellent PR actions and programmes of companies, organizations, institutions and public bodies as well as their consultants and agencies and to promote outstanding public relations ... They are required to submit a summary ... which features the following five points: initial situation, research, planning, implementation and evaluation' (DPRG, 1994). An independent jury, appointed by the DPRG and made up of experts from various professional areas, judges the applications on the basis of a point system.

2  The methods of situation analysis are: (1) survey, (2) interviews/discussions, (3) analysis of target public attitudes, (4) existing data, records or knowledge, (5) analysis of other or previous campaigns, (6) use of statistics, experts, or specialist information, (7) media analysis, (8) focus groups, (9) pilot programme or consultative process, (10) commissioned or market research, (11) meetings or visits, (12) monitoring or tracking, (13) use of literature or research study, (14) media choice or mailing list analysis, (15) client briefing. The methods of evaluation are: (1) response (membership/sales/attendance/inquiries, etc.), (2) media coverage, (3) feedback (employee/government/business, etc. relations/support), (4) survey (formal or informal), (5) proof of objectives achieved, (6) anecdotal evidence, (7) managers' comments.

3  A similar gap between what is said and what is done can be ascertained among the members of the German Public Relations Association, DPRG: while 88 per cent of them consider surveys to be 'important', less than a fifth were able to claim that they regularly carried out analyses (Baerns, 1995: 9–29; Pracht, 1991: 42–3).

4  The correlation coefficient Pearson's $r$ provides us with a measure of association, which produces information about the strength as well as the direction of the presumed relationship. A calculation of the correlation of the quality index with the age of the cases yielded $r = 0.06$.

5  A correlation calculation of this quality index with the age of the cases yielded $r = 0.33$.

6  In order to test the reliability of the constructed quality indexes the internal consistency of the variables (items) used can be calculated. A standard measure for calculating reliability is Cronbach's Alpha, for which values between 0.50 and 0.80 are regarded in the literature as acceptable. With a value of 0.63 the Alpha coefficient lies within the area of the acceptable.

## REFERENCES

Baerns, B. (1991) *Öffentlichkeitsarbeit oder Journalismus? Zum Einfluß im Mediensystem*. Köln: Verl. Wissenschaft und Politik.

Baerns, B. (1995) *PR-Erfolgskontrolle. Messen und Bewerten in der Öffentlichkeitsarbeit. Verfahren, Strategien, Beispiele*. Frankfurt am Main: Inst. für Medienentwicklung und Kommunikation.

Baerns, B. and Luedke, D. (1996) 'Uses and gratifications of a multinational company's attempt to communicate. Case Study of Changes and Latent Barriers of International Public Relations. A Social Responsibility Approach of Research'.

Paper presented to CERP Education and Research Copenhagen Conference on Corporate Social Responsibility and Conflict. Copenhagen, October 24–26.

Bentele, G., Steinmann, H. and Zerfaß, A. (1996) *Dialogorientierte Unternehmenskommunikation. Grundlagen – Praxiserfahrungen – Perspektiven.* Berlin: Vistas.

Bissland, J. (1990) 'Accountability gap. Evaluation practices show improvement', *Public Relations Review*, 16(2): 25–35.

Brody, E.W. and Stone, G.C. (1989) *Public Relations Research.* New York: Praeger.

Deutsche Public Relations-Gesellschaft e.V., DPRG Berufsverband Öffentlichkeitsarbeit (1970) *Auslobung Goldene Brücke 1970.* Bonn.

Deutsche Public Relations-Gesellschaft e.V., DPRG Berufsverband Öffentlichkeitsarbeit (1994) *Auslobung Goldene Brücke 1994.* Bonn.

Deutsche Public Relations-Gesellschaft e.V., DPRG Berufsverband Öffentlichkeitsarbeit (1996) *Das Berufsbild Öffentlichkeitsarbeit/Public Relations.* Bonn.

Deutsche Public Relations-Gesellschaft e.V., DPRG Berufsverband Öffentlichkeitsarbeit and Gesellschaft Public Relations-Agenturen e.V., GPRA Verband führender PR-Agenturen Deutschlands (1990) *Das Berufsbild Öffentlichkeitsarbeit/Public Relations.* Bonn.

Grunig, J., Grunig, L. and Dozier, D. (1996) 'Das situative Modell exzellenter Public Relations. Schlußfolgerungen aus einer internationalen Studie', in G. Bentele, H. Steinmann and A. Zerfaß (eds), *Dialogorientierte Unternehmenskommunikation. Grundlagen – Praxiserfahrung – Perspektiven.* Berlin: Vistas.

Grunig, J., Grunig, L. Dozier, D. and Hunt, T. (1984) *Managing Public Relations.* New York: Holt, Rinehart and Winston.

Pracht, P. (1991) 'Zur Systematik und Fundierung praktischer Öffentlichkeitsarbeit. Ein Soll-Ist-Vergleich', *pr-magazin*, 1991(5): 39–46.

Schuster, S. (1996) 'Mädchen und Jungen haben Durchblick. Die Organon GmbH optimiert ihre Aufklärungsarbeit durch Sozialforschung', in B. Baerns (ed.), *Public Relations 1996: Kampagnen, Trends and Tips.* Düsseldorf.

Walker, G. (1994) 'Communicating public relations research', *Journal of Public Relations Research*, 6(3): 141–61.

# 3 Towards a Theory of Campaigns: The Role of Opinion Leaders

*Michael Schenk and Thomas Döbler*

Air and water pollution and the depletion of raw materials concern not only single groups but whole nations and societies, perhaps even all human beings. Drug and alcohol abuse, social isolation, and incurable diseases are only a few examples of the wide field of social problems (Roehl, 1991). Despite tremendous technological advances that can alleviate these and many other problems, it is doubtful whether most of them can be solved by technology alone; instead, active participation by all members of society is needed. Very often, however, such participation requires a fundamental change in awareness, attitudes, and behaviour. Communication, therefore, plays a major role: without information and communication, change on an individual or societal level cannot be achieved. The aim of communication activities – whether privately funded, partly or entirely state-funded, or supranational – is to cause changes. In the following discussion these activities are called campaigns.

Differentiating between campaigns that are informational and those that are communicative is mostly a linguistic construct. While 'informational' and 'communicative' campaigns are rarely defined explicitly as synonyms (Bonfadelli, 1993: 37), in looking over the literature one notices that the two are implicitly treated as equivalents, in terms of both language and content. Sometimes, however, it is argued that informational campaigns primarily concentrate on the transfer of knowledge, whereas communicative campaigns (quasi as superimposed concept) also aim at changing attitudes and behaviour (Roehl, 1991: 48). Despite the difficulties in proving this analytical distinction empirically, we will make use of it in the following.

Watching the mass media one finds a multitude of campaigns, such as community-sponsored environmental campaigns to conserve valuable raw materials or encourage recycling, citizens' action group campaigns drawing attention to the problem of waste disposal, and AIDS campaigns. Numerous organizations such as Amnesty International, Greenpeace, and churches try to increase awareness or persuade people via campaigns (Pflaum, 1976; Windahl, 1989; Pott et al., 1991; Bonfadelli, 1993; Opitz, 1993; Dorlas and Pitz, 1995 and Schumann et al., 1995).

We can attempt to systematize the multitude of campaigns by dividing them into three categories according to their primary targets of influence: knowledge, attitudes, and behaviour (Roehl, 1991: 87). Campaigns usually aim at changes in

- the cognitive sphere (awareness, knowledge),
- the complex of attitudes or values, or
- behaviour.

*Information campaigns*, which intend a cognitive change or awareness of campaign issues, aim at influencing mental processes concerning certain subjects in a pre-defined way. Examples include campaigns to provide information about AIDS, about the dangers of smoking and alcohol, or about the advantages of tax reform or a single European currency.

Often, *value or attitude campaigns* (without considering the relationships between attitudes and values at this point) touch on areas that are very sensitive and resistant to change. The goals of such campaigns are, for example,

- improving attitudes towards children, the elderly, foreigners, or minority groups,
- accepting women in leadership positions, or
- changing attitudes regarding health (public health).

Influencing such often deeply-rooted values and attitudes is one of the most difficult tasks for a campaign.

Finally, a campaign can aim at influencing behaviour. Examples for the goal of a concrete, specific action are campaigns that appeal for

- blood donations,
- participation in a (population) census or inoculation programmes, or
- donations in case of war, famine, or natural disasters.

In many cases it is useful to consider whether a totally new behaviour is intended (for example, the first inoculation of infants in developing countries) or whether this behaviour is linked to familiar experiences.

A second kind of change in behaviour involves lasting influence on complex behavioural patterns (Kotler, 1978: 287). This kind of campaign aims, for example, at

- changing eating habits,
- encouraging safer and more courteous driving habits,
- encouraging more environmentally aware behaviour, or
- showing support for working women.

In these cases, a general change in behaviour in a certain direction is desired, rather than a single action. Like the lasting behavioural changes they strive to bring about, such campaigns have to be communicated over the long term.

To summarize, one can often observe campaigns setting out from certain social realities perceived as needing improvement and therefore subject to public discussion. But it is still unclear how campaigns should be designed and which rules they must follow to get new ideas across and bring about change as effectively as possible. There are at least two reasons why this is so: first, up to now, campaign research has been strongly influenced by practical questions; no theoretical framework – which many scientists consider necessary – exists yet. Second, the contexts of campaigns vary significantly, making it difficult to elaborate general propositions (Rogers et al., 1987: 841).

Not surprisingly, most campaigns are therefore designed to appeal in a more or less pragmatic way ('If you drink, don't drive'). Often, such campaigns are only successful by chance, and there are many examples in which the target groups evade campaign contact; or perception, interpretation, and memory are very selective (Hyman and Sheatsley, 1947). Hence, there seem to be a number of reasons why campaigns are not successful. For example, the controversial 1987 population census in Germany provided extensive evidence that perceptions of the census campaign were extremely selective: supporters felt that the campaign confirmed their positive opinion of the census, while opponents found that it confirmed their negative views. The campaign failed in its aim of creating broader overall acceptance of the census among the German population.

Of course, in this contribution it is impossible to develop a theory of campaigns. However, in the following discussion we will try to describe some basic aspects of campaign design and performance on a theoretical level. Experience in the field of advertising and public relations has shown that we must distinguish between input, throughput, and outcomes of communication variables. *Input variables* refer to the message, appeals, communicators, etc., while *throughput variables* concentrate on communication channels and user-decoding. *Outcomes* are the named hierarchical effects of the communication campaign on the individual regarding knowledge, attitude, and behavioural change. The throughput variables of communication channels are of special interest to this contribution. We have to differentiate between mass-media channels and interpersonal sources. The role of interpersonal communication in particular within the scope of campaigns seems to have been neglected by previous campaign research, although Paul F. Lazarsfeld (Lazarsfeld et al., 1948) conducted some classic field studies on election campaigns. In these studies we find proof of the assumption that interpersonal channels can be even more effective than the mass media.

Before we concentrate on interpersonal communication and the model of opinion leadership, it is necessary to define campaigns. According to Rice and Atkin (1994: 365; Rogers et al., 1987: 821) campaigns are 'purposive attempts to inform, persuade, or motivate behaviour changes in a relatively well-defined and large audience, generally for non-commercial benefits to the individual and/or society at large, typically within a given time period, by means of organized communication activities involving mass media, and often complemented by interpersonal support'. We draw on this definition but stress the importance of interpersonal communication as a central factor in successfully planning, arranging, and realizing campaigns.

We therefore include campaigns aimed at producing political results, such as advertising to get people involved in government services or activities (family planning, crime prevention, and so on), as well as campaigns designed to influence household behaviour (energy conservation, eating habits, or alcohol consumption) and linked with larger political goals, such as reducing health-care costs, alcohol-related accidents, or dependence on oil imports (Weiss and Tschirhart, 1994: 83).

Many relevant themes for information campaigns are concentrated in the European Union, such as

- health education and health promotion (AIDS information, cancer prevention, prevention of drug and alcohol abuse, information on smoking and health, improved dental health, nutrition, and so on),
- environmental issues such as energy conservation or air pollution,
- consumer behaviour (media behaviour) and business practices,
- safety (road safety, crime prevention or fire prevention), and
- other more specific topics such as family planning, birth control, or child care.

## THE MODEL OF OPINION LEADERSHIP

Usually, within the process of planning, creating, and carrying out campaigns, the media of mass communication are particularly taken into account. Especially in reaction to the extensive propaganda of World War II, politicians and researchers originally believed that the mass media had the power to influence large segments of society. With the help of mass media they expect campaign themes to be announced to the general public or target groups (Rice and Atkin, 1994: 367–8). Following this, further results are expected, especially sympathy to campaign goals, appropriate attitudes and opinions, and finally certain behaviours.

Following hierarchical models of communication effects, campaigns must first attract attention in the population or target groups before changes of opinion are possible. Thus, range, contact, recall, and recognition become the crucial criteria for campaign results. The advantage of mass media is that they can condense the message and reach large populations. However, the effect of mass communication is often overestimated; messages are often perceived selectively, not always correctly understood, or are even rejected. A famous example of overestimating the effectiveness of mass media was provided by the Cincinnati campaign to increase support for the United Nations, which used the slogan: 'Peace Begins with the United Nations – and the United Nations Begins with You'. A respondent questioned about the campaign slogan replied: 'Why, yes. I heard it over and over again.... But I never did find out what it means' (quoted in Rogers et al. 1987: 827). Campaigns such as this one led some researchers to conclude that mass media had no direct effect, because audiences were largely uninterested or showed selective exposure, perception, or retention, while most effects were achieved indirectly through opinion leaders.

The phenomenon of opinion leaders, or those who influence other people via direct interpersonal contact, has been neglected in contemporary campaign designs and studies. Katz and Lazarsfeld (1955) carried out the pioneer study stressing the importance of opinion leadership by examining the effects of the mass media on the attitudes and behaviour of those who listened to radio and television or read a daily newspaper. After presenting a message via the mass media and then measuring the effects of the message, they concluded that most messages produced only slight effects. But when they measured again some weeks later, they found that significant shifts in attitude and opinions had taken place. Seeking an explanation for these unexpected shifts, they suggested that the original message had been received, but that those who later changed their attitudes had talked with other people whose opinions they trusted; Katz and Lazarsfeld called these 'opinion leaders'.

Lazarsfeld and others transformed these empirical results into the 'two-step flow' model of persuasive communication: 'Ideas often flow from radio and print to the opinion leaders and from them to the less active sections of the population' (Lazarsfeld et al., 1948: 151). This model points to the multiplier effect of opinion leaders. In the flow of media communication, personal influence often proved more effective than the actual media messages. Personal communication, especially with opinion leaders, is much more important than (indirect) media communication for making individual decisions or legitimizing a special behaviour. Interpersonal sources are very important in the process of evaluation: in everyday life, individuals often use mutual co-orientation to evaluate messages originally received from the media. Others, especially opinion leaders, are sought out for additional information. Based on given demands, each individual can use both mass media and interpersonal sources, though interpersonal communication has the advantage of allowing new ideas or practices to be evaluated; co-orientation and exchange of opinions in the interpersonal environment determine the real meaning of information and messages from the mass media.

The concept of the opinion leader and its measurement have often been subject to discussion and criticism. One fundamental criticism is that a two-step flow of communication in the information-relaying process could not be proved by follow-up studies; in many cases, mass media reached the audience directly. The social-support functions of opinion leaders appear to be better documented in many studies. A methodological problem in many surveys was the distinction between information and influence: it was implicitly assumed that transmitting the message was the equivalent of influencing the audience (Klingemann, 1986; Schenk, 1989).

Studies dealing with the process of transmitting information found that information about current events passes directly from the mass media to the recipients. According to these studies, personal communication accounts for some transmission of news in the case of events with the highest news value and those which are of interest to a limited number of recipients. Diffusion research also shows that the relaying function of opinion leaders is based on the transmission of additional information. In many cases, the messages first heard from the mass media are soon linked with interpersonal communication, in which additional information is supplied by the opinion leaders. The potential influence of opinion leaders can be seen more in the support of decision-making and in the legitimation of behaviour, which very often are the subject of campaign messages. The advice of opinion leaders is sought particularly when the information spread by mass media differs from the attitudes and the knowledge of the recipients. Uncertainty and the feeling of a higher risk of decision concerning a new action also increases the influence of opinion leaders. Since people tend to seek security in demonstrating a new attitude or behaviour, discussion with informed persons can reduce the social risks associated with new practices. Using reciprocal co-orientation, individuals try to get convergent meanings and exchange opinions about campaign messages first encountered in the mass media.

Thus the opinion leader concept is now a differentiated one. We share Rogers' and Storey's view: for a successful campaign it is necessary to consider the role of interpersonal channels 'including networks triggered by mass media messages in campaigns' (Rogers et al., 1987: 829). Our central hypothesis therefore is that direct interpersonal communication about campaign themes or messages can contribute to the success of a campaign: personal conversation with others leads to a more detailed assessment and judgement of the themes and messages transferred through mass-media channels. In the opinion-leader concept, such personal influences concerning campaigns have been fixed. The opinion leader is regarded as a multiplier who passes on such messages in everyday life, in small networks and groups, and often adds appropriate assessments.

In order to use the opinion-leader concept in designing campaigns or in campaign research, it is necessary to be able to identify these opinion leaders. Our analysis will focus on this question in the following step.

## METHODS TO IDENTIFY OPINION LEADERS

In the past, empirical surveys identifying opinion leaders very often used the following three techniques (Rogers et al., 1971; Eurich, 1976):

- reference person's estimation,
- self-estimation,
- socio-metric analysis.

The first technique is the easiest to use. People with special knowledge of the communicative relations and the influencing process in a social system are asked about people who serve as opinion leaders on certain subjects. This procedure was successfully implemented in family planning campaigns (Rogers et al. 1971), as well as in communication and development studies in local areas. Only after someone had identified the opinion leaders did other persons in the communities follow. This procedure, however, must be seen critically, because within the scope of such interviews usually those people are chosen who belong to a higher social stratum than the average populations, while the opinion-leader concept refers to persons who can be found in all social strata.

In the self-estimation technique, people are asked to what degree they consider themselves opinion leaders. Older studies only used one or two questions to identify opinion leaders (Katz and Lazarsfeld, 1965), whereas recent studies use more questions, as King's and Summer's study shows (Köppler, 1987: 13; Beba, 1988: 60–1) (see Survey 1). An often-criticized disadvantage of this procedure is the possibility that a large number of those interviewed overestimate their influence on others. The technique of self-estimation is already used in communication sociology studies, based on large populations that allow for random samples. Yet this technique seems highly suitable for many of the campaigns mentioned above.

---

SURVEY 1: QUESTIONS TO IDENTIFY OPINION LEADERS

1. 'In general, do you like to talk about subject X with your friends?'
2. 'Do you think that you give your friends very little, average, much, or very much information on subject X?'
3. 'Have you talked with anyone besides your friends about subject X in the last six months?'
4. 'When you discuss subject X with your friends, what role do you mostly play: do you mainly listen to what your friends say or do you try to convince your friends of your own ideas?'
5. 'When you compare yourself with your friends, are you asked for advice about as readily or more or less readily?'
6. 'What happens more often: do you report on subject X to your friends or do they report on it to you?'
7. 'Do you have the impression that your friends/neighbours generally judge you as someone whose advice they are willing to take?'

---

Socio-metric techniques involve asking all members of a social system ('saturation sample') to identify whom they rely on for advice or information. Based on these interviews, communication-network analysis techniques reveal the communication structure of the social system. Opinion-leader roles can easily be identified, as illustrated in the classic example of a survey conducted by Coleman et al. (1966) to determine how physicians living in a small city prescribed a new drug:

• Could you please name three or four doctors with whom you have the most social contacts?
• Name three or four doctors you talk with most often about prescription medicines.
• If you need additional information or advice regarding these medicines, which doctors would you possibly consult?

The members of the group examined who were named most often as the source of advice or information were called opinion leaders. A sociogram helps develop a differentiated picture of the existing relations of advice and information, as well as a measure for the relative influence of these persons. This technique surely is the most reliable since, due to its complex design, it allows the real influential–follower relation to be probed. This socio-metric or network technique is mainly used in small collectives (Eurich, 1976; Rogers et al., 1981).

In the past, the self-estimation method was preferred in many studies. When used in conjunction with socio-metric techniques, it can produce studies with a high degree of reliability and validity (Rogers and Cartano, 1962), and can therefore be used to good effect in campaigns.

Combining the self-designated opinion leadership with modern network analysis can provide a promising expansion for the identification of influential persons (Schenk, 1993). The ego-centred networks of the respondents, collected in regularly representative surveys, reveal the interpersonal environment of respondents or opinion leaders. By using a name generator, the personal networks of the respondents can be determined. Further, name interpreters are needed to describe the alteri of ego, including the information, communication, and exchange relations between ego and alter. This way, one can also analyse the structure of the personal networks (e.g. range, density, homogeneity, etc.).

One of the most common name generators is Burt's (1986), which can also be used in campaigns. His stimulus situation makes it possible to determine personal networks quickly and easily: 'Most people discuss important matters with others. Thinking over the last six months, with whom have you spoken about topics important to you?' For campaigns addressed more to the general public than to a specific target group, recourse to Fischer's name generator (1982, see Survey 2) proves helpful.

---

SURVEY 2: FISCHER'S NAME GENERATOR

1. Who takes care of your apartment when you are away?
2. With whom do you discuss your work affairs?
3. Who helps you with any kind of jobs in your household?
4. In the last three months, with whom have you participated in activities like going out, invitations, and so on?
5. With whom do you usually discuss hobbies or spare-time activities?
6. With whom do you talk about personal things?
7. Whose opinions are important to you?
8. From whom would you borrow money?

---

Ego-centred network analysis makes it possible to describe in detail not only the personal networks of opinion leaders, but also the social background of the members of all target groups at whom campaigns are directed, allowing one to design campaigns that appeal not only to individuals, but also to social groups, scenes, or circles (Reigber, 1993). In many cases group-minded messages can be more effective than messages addressed to individuals. A solid knowledge of the 'interpersonal environment' can be useful for campaigns that try to take advantage of the relaying and multiplying functions of interpersonal communication.

## SOME RESULTS OF EMPIRICAL STUDIES AND FURTHER DEVELOPMENT OF THE OPINION-LEADER CONCEPT

All surveys agree that opinion leaders cannot automatically be called formal leaders or persons with high social prestige. They are instead typical members of a social group or network in frequent contact with other group or network members and aware of the norms or values these members endorse.

Opinion leaders share the same 'milieu' as those they influence, and they operate by influencing those around them. As many studies have shown, opinion leaders have a higher level of social activity or gregariousness and therefore can reach other persons in their environment directly. They display competence, credibility, authority, and self-confidence and make extensive use of media. But they concentrate on those media that supply them with relevant information for their special field of competence. Giving reliable information and advice, opinion leaders often serve as a 'model' for the members of their groups.

Separating influence from status, the opinion-leader concept has an extraordinary position within social research: it demonstrates that people are not persuaded in a simple top-down way. Opinion leaders therefore cannot be detected by an absolute amount of education or social status; these variables are only relative.

It is also not possible to describe opinion leaders more generally because their influence refers to a homogeneous milieu. Further, opinion leaders operate only within a specific sphere of influence and differ with the topic under consideration: a neighbourhood housewife who is asked for her opinion on the latest recipes may not be an opinion leader for new fashions or movies, for example.

To find out more general features of opinion leaders, the publishers of the German news magazine *Der Spiegel* commissioned the Allensbach Institute for Public Opinion Research (Institut für Demoskopie) to develop a new scale to identify influential persons in each social stratum whose influence is not primarily based on their socio-economic status (Noelle-Neumann, 1983). After years of preliminary investigation using different sample tests, the research team under the direction of Elisabeth Noelle-Neumann proposed a 'scale of personality strength', or PS scale. In contrast to the traditional measurement of opinion leadership, the PS scale aims to survey active, influential, and self-assertive persons.

As shown in Survey 3, the scale contains nine self-descriptions for the interviewee to agree or disagree with, along with a multiple-choice question about his or her readiness to give advice. Last, there are three objective items asking about the interviewee's participation or leadership in clubs, political parties, or citizens' action groups in their spare time (base of the reduced scale was a factor analysis on originally 34 items, tested in a representative survey with 3,542 respondents).

Each answer is assigned a certain number of points that are added up in an individual total score ranging between 101 (lowest possible score) and 198 (highest possible score). This allows individuals to be rated on a continuous scale, although in practical analysis this scale is often simplified by dividing the respondents into five groups, ranging from high to low personality strength. Survey 3 shows the 13 stimuli or items and their assigned points. Those scoring at least 163 points are considered persons with a strong personality, while those scoring less than 110 points are considered persons with a weak personality. Three additional groupings distinguish between tendencies to low (111–125 points), medium (126–147 points), and high (148–162 points) levels of personality strength.

---

SURVEY 3: THE 'PERSONALITY STRENGTH' SCALE

Self-description

1. I usually consider my actions to be successful (agree: 13 points/ disagree: 7 points).
2. I am rarely unsure of how to behave (14/7).
3. I like taking responsibility (15/7).
4. I like taking the lead in common projects (17/8).
5. I enjoy persuading other people to share my opinion (15/7).
6. I often realize that other people depend on my behaviour (16/8).
7. I am good at asserting myself against others (14/7).
8. I am often a few steps ahead of the others (18/9).
9. I possess many things which other people are envious of (15/9).
10. I like to give advice or suggestions to others (15/10/5).[1]

Objective items

11. Holding a leading position/being a supervisor in one's profession (16/9).
12. Active in a party, trade union or citizens' action group during leisure time (14/9).
13. Holding an office in an association or organization (16/9).

---

Only a few studies deal with personality strength, but some empirical results can be reported (Noelle-Neumann, 1983, 1985; Weimann, 1992, 1994). Katz and Lazarsfeld (1965) break the influential personality down into the following:

- who one is (personification of values and certain personality characteristics),[2]
- what one knows (competence within the relevant field), and
- whom one knows (ability to communicate; having a strategic position in the social network or group).

We can describe persons with a strong personality as general influentials.

### Personality

Following Noelle-Neumann's concept of influentials, a central feature seems to be that personality strength describes a human quality previously beyond the scope of traditional socio-demography. According to Weimann (1992), personality strength combines many social and individual characteristics. That does not mean that personality strength does not correlate with some demographic features, such as age or education. The very combination of several of these features into a single construct can be seen as an advantage of this scale in measuring influentials or social influence. The personality-strength concept provides a differentiation which traditional features, such as social stratum or social status, fail to do.

For example, in certain situations workers with a strong personality act in ways similar to managerial staff or civil servants and have similar attitudes. Admittedly, managerial staff and civil servants more often agree on given questions concerning job expectations than workers do, looking at professional groups as a whole. But looking separately at persons with a strong personality among the workers, one notes agreement among this segment equal to or higher than the average of managerial staff and civil servants. Thus, the discrepancy in work attitudes or job expectations refers less to specific job classifications than to levels of personality strength.

Similarly, empirical studies display only minor differences in life aims between persons with strong personalities and either high or low socio-economic status (Noelle-Neumann, 1983). Nevertheless, an isolated examination of persons with strong personalities shows that, for a large part of the aims, personality strength is a more significant criterion than status.

It is also apparent that persons with stronger personalities are generally more active than those with weaker personalities, applicable to both leisure (sports, culture, social gatherings) and professional activities.

### Competence

Persons with strong personalities are frequently asked by others for their advice on quite different topics, thus it is important to know what sources of information these influentials use. Persons with strong personalities seem to limit their mass media use; both TV and radio use is rather low among this group, while they use newspapers, news magazines, and books more often. There is no difference between persons of strong personality and the average population with regard to the use of the popular press, magazines, or TV journals. Their use of print media can be described as specific: not all print media are used equally intensively, with newspapers and news- and special-interest magazines typically used most often. Thus, persons with a strong personality show clear preferences in their use of media. These results are comparable to classic opinion-leadership research, which also shows that opinion leaders are characterized by distinctive media consumption.

Similarly, the use of TV concentrates on genres with a high information content: television news, talk shows, political discussions, and documentaries play a special role. Thus, the media use by persons with strong personalities seems related to the general information-seeker covered by audience research. In seeking and using information, the influentials are able to give additional information and opinions to others in different fields of public discussion and indeed to act as a multiplier.

## Social Communication

Like the classic opinion leaders, persons with a strong personality show a crucial ability to communicate and tend to be gregarious. According to Noelle-Neumann, these persons have a large circle of acquaintances, and age and stratum hardly play a role: for example, their circle of acquaintances does not decrease as they get older. It is critical to note that, in principle, one can only make general statements about the social networks of persons with strong personalities. We only know that these influentials have a lot of acquaintances and friends, but cannot determine the total number known, nor differentiate between the contexts of social relations (for instance, between friends, relatives, family, colleagues, etc.). For a more detailed examination of the interpersonal environment, network analysis methods are needed.

However, Weimann's analysis of a total communication network in an Israeli kibbutz (1992) shows that within this communication network persons of strong personality have a central social position and thus are in direct contact with many other people. In comparison, marginal persons or isolates can be classified as persons of weak personality: whereas 58 per cent of those marked as 'centrally positioned' in the network show 'high' personality strength values, only 3 per cent of the marginals are classified as persons with a high level of personality strength.

It was also evident that any close relation between personality strength and communicative behaviour depends on the topics of communication. In contrast to the traditional opinion leader, whose domain of influence is limited to a particular sphere or field, influentials characterized by personality strength often seem to be active in different, overlapping fields. 'Most connections activated with the transmission of messages, consumer information, and influence come from persons with a strong personality' (Weimann, 1992: 98).

## SUMMARY

We consider the PS scale to be a useful approach to discover and describe influentials. According to previous research, the personality-strength concept improves on the old opinion-leader concept. While the classic opinion-leader concept referred to influence exerted in homogeneous small groups, the concept of personality strength enables a change of theoretical perspective, from the small group to social networks containing diverse and heterogeneous social relationships.

The PS scale can be characterized as a survey instrument that enables one to identify influentials generally. It combines social behaviour variables, such as leadership and consultation, with individual psychological traits, such as self-assertiveness, confidence, and responsibility. In contrast to scales that mainly concentrate on consultation and influence, the personality-strength concept seems broader and especially suitable for many campaign studies by identifying influentials who exert multiplying and supporting influences in the social environment.

Considering a study supported by the *Deutsche Forschungsgemeinschaft* (German Science Foundation) on the influence of mass media and interpersonal communication on knowledge of and attitudes toward German reunification (Schenk, 1995), the following additional results appear relevant to the design and planning of campaigns as well as to campaign research: although persons of strong personality were relatively young (under 50 years), male, and had a better education than persons of weaker personality, social stratum did not correlate with personality strength in this study. Persons with a strong personality again showed more involvement in different leisure and political activities. They used modern communication technologies more frequently, and their households were well equipped with these technologies. While respondents with a strong personality showed a less intensive use of the mass media than persons with a weaker personality, the former used mass media more selectively, displaying frequent use of newspapers and a special interest in news magazines, especially *Der Spiegel*.

In this study, egocentric network analyses revealed that persons with a strong personality knew more people than did those with a weak personality. Their social network was clearly larger, including not only their circle of acquaintances, but also friends, colleagues, relatives, etc. Persons with a strong personality had larger networks that often included persons with different levels of education and from different social groups and milieus, leading to the conclusion that these different groups might be linked by the influentials. In contrast to previous research showing that opinion leaders have great influence above all within one group, persons with a strong personality seem to function as bridges between social groups and milieus. Their multiplying effect can be described as 'transborder regression'. Persons with a strong personality often discussed current issues with other persons in their social environment. Their interpersonal communication behaviour was generally remarkable. In holding a superior network position and having special information, one can assume that these influentials pass their knowledge and opinions on to other persons within their environment.

In the study on German reunification, it was notable that both those with stronger and weaker personality types estimated the existing public opinions exactly. In contrast to persons with a weaker personality, whose individual opinions and attitudes corresponded to perceived public opinion, the influentials with a strong personality deviated from public opinion. Influentials obviously hold and communicate opinions in their environment which diverge from the perceived public opinion. The influentials, therefore, play a crucial role in campaign communication. For campaigns to succeed, they must first convince the influentials. Their relaying and supporting functions should not be underestimated because people with a strong personality are willing and able to communicate divergent opinions and can, therefore, limit campaign-communication effects.

People with a strong personality seem to be persons of great charisma who are well-informed about current issues and who can estimate public opinions relatively well. Addressing persons with a strong personality directly and winning them for the campaign seems to be a way to achieve campaign goals.

Finally, we wish to stress that designing and performing campaigns is not a question of choosing between mass communication and interpersonal communication channels. Instead, both communication sources are complementary. In the past, sole concentration on mass media has often failed to change opinions and behaviour of target groups.

Though scientists sometimes adopt the view that interpersonal communication is more effective than mass communication, for example in the context of AIDS prevention (Windahl, 1989: 136), mass-media communication is not useless: it directs our attention to the issues campaigns refer to. It is more likely that interpersonal communication via opinion leaders needs a certain preparation by mass communication in any case (Hausser et al., 1990; Schumann et al., 1995). Mass media can put the issues on the public agenda. The role of opinion leaders lies in assessing and evaluating information seen, heard, or read in the mass media; in this way opinion leaders are an aid to orientation in a confusing, information-overloaded world. In terms of system theory, they often function to reduce complexity. Gaining opinion leaders to stimulate interpersonal contact and to activate interpersonal communication is a major step toward successful campaign communication.

## NOTES

1  Item No. 10 is divided into: Yes/No/(Almost)Never.
2  At first sight, the concept of personality strength seems to have a certain similarity with Rotter's theory of 'locus of control' (Rotter, 1966; for similarity of single items see also Krampen's questionnaire, 1991). In contrast to the personality-strength concept, Rotter concentrates on the alternating effects between individual

and environment that are based on psychological approaches. Rotter describes them as 'internal and external control of reinforcement'. Until now, however, these alternating effects have not been examined in light of their potential influence but more with regard to how they can explain one's own behaviour.

## REFERENCES

Beba, W. (1988) 'Die Bedeutung der interpersonellen Kommunikation: Wandlung des Meinungsführerkonzeptes', *Arbeitspapier Nr. 24, Institut für Marketing der Universität der Bundeswehr*. Hamburg.

Bonfadelli, H. (1993) 'Ökologie als Thema für Informationskampagnen', *Medienwissenschaft Schweiz*, 1: 37–41.

Burt, R. (1986) 'Mass media and interpersonal channels: competitives, convergent or complementary?', in G. Gumpert and R. Cathcart (eds), *InterMedia: Interpersonal Channels in a Media World*. New York: Oxford University Press.

Coleman, J.S., Katz, E. and Menzel, H. (1966) *Medical Innovation: A Diffusion Study*. Indianapolis: Bobbs-Merrill.

Dorlas, A. and Pitz, A. (1995) 'Kampagnen gegen Rassismus und Ausländerfeindlichkeit', in S. Baringhorst (ed.), *Macht der Zeichen – Zeichen der Macht: Neue Strategien politischer Kommunikation*. Frankfurt a. M.: Lang.

Erbslöh, E. (1981) *Die Rolle der Meinungsforschung im öffentlichen Marketing*. Hamburg: Gruner und Jahr.

Eurich, C. (1976) 'Politische Meinungsführer', *Kommunikation und Politik*, 9. München: Sauer.

Fischer, C. (1982) *To Dwell Among Friends: Personal Networks in Town and City*. Chicago: University of Chicago Press.

Hausser, D., Dubois-Arber, F., Lehmann, P., Gutzwiller, F. and Zimmermann, E. (1990) 'Die Evaluation der STOP-AIDS-Kampagne in der Schweiz', *Ergebnisse sozialwissenschaftlicher AIDS-Forschung*, 1: 327–44.

Hyman, H. and Sheatsley, P. (1947) 'Some reasons why information campaigns fail', *Public Opinion Quarterly*: 413–23.

Katz, E. (1980) 'On conceptualizing media effects', *Studies in Communication*, 1: 119–41.

Katz, E. (1988) 'Communication research since Lazarsfeld', *Public Opinion Quarterly*, 51: 25–45.

Katz, E. and Lazarsfeld, P. (1965) *Personal Influence. The Part Played by People in the Flow of Mass Communications*. New York: Free Press.

King, C. and Summers, J. (1970) 'Overlap of opinion leadership across consumer product categories', *Journal of Marketing Research*, 7: 43.

Klingemann, H.-D. (1986) 'Massenkommunikation, interpersonale Kommunikation und politische Einstellungen', in M. Kaase (ed.), *Politische Wissenschaft und politische Ordnung*. Opladen: Westdt. Verlag.

Köppler, K. (1987) *Opinion Leaders*. Hamburg: Heinrich Bauer Verlag.

Kotler, P. (1978) *Marketing für Nonprofit-Organisationen*. Stuttgart: Poeschel.

Krampen, G. (1991) *Fragebogen zur Kompetenz- und Kontrollüberzeugungen (FKK)*. Göttingen: Hoqrefe, Verlag für Psychologie.

Lazarsfeld, P., Berelson, B. and Gaudet, H. (1948) *The People's Choice: How the Voter Makes Up His Mind in a Presidential Campaign*, 2nd edn. New York: Columbia University Press.

McGuire, W. (1989) 'Theoretical foundations of campaigns', in R. Rice and C. Atkin (eds), *Public Communication Campaigns*. Newbury Park, CA: Sage.

Mendelsohn, H. (1973) 'Some reasons why information campaigns can succeed', *Public Opinion Quarterly*, 37: 50–61.

Noelle-Neumann, E. (1983) *Spiegel Dokumentation: Persönlichkeitsstärke.* Hamburg: Spiegel-Verlag Augstein.

Noelle-Neumann, E. (1985) 'Identifying opinion leaders'. *Paper presented at the 38th ESOMAR Conference.* Wiesbaden.

Opitz, P. (1993) 'Kulturelle Vielfalt und Informationskampagnen im Umweltbereich', *Medienwissenschaft Schweiz*, 1: 42–4.

Pflaum, D. (1976) '"Image-Umkehr"-Kampagne gegen Nikotin- und Alkoholmißbrauch bei Jugendlichen', *Markt-Forscher*, 6: 123–7.

Pott, E., Nilson-Giebel, M., Riempp, C., Sandkühler, D. and Troschke, J.v. (1991) 'Ohne Rauch geht's auch: Eine Kampagne der BZgA zur Förderung des Nichtrauchens bei Jugendlichen', *Praevention* 14(3): 92–97.

Reigber, D. (1993) *Social Networks.* Düsseldorf: ECON-Verlag.

Rice, R. and Atkin, C. (1994) 'Principles of successful public communication campaigns', in J. Bryant and D. Zillmann (eds), *Media Effects: Advances in Theory and Research.* Hillsdale, NJ: Erlbaum.

Roehl, S.V. (1991) *Social Marketing Kampagnen: Eine kommunikationswissenschaftliche Analyse am Beispiel der Kampagne zur Volkszählung 1987.* Bergisch Gladbach, Köln: Eul.

Rogers, E. and Cartano, D. (1962) 'Methods of measuring opinion leadership', *Public Opinion Quarterly*, 26: 435–41.

Rogers, E., Cartano, D. and Kincaid, L. (1981) *Communication Networks.* New York: Free Press.

Rogers, E., Cartano, D. and Shoemaker, F. (1971) *Communication of Innovations: A Cross-Cultural Approach.* New York: Free Press.

Rogers, E., Cartano, D. and Storey, D. (1987) 'Communication Campaigns', in C. Berger and S. Chaffee (eds), *Handbook of Communication Science.* Newbury Park, CA: Sage.

Rotter, J. (1966) 'Generalized expectancies for internal versus external control of reinforcement', *Psychological Monographs*, 80(1): 1–28.

Schenk, M. (1984) *Soziale Netzwerke und Kommunikation.* Tübingen: Mohr.

Schenk, M. (1987) *Soziale Netzwerke und Massenmedien. Untersuchungen zum Einfluß der persönlichen Kommunikation.* Tübingen: Mohr.

Schenk, M. (1989) 'Massenkommunikation und interpersonale Kommunikation', in M. Kaase and W. Schultz (eds), *Massenkommunikation: Theorien, Methoden, Befunde.* Opladen: Westdt. Verlag.

Schenk, M. (1993) 'Die Ego-zentrierten Netzwerke von Meinungsbildnern ('Opinion Leaders')', *Kölner Zeitschrift für Soziologie und Sozialpsychologie*, 15.

Schenk, M. (1995) *Soziale Netzwerke und Massenmedien. Untersuchungen zum Einfluß der persönlichen Kommunikation.* Tübingen: Mohr.

Schumann, J., Scherer, K., Bühringer, G. and Kröger, C. (1995) *Evaluation der Kampagne 'KEINE MACHT DEN DROGEN'.* Köln: Bundeszentrale für Gesundheitliche Aufklärung.

Weimann, G. (1982) 'On the importance of marginality: one more step into the two-step-flow of communication', *American Sociological Review*, 47: 764–73.

Weimann, G. (1992) 'Persönlichkeitsstärke: Rückkehr zum Meinungsführer-Konzept?', in J. Wilke (ed.), *Öffentliche Meinung. Theorie, Methoden, Befunde.* Freiburg: Alber.

Weimann, G. (1994) *The Influentials: People who Influence People.* New York: State University of New York Press.

Weiss, J. and Tschirhart, M. (1994) 'Public information campaigns as policy instruments', *Journal for Policy Analysis and Management*, 13(1): 82–119.

Windahl, S. (1989) 'AIDS information: a case for health communication', *Medien Journal*, 13(4): 135–9.

# Part II   PLANNING AND IMPLEMENTING NATIONAL CAMPAIGNS

## 4   The Importance of Research in Planning and Developing Communications Campaigns: The UK Government Home Office Smoke Alarms Campaign

### Malcolm Rigg

The aim of this chapter is to show how research can help to plan and develop a communications campaign. Research here is taken to mean both qualitative methods, such as group discussions and depth interviews, and quantitative surveys. Whilst quantitative research is usually concerned with measurement, qualitative research explores understanding, feelings, and emotions.

The chapter takes as an example a campaign funded by the UK Government Home Office designed to raise awareness of the risks of fire in the home and the value of installing smoke alarms.

Public communications campaigns are designed to achieve one or more of the following kinds of change:

- *cognitive change:* awareness, knowledge, or understanding of an issue
- *action change:* persuading the target audience to take a specific action, such as registering to vote
- *behavioural change:* driving more slowly or giving up smoking
- *value change:* altering or modifying a belief such as prejudice against a group.

It is apparent from these examples that stimulating change through campaigning can vary from the relatively straightforward, where promotion

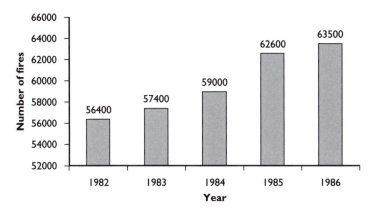

FIGURE 4.1  *Number of fires in England and Wales*
(*Source*: Home Office Statistics Division)

may play a leading role, through to complex and extremely difficult aims where promotion might, at best, support broader longer-term aims or play a minor or just a complementary role in policy implementation.

With a well-designed campaign, we need to know what we are trying to achieve, how best to go about it, and have some idea of how far we have succeeded. Research plays an important role in this process, and I shall illustrate this by describing its use at different stages of the Smoke Alarms campaign.

## CAMPAIGN BACKGROUND

In 1987, sales and use of smoke alarms, which give an audible alert in the presence of smoke, were extremely low. Only 5 per cent of UK households had smoke alarms fitted, and sales of alarms were static. At the same time, fires in the home were rising, as Figure 4.1 illustrates. The number of deaths was also showing signs of rising, as Figure 4.2 illustrates. Half of those who were killed by fires died because they were trapped by a fire that they were not aware of. Over half occurred at night and two-thirds were the result of being overcome by fumes and smoke, often when asleep. Injuries were also rising.

The Home Office appointed an advertising agency, FCO (subsequently merged to form Euro RSCG), to run a test promotions campaign in one region of the UK in order to assess the potential for success in conducting a national campaign which would stimulate people to install alarms.

## UNDERSTANDING THE AUDIENCE

The first stage of research was a qualitative study undertaken by the agency Reflexions to explore people's awareness and understanding of the risks of

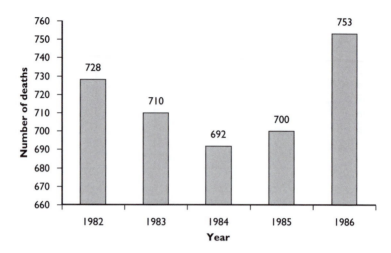

FIGURE 4.2 *Number of deaths caused by fire*
(*Source:* Home Office Statistics Division)

fire, their perceptions of how to deal with fires, and their awareness and understanding of the role, benefits, and costs of smoke alarms. It also explored people's attitudes to the risks of dying by fire.

The research was conducted using group discussions with people of different ages and social classes. This method allows researchers to explore issues in a supportive environment and allows group members to express their feelings and understanding through discussion and interaction with others rather than feeling that they might be being tested on their knowledge, as people sometimes feel when questioned in an individual, more structured interview.

The results provided invaluable information about awareness and understanding as well as about attitudes and emotions related to fires. Most people hardly considered fire a threat, and nearly everyone believed that if a fire broke out they would be aware of it and would be able to take effective action to deal with it. Parents of young children were most likely to acknowledge the risk to their children, but old people were particularly reluctant to think that a risk existed which they could not deal with themselves.

Ignorance of domestic smoke alarms was widespread. The majority were only aware of the type of alarms and sprinkler systems used in hotels, which were perceived to be prohibitively expensive for domestic use and would require specialist fitting. The few who were aware of domestic alarms thought that they were expensive (up to £50 each) and that one was needed for each room.

A dozen concept statements which were possible bases for the advertising were explored. Three of these emerged as a base for building a campaign which could deploy heightened emotions in order to challenge and overcome ignorance and scepticism about the value of alarms.

- The idea of children dying in a fire was particularly emotive.
- The idea of dying in one's sleep and 'just not waking up' horrified people.
- The speed at which smoke and fumes spread was a shock to those who imagined that fires smouldered for hours before spreading rapidly.

## SETTING THE COMMUNICATIONS STRATEGY

The research indicated that the audience most likely to be receptive to a campaign was parents of young children, especially those in higher social grades owning their own homes. Although the risk of fire was greatest in the homes of parents in lower social grades, such parents were more resistant to the idea of installing alarms. Those in higher social grades were, therefore, designated as the prime target for the initial campaign because it was considered essential to achieve a critical mass of awareness and installation and thereby create the base for reaching those most at risk.

The research also pointed to the importance of advertising on television rather than using the press because the advertising needed to be based on the powerful emotional charge which the issue evoked. The budget was too small to permit evening television, and the campaign was planned on the basis of daytime television.

The key message was devised as:

> Only a smoke alarm can buy the precious minutes that can save your family from dying in a fire while they sleep.

Qualitative research is most powerful in the development stage of a public campaign, when its role is to aid understanding of the audience and informing the development of the communications strategy. It is at this early stage that it contributes to the brief for creative advertising development and media planning.

A TV commercial, 'Doll's House', was developed, showing a little girl playing with her dolls in her bedroom, which is later engulfed with smoke as she and her family sleep. Research was carried out by Reflexions using group discussions to check whether the ideas were being communicated clearly. It showed that the key message which the campaign was designed to promote was being communicated effectively, namely:

> You can't be relied upon to avert disaster if you're asleep, so don't take chances, get a smoke alarm.

The research report also indicated that 'the communication that smoke would kill a small child in under a minute came as an unpleasant revelation and emphasized the need for an early warning system'.

The test campaign was run in the Tyne Tees television region of north-east England immediately after Christmas. The advertising agency held briefings with smoke alarm manufacturers and retailers to alert them to the campaign and to promote the availability of alarms. This was reinforced by local Fire

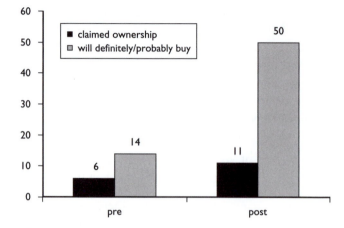

FIGURE 4.3 *Changes in results before and after the advertising*
(*Source*: Millward Brown Omnibus Survey)

Brigade activity. Where a campaign is run to promote action by the target audience it is essential to co-ordinate the associated response mechanisms. If, for instance, the audience is asked to write in or telephone for further information, the mechanisms for dealing with their responses must be in place, otherwise the campaign can result in a negative reaction amongst those who responded.

Quantitative research was commissioned using the Millward Brown national omnibus survey (a survey which is run regularly permitting clients to ask questions on a cost-per-question basis when they require them). The results showed a considerable increase in claimed ownership and in claimed interest in acquisition, as Figure 4.3 demonstrates.

Based on this evidence, and on unprecedented demand for smoke alarms in the area, which led to almost complete sell-outs, the campaign was extended to the London and Granada television areas in December 1988 and then nationally in December 1989.

## MEASURING THE NATIONAL CAMPAIGN

The effectiveness of the national campaign was measured in three ways:

- using annual survey research conducted by BJM to measure reported penetration, awareness, attitudes, and advertising based on a sample of 2,000 respondents;
- using the bi-annual AGB Home Audit in order to measure actual penetration of smoke alarms in homes;
- sales data acquired from retail audit panels undertaken by AC Nielsen.

The success of the campaign had led to considerable sales for manufacturers and retailers so that what was being measured by the home audit and

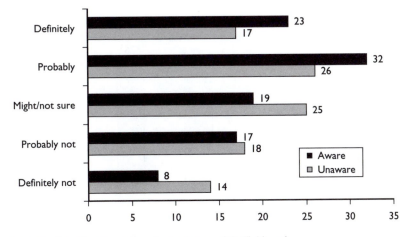

FIGURE 4.4  *Intention to purchase by awareness of 'Doll's House'*
*advertisement (non-owners)*
*(Source:* BJM)

sales data was overall effectiveness of the marketing and promotion by all
interested parties, not just the effect of the Home Office campaign.
Nevertheless, the Home Office campaign was the dominant source of publicity from 1988 to 1990.

The BJM quantitative survey, however, was designed to assess the association between the campaign and attitudes and behaviour. It showed that
awareness of the campaign was 61 per cent of the adult population in 1990,
rising to 69 per cent awareness of the 'Doll's House' advertisement after
prompting respondents with illustrations from the advertisement.

The research indicated a strong association between advertising recall and
actual or intended purchase of smoke alarms. There was a significant difference between those aware and not aware of 'Doll's House' which suggested a strong advertising effect, as Figure 4.4 shows. The changes in
household ownership are shown in Figure 4.5. The rate of growth was twice
as fast in households with young children. Penetration of smoke alarms was
also highest among higher social grades. The results also showed that the
elderly were less likely to acquire smoke alarms, which was a particular
cause of concern because they accounted for nearly half of all fatalities. The
pattern of ownership is illustrated in Figure 4.6.

## OPTIMIZING THE CAMPAIGN

These results further indicated that ownership remained low among some
groups who were vulnerable to fire. Penetration amongst DE social grades
aged 55 and over was only 20 per cent. Only 26 per cent of non-owners in
this group said they intended to buy, compared with 51 per cent of the population as a whole.

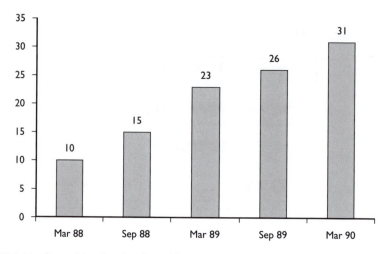

FIGURE 4.5   *Ownership of smoke alarms(%)*
(*Source:* AGB)

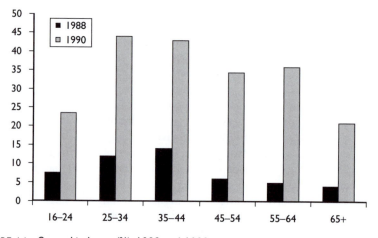

FIGURE 4.6   *Ownership by age(%), 1988 and 1990*
(*Source:* AGB)

Qualitative research amongst the elderly, conducted by Research Perspectives in June 1989 and consisting of group discussion, had shown that they:

- were less aware of alarms
- over-estimated their cost
- perceived alarms to be complex and difficult to install
- felt themselves to be 'immune' to the threat of fire.

Based on this, the key message for the next phase of advertising was expressed as:

*Smoke and fumes can kill anyone while they sleep. The elderly are particularly vulnerable. Only a smoke alarm can keep watch on you.*

A new advertisement, 'Dying', was devised to:

- directly address the elderly
- demonstrate the speed and lethal effect of smoke
- remove the misapprehension that something would wake you in a fire (the BJM survey research showed that a quarter of respondents relied on their pets)
- draw attention to the affordability of a smoke alarm.

The advertisement was evaluated in animatic form in qualitative research (group discussions) by Andrew Irving Associates amongst elderly people and their near and distant friends. The report spoke of the 'stunned silence' that met the animatic and concluded:

> Overall this approach suggests that the high-impact, emotional route adopted for this campaign is both appropriate and likely to be effective in:
>
> - persuading some to take action
> - making others more conscious of/interested in the idea of installing an alarm.

During this period, the Home Office campaign accounted for at least two-thirds of all advertising expenditure. Ownership of alarms amongst the elderly increased from 24 per cent to 40 per cent. This demonstrated clearly that successively targeting the message at different groups can be highly effective in optimizing a campaign.

The approach illustrated here was then continued by tracking awareness, attitudes, and behaviour over several more years and refining the campaign to address more resistant segments of the audience. The success of this strategy was demonstrated by the continuing increase in penetration of alarms and the continuing improvements in survey results regarding intentions to purchase amongst non-owners.

## SUMMARY

This chapter has sought to describe the role of research in planning communications campaigns. In doing so, it has drawn heavily on the results of qualitative research. One UK practitioner explains the role of group discussions and depth interviews as follows:

> Qualitative research is best used for problems where the results will increase understanding, expand knowledge, clarify the real issues, generate hypotheses, identify a range of behaviour, explore and explain consumer motivation, attitudes and behaviour, identify distinctive behavioural groups, provide input to a future stage of research or development.

The authors explain that

qualitative research:

- involves small samples of consumers which are not necessarily representative of larger populations
- employs a wide variety of techniques to collect data, not simply a structured question-and-answer format
- relies on interpretation of the findings, which is an integral part of the data collection ...
- allows access to the ways in which consumers express themselves.

This last point can be extremely important because it can provide indications of the kind of language that is appropriate to the audience.

Qualitative research is most powerful in the development stage of a public campaign, when its primary role is aiding understanding of the audience and informing the development of the communications strategy. It is at this early stage that it contributes to the brief for creative advertising development and media planning. The chapter showed how the brief for creative development was drawn from the qualitative research, namely:

*Only a smoke alarm can buy the precious minutes that can save your family from dying in a fire while they sleep.*

In addition, qualitative research can play an important role in checking communications in draft or final form in order to test whether the approach is succeeding in conveying the messages which the communicator intends to convey.

### REFERENCE

Gordon, G. and Langmaid, R. (1988) *Qualitative Market Research: A Practitioner's and Buyer's Guide*. Aldershot: Gower.

# 5 Planning and Implementing a National Campaign: Two Campaigns by the National Farmers Union

*Simon Rayner*

This chapter provides practical examples of how survey research can help a national campaign to more readily achieve its objectives. The contribution is primarily concerned with the planning and implementation phases of the campaign; however, as effective planning has a major impact on a campaign's results and the ease of evaluation, the contribution is also relevant to the final stages of the campaign. Its approach is intended to be practical and thought-provoking. It sets out two golden rules to remember when starting to prepare a campaign. They address the need for realistic, honest, and clearly defined objectives. These basic guidelines will help campaigns remain on course and ensure that any survey work done to support the campaign is relevant and cost effective.

The possible use of survey research in the planning and implementation stages of campaigns is demonstrated via two case studies. The first case study looks at the use of market research in the early stages of a campaign to test the effectiveness of the campaign's creative concept prior to its launch. For the purpose of this contribution, the creative concept is defined as the combination of artwork and text that will ultimately be presented to the public to attract their attention and communicate the principal campaign messages. The second case study is an example of how a survey can be used in the implementation stages of a campaign. Although this is not the typical use of survey research, it has been included to demonstrate how survey research can also be effectively used throughout the whole campaign procedure. For this case study a survey provided the ideal way of involving people in the campaign, generating media coverage, and creating direct pressure on the government.

Most academic textbooks paint a fairly clinical picture of the planning, implementation, and evaluation phases of a campaign. Unfortunately in the real world these processes do not always flow as smoothly as textbooks suggest: time and budget constraints, egos, and company politics can all cause a campaign to head off in the wrong direction. Books alone will not stop mistakes from happening, and the experience of practising campaign managers is invaluable in the early stages of a campaign.

Evaluating the success of a campaign can sometimes be a sobering experience. Despite a flurry of press releases, glossy publications, and even column inches the target audience can remain blissfully unaware of the efforts. Although few campaign managers would admit it, writing a report to the board on a campaign's achievements can often be the most creative part of the campaign. Too many campaign evaluations are nothing more than a list of actions, for example: printed 10,000 leaflets, sent out 10 press releases, or 1,000 people attended a launch event. So how can we, as practitioners, avoid these pitfalls and what should we do in the planning and implementation stages of a campaign to stop campaigns from heading off in the wrong direction? Two of the most important points that I have learnt from past experience are the need for honesty and clarity. Why?

We need to be honest about what we can realistically achieve through a campaign and honest about what we are really trying to achieve. If we want to improve our effectiveness we also need to be more honest about what we have achieved.

When pitching for business or trying to convince the Chief Executive to agree to a campaign proposal, it is all too easy to promise the earth. But in reality changing the public's habits and behaviour takes time and money. If the budget is only £10,000 and the deadline for the launch is a month away, be honest about what you are going to achieve. Don't pretend you are going to solve the world's problems overnight. By being realistic when planning your campaign goals you will also avoid unfair criticism at a later stage.

Campaigns very often have a large number of objectives, not only the publicly stated objectives such as increasing public awareness, but also private or hidden agendas. A conservation charity may launch a campaign to save a forest from destruction, but it may also be trying to outshine other similar charities and increase its total revenue. If we are not honest about our real aims and objectives, at least within the planning meetings for the campaign or when briefing designers, we will never develop a truly effective action plan. The campaign will be designed to satisfy one set of criteria and then ultimately judged on another.

A second important criterion for a campaign proposal is clarity. If you are not clear about what you are trying to achieve you are unlikely to achieve it and will probably not be able to tell when you have achieved it. It sounds like common sense but I frequently find myself writing objectives such as increasing the public's level of understanding about the importance of a healthy diet, or increasing the public's awareness about the work of my organization. Objectives like these are impossible to measure. That might be why so many public relations professionals like them so much. If, however, we are going to change anything, we need to be clearer about where we are starting from and where we want to end up. We should set down a time and money target and we need to be as clear as possible about our audience. A better way of writing the above objective would be to increase a representative sample of exciting and potential customers' understanding of the work of my organization by 10 per cent between now and the same time next year – and do that within a budget of £60,000.

Most campaigns run for at least six months or more. During this time a great deal can change both inside and outside an organization. The political environment in which we operate changes, and consequently corporate objectives and goals change. You, however, may still be in the middle of your campaign. It is all too easy for a campaign to acquire goals that were not set out in the original strategy. Once again, if you are not clear about what your original goals were you can get spun off in all sorts of directions and ultimately be judged against goals you never set out to achieve. Never start a campaign without a list of objectives by which the campaign will ultimately be measured. Make sure your client or chief executive agrees and appreciates what they are.

Clear objectives will also help identify any hidden agendas. If your chief executive has a hidden agenda to raise his or her own personal profile through the campaign, he/she has no right to complain later, unless he/she 'comes clean' when agreeing to the objectives by which the success of the campaign will be judged.

The following two case studies illustrate some of the points made above. They are real-life examples of how two campaigns were put together. They are not perfect examples of how campaigns should be run, but rather illustrations of difficulties you might face and the compromises that have to be made in the real world of campaigning.

## CASE STUDY ONE: 'WELCOME TO THE COUNTRYSIDE CAMPAIGN – A CONCEPT TEST'

### Overview

A national survey conducted by MORI in May 1994 on behalf of the National Farmers Union (NFU) on the public image of farming concluded that although the public had an overall favourable attitude towards farmers, many felt that the priorities were misplaced and that they were poor providers of information. This apparent lack of information generated a feeling of secrecy and mistrust. As a result of this survey, in 1995, the NFU launched a major public information campaign about farming.

The campaign focused on welcoming people onto farms and showing them what actually happens, showing people that farmers are doing a good job, and that people can come and see for themselves.

### Aims

The aims of the campaign were:

- to raise the profile of the positive aspects of British agriculture in national and local media;
- to create a better understanding of the role of the farmer;
- to strengthen public trust in farming.

It was felt that an advertising programme in national newspapers would be a valuable means of bringing this work to the attention of the key audiences and give the campaign a tremendous boost.

The campaign team was then faced with a problem: what was the most effective way of presenting this to the target audience? What should the adverts look like and what should they say? This is known as the creative concept, and deciding what it should be can be a nightmare. Further, once you have decided how to present your campaign, how do you know that it will get noticed and not offend your target audience?

The creative concept had to present an industry that was transparent and open to public inspection. It had to address key issues of concern to the public and get people to attend the special farm open days.

The creative concept used in any campaign is almost always an issue of hot debate; it sometimes seems that everybody from the managing director to the cleaner has a different opinion. It can be extremely difficult for a campaign manager to satisfy all the different demands. Too often organizations produce campaign literature that is solely based on what they want to tell the world. This approach often fails to address the key concerns of the target audience or results in a campaign that fails to grab people's attention. A concept test is an essential part of any campaign planning stage. The results are also an invaluable tool when justifying a particular creative strategy.

However, the decision to conduct research is not always that simple. It was not cheap and in this instance represented a large proportion of the overall budget. The cost of the research would have paid for a number of prime slots in national newspapers. This trade-off is one that many campaign managers will face: whether to use your budget to buy more space for a potentially poor advert or to test the advert's effectiveness and reduce the amount of exposure you can afford to give it. In this instance it is obvious that the research identified a number of ways to considerably improve the campaign material.

The concept test provided invaluable feedback for the design of the final campaign advertisement and literature. Without this information we could have produced literature that was ineffective or, worse, caused a hostile response from the public.

To make sure the campaign had maximum impact with the target audience, the draft promotional literature for 'Welcome to the Countryside' was shown to a representative sample of 150 people consistent with other creative concept tests of this type. The survey work was conducted by MORI.

The research objectives were as follows:

- How appealing is the concept?
- What does it communicate about farmers?
- Which of these communications generate the concept appeal?
- Which communication blocks or inhibits concept appeal?

The 150 interviews were conducted with people aged 20–55 and from social grades ABC1. Quotas also applied to sex, age, social grade, and work status. The interviewees were given boards with the promotional literature and creative concept presented on them. They were allowed to look at them for as long as they wished; the boards were then taken away and they were asked questions on the following topics:

- understanding of the concept;
- level of desirability and commitment generated by the concept;
- likes and dislikes;
- likelihood of calling a hotline/visiting a farm;
- confusion or credibility problems;
- attitudes towards farmers.

## The Results

### HOW APPEALING WAS THE CONCEPT?

The draft advertisement invoked a measurable response from 74 per cent of the people asked. A third of them were strongly committed to the key messages. This is an average result for this type of test. The concept was more appealing to women than to men, and to older people than younger people.

### WHAT DID PEOPLE REMEMBER MOST ABOUT THE ADVERTISEMENT AFTERWARDS?

The main message that people picked up from the promotional literature was farmers' commitment to conservation. Nine out of ten people recalled the message that farmers care about the environment.

Other messages that had a strong impact on people, with between six and seven out of ten people registering each message, were

- farmers care for animals and treat them well;
- the invitation to visit a farm;
- ideas about food quality;
- farmers are working to reduce pesticide use.

What are the most appealing aspects of the advertisement and how are these most effectively expressed?

### CONSERVATION

The idea that farmers are concerned about the environment and are acting to do something about it was a key contributor to the appeal of the concept. The most effective way of expressing this was:

- the idea of planting trees, hedgerows, shrublands, or flora, particularly if this is a voluntary activity;
- working with leading conservation charities to protect wildlife.

### ANIMAL WELFARE

The idea that farmers are a positive force for animal welfare was an appealing one. The most effective way of expressing this was:

- farmers care about animals;
- working with the leading animal welfare charities to improve standards;
- belief in the rights of animals from the animals' point of view.

### VISITING A FARM
The expression of this idea was readily received so that people could find out more about how a farm operates. It was more oriented towards education rather than entertainment.

### FOOD QUALITY
The idea that farmers provide healthy, fresh food, listen to and are responsive to consumers and produce milk to high quality-controlled standards are those that were most appealing.

### REDUCING PESTICIDE USE
Although people remembered this message it was not appealing and did not contribute to the overall appeal of the concept.

The promotional material also communicated a number of other ideas about farming which had potential to generate appeal if expressed more strongly:

- farmers work hard for a living;
- farming is an important part of the economy.

### WHAT PEOPLE DID NOT LIKE
Most of the key communications generated some level of incredibility. Conservation, animal welfare, pesticide reduction, and food quality claims were all challenged. However, it does not appear that any particular thing that was said in the concept caused the polarized response. Rather, there are indications that these claims of incredibility were based on the existing attitudes of respondents.

### RECOMMENDATIONS
The research made a number of key recommendations on how to maximize the campaign's impact on the target audience. It concluded that the campaign should be built around a number of key ideas.

- That farmers care about the countryside and work to look after the environment. Supporting evidence should be based on planting and wildlife conservation activities, highlighting links with other leading conservation organizations.
- That farmers have empathy for and understanding of animals, they respect their wishes and feelings, leading to humane and caring animal welfare practices. Any affiliation with leading animal welfare charities would strengthen this element of the campaign.
- That farming is an important part of the economy, vital for feeding the nation, and farmers work hard to be successful in this difficult and vital industry.

- That farmers produce our food, the fresh, healthy produce which we rely on having on our tables.
- There may be more to farming than people are aware of; maybe they should think about visiting a farm to see it for themselves.

With the recommendations of the market research, the campaign team was able to decide the best possible design for the advert with the confidence that its messages would have maximum impact on the target audience. Without this information we could have produced literature that was ineffective or, worse, caused a hostile response from the public.

## CASE STUDY TWO: THE NFU RURAL CRIME CAMPAIGN

### Overview

The National Farmers' Union (NFU) has been working to prevent rural crime for many years, but in early 1995 local membership groups started to report an increase in the incidence of crime. This was accompanied by an increase in the number of claims registered with the NFU Mutual insurance company and by the frustration of members at the lack of action by the Government and the police.

As a result the NFU decided to scale up its own level of activity to prevent crime. If we were to achieve our aims, we had to generate large-scale media interest in rural crime and generate pressure on the government for urgent action. The aim of the NFU was to act as the catalyst for action. The resources available for the initiative were extremely limited; we had to find a low-cost way of stirring up the issue. And as the NFU is paid for and answerable to its membership we had to find a way of involving them.

Official information on the level of rural crime was scarce and misleading, so the NFU decided to carry out its own nation-wide survey into the scope and scale of rural crime and use this as the basis of a national campaign.

This case study is not an example of how to conduct a nation-wide survey, but rather an example of how a survey can be used in the implementation stages of a campaign to help you achieve your aims. The survey academics may well raise their eyebrows at the sampling techniques used for the survey, but on a limited budget a truly representative survey was too expensive. In this instance the survey became the campaign strategy.

For the purpose of this campaign the announcement that we were going to conduct the campaign was a valuable lobbying tool in its own right.

### Aims

The aims of the campaign were:

- to raise the profile of rural crime;
- to apply pressure on both the Government and the police for increased funding and innovation to solve the problem of rural crime;
- to continue to position the NFU as the leading organization working for a living countryside.

Accurate information on the scale of rural crime is scarce. Official government statistics released in April showed a sharp increase in recorded crime over the past ten years.

But these figures can be misleading as they do not break down the incidence into areas small enough to be an effective measure. Furthermore, the Government's own surveys show that nationally, over 70 per cent of crimes are not reported by the statistics because they are not reported by the public. The NFU could lobby Government and the police effectively only if we could clearly demonstrate the size and nature of the problem.

The NFU launched its Rural Crime Survey in June. It was sent to members through the in-house corporate magazine, *British Farmer*. The survey was supported by an article on crime, and a £100 prize draw was included as an incentive. The survey asked members:

- if they had been a victim of crime;
- the nature and time of the crimes;
- the cost of the crime;
- their action to prevent crime;
- whether they thought enough was being done to prevent crime by the police/and Government; and
- what action would they like to see taken to prevent crime.

The survey seemed to touch a raw nerve, and over 1,200 farmers responded, making it one of the most comprehensive surveys of rural crime ever undertaken. The results were surprising and revealing. Eight out of every ten farmers have been the victims of crime in the past three years. And the incidence of criminal activity in our countryside is increasing all the time.

Through the survey we heard of small family farms which have been virtually forced out of business as a result of vandalism and arson; how farmers have had to spend thousands on security systems; and of some criminal incidents where joyriders have killed livestock and destroyed growing crops. Incidents range from the cruel and devious to the outright bizarre. One member woke up to find his entire field of potatoes had disappeared overnight.

Our survey revealed that fly tipping and theft of farm equipment accounts for nearly half of all crimes suffered by farmers and growers. Vandalism and burglary from farm outbuildings make up one in three incidents, with theft of vehicles, burglary from home, theft of farm gates, and arson all close behind on the list of top crimes. The fastest growing types of crime are waste dumping and vandalism, both of which, according to the survey, have more than doubled in the past three years. Incidents of vandalism include breaking down hedgerows and fences, joyriding through crops, and damage to farm machinery. One farmer was prompted to remark that 'If I fail to get my hay bales under cover within four hours after harvesting, they are almost guaranteed to be slashed, rolled or burnt.'

Over 90 per cent of the survey respondents felt that more could be done by the Government to prevent crime, and 18 per cent felt the police should do more. Time after time farmers reported 'a lack of interest from the local police when they report criminal incidents'. Over two-thirds of respondents called for more visible policing of countryside areas, followed by tougher sentences for criminals and an increased number of farmwatch schemes.

The results of the survey were press released and an article was published in *British Farmer*, resulting in extensive national and local media coverage. The effect was strengthened by the fact that we were able to provide a wide range of victims and breakdown of rural crime by county. More importantly, the Minister was called to give a radio interview and made to answer to the criticism that over 90 per cent of UK farmers felt the Government should do more. From then on they were forced to defend their performance record on crime. The Minister agreed to meet the President of the NFU to discuss the issue and also agreed to speak at a conference which the NFU ran together with Crime Concern.

The campaign is continuing, but we have recently heard encouraging news from the Government that next year's funding for police forces will take into account the particular problems of rural areas. So far an increase of £240 million has been proposed.

## CONCLUSION

Understanding why campaigns go wrong is extremely important if the communications industry is to move forward. Case studies have a vital part to play in that learning process. Real-life examples of how academic principles are applied in practice are the best guide to what works and what does not in the real world. In this contribution the case studies demonstrate the role survey research can play in shaping and sharpening a campaign in both the planning and implementation stages.

It would be easy for the campaign manager to try to save money and not conduct research, but as the first example demonstrates, working on instinct alone can be dangerous and ultimately reduce the effectiveness of the campaign. The second case study explores the broader use of surveys in campaigns and shows that they can also have a part to play in the implementation stages of a campaign.

# 6 Public Opinion Information and Campaign Strategies: An American Case Study

## Ronald L. Holzhacker

Campaign strategists need a great deal of information about their electoral environment to plan an effective, winning campaign for a candidate. They certainly need to understand the strengths and weaknesses of their own candidate, including his public character and the kinds of issue stances the candidate has taken publicly before. The strategist must also know everything possible about their candidate's competitors, their strengths and weaknesses, their character traits, and their previously taken issue stances. But most importantly, the strategist needs to know an awful lot about the public or – more narrowly and more importantly in the American case because of low rates of voter turnout – the prospective voters in the upcoming election. It is necessary to judge the attitudes and perspectives of the voters in a variety of areas: what issues does the public view as most important, what does it think should be done about these issues, what image does it have of the candidate and his competitors? But one is not often so interested in the attitudes of the average voter toward these questions, but the attitudes of various identifiable groups in the electorate to whom a candidate may be able to appeal by tailoring a message to them.

This essay will focus on the use of public opinion information in the planning and implementation of strategic communication during election campaigns in the United States. It will discuss the various instruments for measuring and gauging public opinion at different stages of an election campaign and the strategic use of this information for a campaign, especially the development of effective campaign communication. After a brief review of the use of public opinion information in election campaigns in the USA and the assistance which national campaigns may provide to state and local campaigns, the essay will focus on the use of polls in a recent American election campaign at the state level. The setting is the 1998 governor's race in Minnesota, presented as a strategically complex 'game' involving three close competitors.

If one views a campaign in a game theoretic perspective, one may analyse the sequence of moves and countermoves by the competing candidates in terms of players, strategies, and payoffs. Campaigns may be viewed as a sequential game of move and countermove by the players, culminating on election day with the winner decided upon by the choice of the electorate. Campaigns are designed to secure one's core constituencies, persuade undecided swing voters, and turn both groups of voters out on election day to vote. The role of polling and other forms of public information during the campaign is to provide information to inform strategy based on the current attitudes of the electorate, and secondly to inform the campaign about expected payoffs in terms of electoral support if a given strategy is pursued.

The central theme of this article is that contemporary political campaigns use a variety of information sources about the electorate to make strategic decisions about their communication with the electorate. Such information has become increasingly important as campaigns pursue a strategy of priming the electorate. The emphasis on priming proposes that candidates do not primarily attempt to change the attitudes, values, or issue preferences of voters during a campaign, but attempt to focus the attention of the electorate on a chosen agenda and make the issues salient in the voter's mind. The concept of priming developed from social psychologists' analysis of the role of attitudes and information in decision making. Individuals are presumed to have a set of enduring attitudes, but whether these attitudes will have an impact when a decision must be made is dependent on whether these attitudes are retrieved from memory (Iyengar and Kinder, 1987; Aldrich et al., 1989; Iyengar, 1990; Krosnick and Kinder, 1990; Lavine et al., 1992). In order for this technique to be successful, the candidate must capitalize on existing perceptions of the electorate toward candidate and opponent, as well as their views toward issues by reinforcing and amplifying existing held beliefs and attitudes.

Candidates have a variety of ways to communicate messages to the potential electorate, including free and paid mass communication, campaign rallies and appearances before groups, and direct mail. Modern American election campaigns are struggles fought primarily through the mass media. Candidates seek to present favourable images of themselves and their approach to issues to the voter through the mass media. The mass communication of campaigns is focused in two directions:

1 attempts to influence the media agenda, and thus to reach voters who attend to news and information sources, so-called *free media*, and
2 the direct communication of candidates which reaches the voters unmediated, which is traditionally called *paid media*.

Candidates have complete control over their paid media, but their efforts to reach voters through the free media is filtered and mediated by journalists before reaching the voters. (The exception to this is a candidate's participation in televised debates, where candidates may reach voters at no cost, but they may speak directly to voters.) Candidates may use traditional forms of direct communication with voters which are heavily dependent on local party organization involvement, such as door-to-door campaigning or distributing party leaflets, or they may utilize forms of mass communication such as newspaper advertisements, billboards, radio, and above all else in modern campaigns, television commercials to reach the broadest possible audience.

Campaigns have various instruments for gauging and scientifically measuring public opinion in order to reach strategic decisions in the campaign and to design effective campaign communication. A well-designed, scientific public opinion poll using random sampling provides a basis for understanding a population based on interviews with a selected few. This is the best assurance that the information gained is relevant to the electorate as a whole and allows one to also systematically analyse important segments within the electorate that a candidate may wish to communicate. But a very different kind of technique for gauging public opinion, posing questions to a focus group, may also be helpful in assessing the progress of a campaign and to judge proposed campaign communication before airing.

Knowledge about public opinion, gained through scientific polling and increasingly supplemented by focus groups, can be effectively used to:

1 determine the current strengths and weakness of a candidate and those of competitors,
2 determine the most important issues in the voters' minds and their present position on those issues,
3 determine the demographics of the electorate and the accessibility to the campaign of important segments of the electorate, and to
4 identify core supporters and what they need to hear from a candidate, and how to reach out and win the support of undecided voters.

## TYPES OF POLLS AND FOCUS GROUPS

Polling consultants routinely design different kinds of polls to discover information about potential voters on which to base decisions during different phases of a campaign. For example, a pre-decision poll may be used by a candidate to decide whether or not he wants to seek a particular office. Such polls typically measure the name recognition of a potential candidate and may offer a thumbnail sketch of the public's positive and negative views toward the person. A pre-decision poll may also be used by referendum organizers to decide whether or not they should mount a referendum campaign on a given issue. These pre-decision polls may be used to approach potential financial donors, who may be interested in the name recognition of a potential candidate and how favourably the public sees him or her, in order to gauge the probability that the candidate can mount a successful campaign and win.

Once a decision has been made whether to run for office or mount a referendum initiative, campaigns often then commission a more extensive bench-mark poll done immediately before the organization begins to campaign and communicate earnestly with the broader public. These bench-mark polls typically include questions concerning the level of candidate support, candidate image and that of competitors, attitudes and positions on issues, and demographic data on the respondents. The polls typically also include a type of question that distinguishes them markedly from the kind of polling performed by the news media or academics. These are 'push' questions, hypothetical questions which ask how, if the respondent had a particular piece of additional information about a candidate or his or her competitors, this might effect their evaluation of the candidate. These questions allow a candidate to attempt to judge the impact of communicating a given message to the electorate before actually uttering the words in a speech or purchasing advertising to send the message. The final type of poll is the tracking poll designed to gauge the changing levels of support for the various candidates during the course of the campaign. These polls are typically conducted every evening, and a rolling three day average is presented to the campaign strategists to determine the current level of support for the candidate. Strategists may use these to see what impact the last few days of media reports, debates, or advertising are having on the public's support for the various candidates in the race.

In addition to scientific polling using random samples, campaigns also use focus groups to attempt to gauge public opinion in a more informal way. Focus groups typically consist of a small group of people (typically 10–20 individuals) brought together in a room to discuss questions presented to them by a trained facilitator. The discussants in the room often share either a demographic characteristic, for example, senior citizens in a given state, or share a political attribute, for example, registered voters undecided in the current race. Nonetheless, because the focus group participants are not drawn from a random sample, there is no way to determine how representative the group is to a wider population one might be interested in. But focus groups are often heralded by campaign strategists for providing qualitative information about the progress of a campaign, the important issues in the race, and how the personal traits of the candidates are perceived by potential voters. Strategists may feel they can gain a more intuitive understanding of a race through these in-depth group conversations than they can from reading polling results alone.

In addition to providing this kind of qualitative information about the campaign from ordinary voters, focus groups are very good for two additional purposes to a campaign. Focus groups may be used to develop questions which can be used in scientific polling. Thus, campaign strategists may develop an insight about a race that they then may wish to measure scientifically through polling. Finally, focus groups may be used appropriately to test campaign communication before it is broadcasted or printed. For example, often new television campaign commercials will be tested before a focus group to test the reaction of the audience and to judge its effectiveness at communicating the desired message.

A new kind of very informal focus group has also emerged in the last few election cycles in the USA. These are called 'mall-intercepts' and involve people being asked individually at a shopping mall if they would mind answering a few questions about a current political campaign or giving their reaction to proposed campaign communication. The idea is to inexpensively and quickly gather brief impressions from suburban households about the course of a campaign. It may be argued that a harried shopper going about his or her normal routine is giving the same kind of brief attention to these matters that they do to politics generally, and thus their responses are a more spontaneous (perhaps more genuine?) reaction than occurs during participation in a lengthy poll or a traditional focus group. Of course, one is reaching only a certain kind of voter in these mall environments, and one has no idea how representative the person standing before one is of a certain group.

## THE NATURE OF PUBLIC OPINION AND THE IMPACT OF ELECTION CAMPAIGNS

Before considering more precisely how campaign strategists use public opinion information, it is helpful to be aware of the general structure of public opinion in the USA. A constant theme of public opinion research has been the relative ignorance of the majority of Americans toward political issues (see e.g. Converse, 1964). In a view summarized by scholars of a recent book on political campaigns: 'Superficiality in issue constructs, inattentiveness to current events, and wildly fluctuating viewpoints gave scholars reason to distrust the rationality of the average American voter' (Johnson-Cartee and Copeland, 1997). Scholars such as these divide the American electorate into four groups: (1) the chronic know-nothings, who are not interested in political issues and do not seek information about them, making up about 4 per cent of the population (Sego, 1977); (2) the general public, making up about 70–75 per cent of the American population, who have very little interest in politics and do not actively seek information about the political process; (3) an attentive public, made up of individuals interested in political issues who actively seek information about politics, discuss matters with their family, friends, and colleagues, and may join political groups, who make up between 10 and 17 per cent of the population depending on the issue; and (4) the opinion-making elite, who share the general characteristics of the attentive public, but are actively engaged in the day-to-day political process, including office-holders, lobbyists, consultants, and news reporters, making up a miniscule part of the whole electorate (Johnson-Cartee and Copeland, 1997: 57). These authors conclude that in the final analysis, public opinion 'is not opinion *of* the public or of publics, but opinion *made* (emphasis in original) public' (Johnson-Cartee and Copeland, 1997: 57, citing Vatz, 1976: 206). This approach focuses on the power of an elite to help form and guide public opinion.

This picture of a relatively inattentive and disinterested electorate has always raised concerns about the impact that campaign communication may have on the electorate. Early electoral research conducted by the Columbia Group (Lazarsfeld et al., 1944; Berelson et al., 1954) in the USA was concerned about the potential impact of the use of new forms of mass communication following the experience of propaganda in World War II.

The scholars were relieved to find little evidence of persuasion over the short period of a campaign. The group's research indicated that the main effects of campaigns are to 'activate' the underlying attitudes, values, and partisan dispositions of the electorate and make them relevant for elections. A substantial portion of subsequent campaign research has supported these findings (e.g. Patterson, 1980; Miller and Shanks, 1982; Markus, 1988; Finkel, 1993; Finkel and Schrott, 1995).

Great effort has been expended to discover the determinants of these underlying attitudes and values of the American, as well as other Western electorates. Research began to focus on such determinants of voting as class and religious cleavages in society (Lipset and Rokkan, 1967) and the impact which party identification has on the vote (Campbell et al., 1960). The great importance of social cleavages and party identification on vote choice has been shown in many Western democracies. The development of statistical models able to predict the outcome of elections even before the campaign begins lends credence to the continuing power of these concepts for vote choice (Rosenstone, 1983; Markus, 1988; Bartels, 1992; Gelman and King, 1993).

These traditional approaches left little room for campaign effects on voting. However, campaigns have become much more important to the electoral success of political parties and candidates over the past two decades due to the impact of societal change on the electorates in the USA and other advanced industrial democracies. Evidence of weakening attachments to parties began in the United States (Converse, 1976; Nie et al., 1979) and soon appeared in many European party systems (Dalton et al., 1984; Crewe and Denver, 1985). Evidence of a decline in party identification has been generalized into a hypothesis of partisan dealignment in these democracies (Dalton, 1984; Dalton et al., 1984; Inglehart, 1990). This hypothesis traces the decline in attachments to political parties to general trends associated with social and political modernization.

Dealignment is caused by both macro-level changes which have changed the role of political parties in democratic society and to micro-level changes occurring within the electorates of advanced industrial democracies. In terms of the macro-level, whereas political parties once had more control over the information reaching voters, today mass media play a larger role in informing the electorate about politics. Thus, instead of learning about the choices confronting a voter at a campaign rally or from party volunteers, television and newspapers have become the primary sources of campaign information for most voters (Dalton, 1997). This information includes both television news programming and newspaper stories, the content of which is under the control of the media, and campaign advertising, which is under the control of the candidates. In terms of micro-level changes occurring in the electorates of advanced industrial societies, increasing educational levels have improved the political and cognitive resources of these electorates. More political information available to a more educated electorate means citizens are less likely to defer to party elites or to support a party's candidate merely out of habit

(Dalton, 1984, 1997; Inglehart, 1990). Dalton concludes that as the influence of long-term sources of partisanship erode, other factors will likely play a larger role in voter choice. He states that this might 'encourage the public to judge candidates and parties on their policies and governmental performance – producing a deliberative public that more closely proximates the classic democratic ideal. However, he notes that on the other hand, 'the lack of long-standing partisan loyalties may also make electorates more vulnerable to manipulation and demagogic appeals' (Dalton, 1997: 15, citing Holmberg, 1994: 113–14).

It is clear from existing campaign research that the impact of campaigns on voter activation and reinforcement are very important to the electoral success of candidates (Kinder, 1996). The lessons of campaigns learned from the Columbia group's landmark study of the 1940 American Presidential race continue to be validated: the reassembly of old coalitions (Huckfeldt and Sprague, 1995; Johnston et al., 1992), providing information to the electorate (Gelman and King, 1993), and priming vote choice (Iyengar and Kinder, 1987; Jacobs and Shapiro, 1994).

More recent research indicates that election campaigns have impacts other than the main effects of activation and reinforcement, especially among undecided floating voters who decide late which candidate to cast their vote for. In the American case, research has demonstrated that campaigns not only reinforce and activate latent partisan dispositions, they also are able to persuade and convert some voters (Holbrook, 1996). In elections abroad, a study of the 1990 election for the German parliament found a clear shift in evaluation of the top candidates and their parties over the final six weeks of the campaign and demonstrated that this was a consequence of exposure to information during the campaign (Semetko and Schoenbach, 1994). Another study of the same election campaign found that one in eight voters reacted to the campaign in ways that were not predictable from their predispositions toward a party or their prior preferences. The study concluded that in close elections these voters hold the key to the outcome and that successful campaign efforts can win the support of up to two-thirds of these voters (Finkel and Schrott, 1993: 30). These studies on campaigns and elections suggest that it is useful to analyse how candidates use campaign communication to both activate the prior attitudes, values, and partisan dispositions of the greater part of the electorate, and to appeal to the smaller, yet growing percentage of late-deciding voters who make up their mind during the campaign itself.

The rise of television has had an extremely important impact on modern election campaigns. Television's dominance as a communication tool for campaigns in the United States is well known (Diamond and Bates, 1984), and presidential candidates now spend well over half of their money on producing and broadcasting television campaign commercials (Devlin, 1995). In a pace-setting book on election campaigns, *The Unseeing Eye*, Patterson and McClure (1976) took an early look at the impact television was having on American elections. Research in the USA suggests that voters receive and remember much more information concerning issues from television commercials than they do from network news broadcasts (Patterson and McClure, 1976: 104). This was particularly true of those who do not read newspapers or were poorly informed. Others conducted research into those most likely to be impacted by such advertisements. 'Uncommitted voters, highly interested voters, and partisans of the advertised candidate are most likely to absorb the content of campaign commercials' (Owen, 1991: 25). These commercials allow the campaign strategists to bypass the media filter, applicable to news broadcasts and newspaper coverage of the campaign, which may change, alter, distort, or interpret the candidate's desired message. As the power of campaign advertising to deliver votes has increased, the value of careful analysis of public opinion information to plan and implement this communication has grown immensely.

## SEGMENTATION OF THE ELECTORATE
## FOR THE PURPOSES OF TARGETING

What candidates are especially interested in gaining from survey research is a deep understanding of 'Who are my potential voters?'. Understanding the electorate through a process of segmentation, of splitting the electorate into identifiable groups characterized by relevant characteristics – socio-economic, age cohort, geography, or issue orientation – can be used to develop appropriate messages and to concentrate communication and persuasive efforts where there is most to gain. Market segmentation in election research is the search for different subsets in the electorate in which various communication strategies may be developed to reach, persuade, and mobilize a particular part of the electorate. The usefulness of electoral market segments to the campaign strategists depends on the accessibility and size of the segment and their differentiation from one another (Niemöller, 1998). The segments should be defined on the basis of common characteristics which can be reached through the media and which are sufficiently large to allow them to be reached in an economical way.

A number of different kinds of segmentation of the electorate are possible:

1  geographical segmentation – regional differences are often the basis of segmentation. This is especially important in US presidential campaigns where the electoral college drives campaigns to concentrate their efforts on large states where the election may be close;
2  demographic segmentation – segmentation based on characteristics of voters such as socio-economic class, occupation, age, sex, religion, education, or ethnicity;
3  life-style segmentation – general value orientations of groups of voters, such as rural traditionalists, suburban families, or college students;
4  issue segmentation – voters who feel especially strongly about an issue or a given set of issues.

It should be kept in mind that it is not possible through mass media to communicate exclusively with a single segment which one may have identified in the electorate.

One can use vehicles which will be extremely efficient (cost versus number of people in the segment reached), but the message will also reach individuals who do not belong to the segment. Thus, it is important that the message does not alienate other segments important to the candidate, and if the message has at least some resonance with other segments then all the better. An additional consideration is that one may not want to provoke a strong negative reaction to the message developed for a particular segment, which may act as a catalyst to mobilize supporters of competitors. Finally, while it is appropriate that messages developed for different segments emphasize different parts of a candidate's issue or image profile, fundamental conflicts in the messages sent to various segments will be picked up immediately by the media and amplified to the detriment of the candidate.

## THE DEVELOPMENT OF POLLING TO GUIDE CAMPAIGN STRATEGY

The use of scientific public opinion surveys in the USA to understand the nature of public opinion began in the late 1940s, although three early practitioners of scientific polling, George Gallup, Archibald Crossley, and Elmo Roper, practised their craft to correctly predict the victory of Franklin Roosevelt for President in 1936. The scholarly interest in measuring and quantifying public opinion had been awakened in the USA from the experience on both sides of the Atlantic during World War II.

It was not long before candidates realized that these new scientific techniques could be used successfully in helping them make strategic decisions in a campaign. In 1946, Elmo Roper used polling to assist New York congressional candidate Jacob Javits. Javits attributed part of his success to the poll and explained he used it, not to arrive at his issue positions in the campaign, but to demonstrate to the voters that there was 'substantial agreement on the major issues' with the voters (Friedenberg, 1997: 32). The first time polling services were used in a presidential campaign was that of General Dwight Eisenhower in 1952. Here polling was used to help determine the themes for the limited number of television spots that the campaign aired that year.

But it was not until 1960 and the presidential campaign of John F. Kennedy that modern scientific polling was used broadly in all phases of the strategic planning of a campaign. Jacobs and Shapiro (1994) analysed Kennedy's 1960 campaign and were particularly interested in how the innovative public opinion surveys produced by Louis Harris 'heightened the Kennedy campaign's interest and skill in using position taking to shape the candidate's image' (Jacobs and Shapiro, 1994: 528). The research suggests that a candidate may use popular policy stances on issues to 'prime' the electorate's standards for evaluating the candidates.

Harris was considered an integral part of the Kennedy campaign, conducting 66 polls during the primary and general election campaign, and reporting his results to the campaign through both written accounts and frequent meetings with the candidate. These polls were focused both on the issue concerns of the public and their perceptions of Kennedy. Harris's surveys asked not only about the most important problem facing the country, but also tracked the public's preferred policy direction in alleviating the problem. In addition, the polling gave the campaign important information about the public's perception of Kennedy's image. Recent interviews and archival research has shown that the campaign viewed Kennedy's policy positions and the public's perception of his personal image as interconnected strategic concerns. Thus, when polling was showing that Kennedy was seen as 'too slick' and 'lack(ing) depth' the campaign recommended that a 'Kennedy-identified program' be developed that would appeal to two groups of voters: party activists and more moderate centrist voters (Jacobs and Shapiro, 1994: 531). The objective was to identify Kennedy with new and dynamic approaches to the country while tying Richard Nixon to the 'do-nothingism' of the last eight years of Republican leadership in the White House. 'Campaign officials calculated that emphasizing Kennedy's proposals for addressing several highly salient issues would serve as a "campaign tool" for creating an appealing image' (Jacobs and Shapiro, 1994: 531). The authors of the study concluded that the campaign not only *responded* to public opinion, but also *directed* voters' evaluations of Kennedy's personal character by strategically raising certain issues to prime the electorate.

As the 1960s progressed, the use of polling to guide campaign strategy spread from Presidential and Congressional races to state and local races as well. This information was increasingly used to aid in the development of campaign messages as television entered more and more people's homes and politics was transformed by this new medium. Public opinion information has become increasingly valuable in setting campaign strategy since the early 1970s due to (1) a decline in party identification and an increase in undecided, independent voters, (2) changes in the role of political parties, especially in the nominating processes of the major parties, (3) changes in communication technologies, specifically the ability to send repetitive messages into people's homes via television (Friedenberg, 1997). These changes mean the main campaign strategy has shifted from one based on sending group cues to the core constituencies of a political party, to one based on priming designed to appeal to undecided voters who may swing from candidate to candidate, and to get these voters to the ballot box on election day. This change in campaign strategy makes having reliable information about the attitudes and perceptions of the electorate essential to figure out how to appeal to these undecided voters. Whereas previously, messages could be formulated based on the need to mobilize core groups and be of the rather simple form 'I support your group and what it stands for', today's messages must be tailored from campaign to campaign and are much more dependent on the vagaries of the current situation felt by undecided voters.

## NATIONAL CAMPAIGNS AS A PROVIDER OF
## INFORMATION AND SUPPORT TO STATE CAMPAIGNS

National campaigns have traditionally played a role in state campaigns as a provider of information about the electorate. This sharing of information is a way for state candidates to use the greater resources of national campaigns, and provide the national campaigns with something they can trade for endorsements or assistance by the state campaigns. The national campaign might share or co-operate in the production of two different types of information about the electorate: first, state polling data and second, individual voter identification. Voter identification operations are run by national campaigns in key states, consisting of volunteers telephoning people two or three months before an election and asking what issues are the most important to them for the upcoming election and whether they have firmly decided which candidate to support or are leaning toward. The campaign then follows up by periodically mailing undecided voters and those leaning toward their candidate with direct mail geared to the issues the potential voter has identified as the most important to him or her.

But there is evidence that national campaigns are beginning to be less involved in these voter identification operations. Take for example the case of the 1996 Clinton/Gore campaign in the state of Ohio. There, the state director for the campaign, Jim DeMay, explained that his most important tasks were to win over local politicians and bring them on board in supporting the campaign, and secondly, to establish a get-out-the-vote apparatus to reach out to the base democratic vote (white ethnics and urban minority groups) and turn them out to vote.[1] The campaign at the state field level also had a persuasive component, trying to win over undecided voters. The field campaign attempted to reach such voters through direct mail, efforts to attract free media, and campaign rallies and other events. But in 1996, the Clinton campaign in Ohio and many other states did not use the traditional method of identifying individual voters by telephone and then sending them targeted mail to persuade them. Instead the campaign relied on national public opinion polling that let them know about the thinking of identifiable groups in the electorate. So, for example, when they decided they needed to target women in the campaign, they bought commercially available lists of women of a certain age group, residing in suburban counties in the state, and mailed them a letter on an issue identified in the national polling as especially important and relevant to this group in their vote decision. Thus the campaign shifted its information source for decision making from individual identification by telephone based on voting history, issue interest, and current commitment to a candidate, to a national analysis of public opinion polling used in conjunction with commercial lists organized by demographic characteristics.

National campaigns may also typically be helpful to state races by arranging a campaign appearance by a national leader or surrogate (often the spouse or a member of the cabinet) with the state candidate. The Deputy White House Political Director in the Clinton administration, Linda Moore, explained that polling information is used to help decide where a visit by the President may be helpful.[2] Polling data helps the White House decide where a campaign visit by the President may help a state candidate and where it may not. In some cases, the White House explains to candidates in particular districts that they may be better off distancing themselves a bit from the President. The White House explained that polling provides the campaign with information about how a particular message is being received by various demographic groups in the electorate and assists in the process of modifying the message to firm up support among groups whose support may be slipping.

Moore explained that polling is useful to 'find areas where you are experiencing weak links in the demographic chain and then to identify issues to play to them and buck up the parts where you are weaker'. With this information, strategic decisions can be reached in deploying resources of the campaign, both in terms of money for the state's media purchases and candidate time. Moore also explained how a strategy of issue priming refines and strengthens the public's perception of a candidate's image. Moore said that although the 1996 Clinton campaign found it unnecessary to dwell much on the President's image, they nevertheless thought that 'when you buck up parts of his policies, or bring forward those policies which really talk responsibility and being tough, that will then say something about him as a person'. She cited an example of how one might want to reach a particular group, say senior citizen voters. If you want to appeal to this group you might talk about issues like Social Security and Medicare, but this group of voters also wants to hear something about defence because they want to be able to think about the President in terms of a leader they feel comfortable with as Commander in Chief. Voters also often feel more positive toward leaders who they think are sympathetic toward people like themselves. The White House explained that the most important thing about President Clinton's image and the reason he keeps solid public approval numbers is that people give him high ratings for the assertion 'He cares for people like me'.

## THE USE OF PUBLIC OPINION FOR STRATEGIC ACTION IN A THREE-CANDIDATE RACE

A look at the 1998 Minnesota race for Governor, although unique in many respects, may be insightful in understanding certain aspects of contemporary campaigns in the USA. The three persons in the race were: (1) Hubert 'Skip' Humphrey III, who had emerged as the Democratic-Farmer-Labor party (the Democratic party in Minnesota) candidate after a bruising primary competing against other prominent sons of former politicians in the state, (2) a Republican candidate, Mayor Norm Coleman of the City of St. Paul, who had recently switched from the Democratic Party, and (3) Jesse Ventura, best known in the state as a television pro-wrestling star and running as the Reform Party candidate. The campaign may be a harbinger of future campaigns in the USA in which populist figures who already have media fame are able to achieve political success by using an anti-politician, anti-traditional party message to turn out disenchanted voters.

Campaigns are usually two-person games, and strategies are pursued to maximize one's own vote and minimize the votes of one's competitor. Part of the public opinion collection during a campaign is designed to test various messages and see whether real world use of the message will be beneficial in attracting more voters than it repels. The problem in a three-person race is that it is difficult to determine whether, by pushing down another's level of support – for example, by raising certain issues and going on the attack – those voters will be attracted to the one going on the attack or to the third candidate in the race. This makes it difficult for the campaign to know what the payoffs will be for a given set of actions during the campaign. To analyse the race in Minnesota, I interviewed the campaign managers for each of the three candidates a few months after the election. Of special interest was the kind of information they acquired about the public opinion and how they used their analysis of this information to make strategic decisions in the campaign, especially in setting their free and paid media strategies. These interviews demonstrate that a great deal of information about public opinion is often available free to a campaign for free from public sources, and can be used quite effectively by insurgent, under-funded candidates. Secondly, the interviews suggest that polling data must be carefully interpreted in a true three-person race, because it is both difficult to judge the level of support for third-party candidates and to judge which candidate will benefit the most by raising certain issues.

Hubert Humphrey's campaign managers, Eric Johnson and Amy Finken, needed to turn their candidate's long-running success as Attorney General of the State into electoral victory in the race for Governor.[3] The strategists had access to a wide array of private polling and information from focus groups; a quell of information stretching back over his years as a state-wide candidate and office holder. The polls had been conducted each year or so over decades. The strategists thus knew a great deal about how the electorate's view of Humphrey had developed over a long period of time. Immediately before the campaign started in earnest the campaign did a baseline survey and also conducted focus groups consisting of separate groups of traditionally Democratic voting men and women. Even at this stage of the campaign, the strategists were interested in how to set-up the battle with Norm Coleman, the likely Republican candidate in the general election race. In fact throughout the campaign, the strategists admitted that they had 'focused like a laser beam on Norm Coleman and largely ignored Jesse Ventura'.[4] This persistent focus on the Republican candidate, in terms of polling, campaign strategy, and campaign advertising would lead in the end to the surprising victory of the third-party candidate in the race.

The main issue emphases and themes of the general election campaign were based on this early public opinion information. The campaign used the response to the question 'What are the most important issues facing the state?' to help decide which issues to make salient during the campaign. The strategists tested tax issues early because they knew the Republican candidate would raise these issues to attempt to exploit the public's perception of the Humphrey name as an 'old-fashioned, tax and spend liberal' (in the Republican rhetoric). The campaign thus tested the public's response to different kinds of tax cuts to see which one sounded the most appealing. The different proposals all had the same impact on the state treasury, but were alternatively worded to either emphasize a large total dollar figure of the tax or the amount that each family would be expected to save under a tax cut of that amount.

In addition to the proposal to cut taxes as a way to disburse the state's considerable revenue surplus, the campaign decided to emphasize Humphrey's 'significant policy achievements' for the state. Here, Humphrey's widely touted recent achievement in winning a multi-billion dollar settlement from the tobacco industry for the state a few months before the campaign began was fairly straightforward, but the sometimes arcane achievements of a state Attorney General, the chief lawyer representing the state, proved difficult to discuss and communicate in the campaign. In the end, the strategists conceded that they had focused on too many issues and that they were 'not successful in getting voters to know him deeply on any one topic'.[5] The campaign at times veered dangerously close to presenting the candidate as deserving to be governor because of his long service to the state and his family legacy, while failing to present a concrete vision for the future.

Weekly polling by the Humphrey campaign began eight weeks before election day. This polling no longer focused much on issues, but on favourability ratings of the candidates and how 'hot and cold' the public viewed the candidates. The campaign also used the polls to test an argument or two and to see how voters might respond to it. These questions were in the form, if a candidate says X, will you think more or less of him? Focus groups were also conducted during this period, and participants were targeted to hear from swing voters, especially men between 39 and 55. Polling results had shown Humphrey stronger among women voters, so the campaign used focus groups of 10–12 middle aged voters from the suburban areas of the Twin-Cities (Minneapolis and St. Paul) metropolitan area, to find out what their perceptions were and what they needed to hear from Humphrey to win their vote. Once again, separate focus groups of men and women were assembled, to try to qualitatively understand the differences in thinking between the genders that had become apparent from the polling data.

The Humphrey strategists used the focus groups to get a feeling not only for how issues were coming across in the campaign, but also for Humphrey's image. They asked the focus groups: if they were invited over to Humphrey's house for dinner, what did they think they would be served? The responses were typically native Minnesota dishes like Walleye fish and the favourite of Sunday church socials – hot-dish casserole. But the campaign found it difficult to figure out 'how to communicate with people about his

Minnesota values'. Humphrey's campaign slogan 'Believe in Minnesota' tried to capture these feelings that Humphrey was part of the state's identity. In the end, both Humphrey's polling information and his campaign communication were focused on what he had accomplished for the state, instead of offering a vision of the future guided by his deep understanding of Minnesota values.

The campaign strategist for Norm Coleman, George Georgacas[6] began polling two months before the election and included questions in five areas: (1) likelihood to vote – including questions whether respondent is registered to vote, interest in the election, self-appraisal of whether one will go to the polls; (2) general feeling toward the direction the state is currently moving; (3) general impressions of the candidate and competitors in the race; (4) open response questions concerning what the respondent had heard in the media (newspapers, television reports, and television advertisements) and the impact of this information on the respondent; and (5) testing various messages on the respondents, in the form of 'If we say X in the campaign, are you more likely to vote for Coleman or Humphrey?'.

The Coleman campaign used their polling data to decide that they needed to connect the public's concern about taxes and spending with their decision on whom to support in the race for governor. The polling had revealed that many voters believed that cutting taxes and holding down spending deserved the greatest or the second greatest attention in the race and believed that Coleman would be better than Humphrey on the issue, but were not yet supporting Coleman. These voters were labelled 'opportunity voters'; Coleman needed to reach them and win their support. The campaign initially thought that raising various moral issues might be beneficial to the campaign, but the polling revealed that, although raising these issues would be welcomed by some of their conservative Republican core-voters, Coleman's opportunity voters in terms of taxes and spending were split on these moral issues. In fact the polling indicated that raising these issues would slightly benefit Humphrey over Coleman.

However, as the campaign increasingly looked like a close three-person race by the third week of October, and all three candidates were trying to appeal to the undecided middle of the road voter discussing taxing and spending issues, the Coleman campaign decided it would be beneficial to develop messages designed to appeal to conservative moral value voters. Polling had revealed that if Coleman campaigned on the issue of his opposition to gay marriage, 16 per cent of the respondents would be more likely to support him, with only 6 per cent driven away, for a net gain of 10 per cent. Coleman had decided that he had gotten all the support he could out of his emphasis on tax issues, and now he would focus on a new issue, but carefully targeted to reach only those receptive to the message. The campaign did this by purchasing radio time in conservative rural areas of the state to beam in his opposition toward gay marriage. Coleman did not raise the issue in his free media, and the metropolitan Twin-Cities-based journalists of the state did not pick up on the fact that Coleman had decided to emphasize this issue in only selected parts of the state in the closing few days of the campaign. It was a desperate move to increase the voter turn-out of social-value conservatives in the state, as the campaign felt there were no more votes that could be won in the crowded middle in the three person race.

The tricky nature of a three-way race is evident when one sees how the horse-race data were analysed and interpreted by the Coleman campaign in the final few days before the election. The pollster for the campaign presented the level of support results from the surveys using four different models of likely voters. It is especially important in American elections to look at the results of likely voters because many members of the eligible electorate simply do not participate and vote. The pollster provided levels of support percentages for the candidates using four models of voters: one based on the pure results from all participating in the poll and the remaining three using various screens to determine the most likely voters. These models which screened the voters used either past voter turn-out, current interest expressed in the election, or a combination of the two questions to predict participation in the election. To illustrate the wide variation in levels of support these models produced in this race, consider the results of the Coleman poll conducted between October 26–28, a few days before the November election. The pure results from the survey showed Coleman with support of 33 per cent of the respondents, 30 per cent for Humphrey, 27 per cent for Ventura, and a large 10 per cent still undecided. Using the combination model above to screen for the most likely voters resulted in 36 per cent for Coleman, 33 per cent for Humphrey, but only 22 per cent for Ventura, with 9 per cent undecided. While the pollster reported to the campaign that past experience demonstrated that the fourth model was the most accurate predictor of levels of support, the reality in this race was that a model which effectively screens out past non-voters and first time voters was underestimating support for the non-traditional, insurgent campaign of the third-party candidate, Jesse Ventura. The campaign's acceptance of the traditional screen for most likely voters meant that they failed to fully realize the significant challenge that Ventura had become in the closing weeks of the campaign and concentrated too much of their communication effort on Humphrey instead of attacking Ventura. This miscalculation also bedevilled the Humphrey campaign – 'we didn't see Ventura coming … the polling had screened out the unlikely voters'.[7]

The Ventura campaign, led by Dean Barkley,[8] had an atypical candidate, who had taken his fame from being a professional television wrestler to being a mayor of a small Twin-Cities suburb and a controversial local talk radio host, and ran a surprisingly successful third-party insurgent campaign. Part of Ventura's appeal was reflected in a stark black T-shirt he sported during the campaign proclaiming 'Retaliate in '98'. Ventura was challenging both the establishment candidates of the major parties and politics as usual in the state. Perhaps most surprising for this research about the role and importance of public opinion in a successful campaign, Ventura won the race without commissioning any of his own polls. The campaign simply did not have enough money early on to pay for them and doubted their benefit. Later as the race tightened and the campaign coffers filled a bit, the decision was made that polling would not overly assist the campaign and resources were better spent elsewhere.

The campaign nonetheless had good access to public opinion information that it could use. They simply read the very well regarded Minnesota Poll which appears periodically in the Minneapolis Star and Tribune. This publicly available information, used in conjunction with demographic data assembled by campaign consultants and a marketing service of the advertising section of the Star and Tribune, allowed the campaign to reach the demographic groups it wished to reach. The campaign used the polling information to decide two things: (1) which additional issues should be the focus of the campaign in addition to the theme of cutting taxes, and (2) the kind of running-mate who would fill the position of Lieutenant Governor if the team were elected. The importance that education registered in the Minnesota Poll led to the decision that education would not only be one of the main issues raised in the campaign, but would also drive the selection of a running-mate. The selection of Mae Schunk, a former school teacher, was designed to highlight the education issue and to provide an authoritative public voice on the subject to the electorate. The choice of Schunk was also designed to close the gender imbalance in Ventura's support. In the words of Doug Friedline, a campaign manager for Ventura, 'The (Minnesota) poll told us we needed an educator. Because Jesse's support was 3–1 male we needed a female' as Ventura's running mate.[9]

The Ventura campaign took great advantage of the free exposure that its candidate received during the many televised debates held, and saved their limited funds for a final 10-day television advertising campaign featuring an off-beat and irreverent candidate. The increased importance of televised debates during election campaigns is being seen across the USA in a variety of races. News stories concerning the US presidential primaries in 2000 have focused on the candidates taking part in the debates and their impact. Tony Fabrizio, former pollster for Bob Dole, the Republican presidential nominee four years ago, commented that in the presidential race in 1996 'you had a situation where the ads – and responds ads – were dictating the terms of the campaign. Now it's the debates'. In addition, while many of the debates have relatively few viewers '… there is a larger microphone from the press to the public on these debates than there ever has been before'.[10]

Greta Lilleodden Unowsky, a media consultant to the Ventura campaign, explained the three communication goals the campaign pursued: (1) to 'legitimize' the candidate for the voters, letting them know that Ventura wanted to win the governorship (and not just offer an entertaining campaign), by having him participate constructively in the debates with the other candidates; (2) to counter the wasted-vote syndrome by launching the slogan 'Don't waste your vote on politics as usual'; and (3) communicating a feeling of momentum to drive their typically non-participating voters to the polls by launching a 72-hour 'Drive to Victory' bus tour.[11] This was designed to attract a lot of free media attention to get out the vote – especially important to the Ventura campaign because they lacked the traditional party field organization to turn out their voters.

## CONCLUSION

The two major party candidates for the 1998 Minnesota Governor's race, Humphrey the Democrat and Coleman the Republican, had a great deal of public opinion information gathered through private polling and focus groups to guide strategy and create effective communication in their campaigns. However, the polling and the interpretation of this polling failed to adequately alert the campaigns to the meteoric rise of Ventura in the closing couple weeks of the campaign. Although the raw polling data showed some indication of a final surge for Ventura, the pollsters' screen for most likely voters dampened the perceived threat. The polling also failed to provide adequate information on how the electorate viewed Ventura's image – information which would have given the campaigns insight into how to develop campaign messages to blunt his challenge. Fred Steeper, a pollster for the Coleman campaign, argues that Ventura was given a free ride in the campaign and that the other campaigns allowed him to run as a populist 'instead of either campaign defining him as the extreme libertarian that he was'.[12] But Coleman and Humphrey were always reluctant to attack Ventura. They were following the conventional wisdom that the one who attacks the third candidate only hurts oneself because in the end potential supporters of the third-party candidate will decide not to waste their vote but to cast it for one of the major party candidates.

The campaign strategists for the major party candidates were prepared for a typical Minnesota campaign, discussing the past records of their seasoned politicians and sparring over an array of issues with their opponent from the other party. The Ventura campaign had an entirely different game plan. Ventura used publicly available polling data to focus during the televised debates on a few key issues identified as important issues facing the state by the electorate and ran irreverent campaign commercials mocking politics as usual. In the end, many undecided voters and first-time voters were enthralled and entertained by Ventura's 'no more politics as usual' campaign message, tipping the scales in the three-way race in Ventura's favour.

## NOTES

1  Interview with Jim DeMay, State Director for the 1996 Clinton for President campaign in Ohio, 2 March 1999 in St Paul, Minnesota.
2  Interview with Linda Moore, Deputy White House Political Director, 23 February 1999, in Washington, DC.
3  Interview with Amy Finken, one of the campaign managers for Hubert Humphrey, 6 March 1999 by telephone from Minneapolis.

4   Eric Johnson, one of the campaign managers for Hubert Humphrey, spoke during a videotaped conference 'Minnesota Gubernatorial Election and Implications for the Body Politics,' at the Hubert H. Humphrey Institute of Public Affairs, University of Minnesota, 14 January 1999.
5   Amy Finken, Ibid.
6   Interview with George Georgacas, campaign manager for Norm Coleman, 1 March 1999 in St Paul, Minnesota.
7   Eric Johnson, Ibid.
8   Interview with Dean Barkley, campaign manager for Jesse Ventura, 2 March 1999 in St Paul, Minnesota.
9   Doug Friedline, a campaign manager for Ventura, as cited in the Minneapolis Star and Tribune, 'Smaller parties have trouble getting media's attention', 27 December 1998, p. 29A.
10  Tony Fabrizio, International Herald Tribune, 20 January 2000 'Few watched, but the debates have been crucial', p. 3.
11  Ibid. Humphrey Institute conference.
12  Fred Steeper, pollster for Norm Coleman, Ibid. Humphrey Institute Conference.

## REFERENCES

Aldrich, J.H., Sullivan, J. and Borgida, E. (1989) 'Foreign affairs and issue voting: Do Presidential candidates waltz before a blind audience?', *American Political Science Association*, 83: 123–41.

Bartels, L. (1992) 'Stability and change in American electoral politics', in David Butler and Austin Ranney (eds), *Electioneering*. New York: Oxford University Press.

Berelson, B.R., Lazarsfeld, P.F. and McPhee, W.N. (1954) *Voting: A Study of Opinion Formation in a Presidential Campaign*. Chicago: University of Chicago Press.

Campbell, A., Converse, P.E., Miller, W.E. and Stokes, D.E. (1960) *The American Voter*. New York: Wiley.

Converse, P. (1964) 'The nature of belief systems in a mass public', in D.E. Apter (ed.), *Ideology and Discontent*. New York: Free Press.

Converse, P. (1976) *The Dynamics of Party Support*. Beverly Hills, CA: Sage.

Crewe, I. and Denver, D. (1985) *Electoral Change in Western Democracies*. London: Croom Helm.

Dalton, R.J. (1984) 'Cognitive mobilization and partisan dealignment in advanced industrial democracies', *Journal of Politics*, 46: 264–84.

Dalton, R.J. (1997) 'Parties without partisans: the decline of party identifications among democratic publics', *paper presented at the workshop 'Change in the Relationship of Parties and Democracy'*. Texas A&M University, April.

Dalton, R.J., Flanagan, S. and Beck, P. (1984) *Electoral Change in Advanced Industrial Democracies: Realignment or Dealignment*. Princeton, NJ: Princeton University Press.

Devlin, P.L. (1995) 'Political commercials in American Presidential elections', in L. Lee Kaid and C. Holtz-Bacha (eds), *Political Advertising in Western Democracies: Parties & Candidates on Television*. Thousand Oaks, CA: Sage. pp. 186–205.

Diamond, E. and Bates, S. (1984) *The Spot*. Cambridge, MA: MIT Press.

Finkel, S. (1993) 'Rexamining the "minimal effects" model in recent Presidential campaigns', *Journal of Politics*, 55: 1–21.

Finkel, S. and Schrott, P.R. (1993) 'Campaign effects on voter choice in the German election of 1990', *presented at the annual meeting of the American Political Science Association*. Washington.

Friedenberg, R. (1997) *Communication Consultants in Political Campaigns: Ballot Box Warriors*. Westport, CT: Praeger.

Gelman, A. and King, G. (1993) 'Why are American presidential election campaign polls so variable when voters are so predictable?', *British Journal of Political Science*, 93: 409–51.

Holbrook, T.M. (1996) *Do Campaigns Matter?* Thousand Oaks, CA: Sage.

Holmberg, S. (1994) 'Party identification compared across the Atlantic', in M.K. Jennings and T. Mann (eds), *Elections at Home and Abroad*. Ann Arbor: University of Michigan Press.

Huckfeldt, R. and Sprague, J. (1995) 'Citizens, contexts, and politics', in Ada Finifter (ed.), *Political Science: The State of the Discipline II*. Washington, DC: American Political Science Association.

Inglehart, R. (1990) *Culture Shift in Advanced Industrial Society*. Princeton, NJ: Princeton University Press.

Iyengar, S. (1990) 'Shortcuts to political knowledge: the role of selective attention and accessibility', in J.A. Ferejohn and J.H. Kuklinski (eds), *Information and Democratic Processes*. Urbana: University of Illinois Press.

Iyengar, S. and Kinder, D.R. (1987) *News that Matters*. Chicago: University of Chicago Press.

Jacobs, L.R. and Shapiro, R.Y. (1994) 'Issues, candidate image, and priming: the use of private polls in Kennedy's 1960 Presidential campaign', *American Political Science Review*, 88: 527–40.

Johnson-Cartee, K.S. and Copeland, G.A. (1997) *Inside Political Campaigns: Theory and Practice*. Westport, CT: Praeger.

Johnston, R., Blais, A., Brady, H.E. and Crete, J. (1992) *Letting the People Decide: Dynamics of a Canadian Election*. Stanford, CA: Stanford University Press.

Kinder, D.R. (1996) 'Opinion and action in the realm of politics', in D. Gilbert, S. Fiske and G. Lindzey (eds), *The Handbook of Social Psychology*. New York: Random House.

Krosnick, J. and Kinder, D. (1990) 'Altering the foundations of support for the President through priming', *American Political Science Review*, 84: 497–512.

Lavine, H., Sullivan, J., Borgida, E. and Thomsen, C. (1992) 'The Relationship of National and Personal Issue Salience to Attitude Accessibility on Foreign and Domestic Policy Issues'. University of Minnesota Manuscript.

Lazarsfeld, P.F., Berelson, B.R. and Gaudet, H. (1944) *The People's Choice*. New York: Duell, Sloan and Pierce.

Lipset, S.M. and Rokkan, Stein (1967) *Party Systems and Voter Alignments: Cross-National Perspectives*. New York: Free Press.

Markus, G.B. (1988) 'The Impact of personal and national economic conditions in the presidential vote: a pooled cross-sectional analysis', *American Journal of Political Science*, 32: 137–54.

Miller, W.E. and Shanks, M.J. (1982) 'Policy directions and presidential leadership: Alternative interpretations of the 1980 presidential election', *British Journal of Political Science*, 12: 299–356.

Nie, N., Verba, S. and Petrocik, J. (1979) *The Changing American Voter*. Chicago: University of Chicago Press.

Niemöller, K. (1998) 'Divide et impera? Segmentation of the electorate', in M. Fennema, C. van der Eijk and H. Schijf (eds), *Search of Structure: Essays in Social Science and Methodology*. Amsterdam: Het Spinhuis.

Owen, D. (1991) *Media Messages in American Presidential Campaigns*. Westport, CT: Greenwood Press.

Patterson, T.E. (1980) *The Mass Media Election*. New York: Praeger.

Patterson, T.E. and McClure, Robert D. (1976) *The Unseeing Eye: The Myth of Television Power in National Politics*. New York: G.P. Putnam and Sons.

Rosenstone, S.J. (1983) *Forecasting Presidential Elections*. New Haven, CT: Yale University Press.

Sego, M.A. (1977) *Who Gets the Cookies? III*. Brunswick, OH: King's Court Communications.

Semetko, H.A. and Schoenbach, K. (1994) *Germany's Unity Election: Voters and the Media*. Creskill, NJ: Hampton Press.

Stempel, G.H. (1994) *The Practice of Political Communication*. Englewood Cliffs, NJ: Prentice-Hall.

Vatz, R. (1976) 'Public opinion and presidential ethos', *Western Speech Communication*, 40: 196–206.

# Part III   PLANNING AND IMPLEMENTING INTERNATIONAL CAMPAIGNS

## 7

### Communicating 'Europe': Implications for Multi-Level Governance in the European Union

*Hans-Dieter Klingemann*
*and Andrea Römmele*

#### INTRODUCTION AND APPROACH

The introduction of the Euro in almost all member-countries of the European Union is yet another sign of the increasing influence that European politics has on the daily life of citizens. The growing significance of European politics (compared with politics at the national level) is becoming more evident than ever before, putting the relationship between European citizens and political actors at the European level in a new light and raising new problems and challenges to governing in the European multi-level system. In this context, the aggregation of citizens' political preferences and the extent of their information about European politics take on central importance.

In modern representative democracies, citizens' demands are aggregated and processed by intermediary organizations, above all political parties. The voters are informed about what the parties offer and make a decision based on their general political predisposition and information about the political alternatives. In each election, the voter has a new opportunity to express his or her approval or rejection of government policy and of the policies and candidates offered by the competing parties. This is a brief summary of how citizens give a political mandate and demand accountability from parties. In doing so, it is essential in a representative democracy that citizens are informed about the political alternatives, and that parties have access to information about citizens' preferences and interests.

This study focuses on the European multi-level political system and the question of how European citizens gain information about European politics. The political preferences of European citizens can only be articulated and aggregated in the European multi-level system on the basis of existing political predispositions and information about policy issues. Particularly with regard to European Union issues, citizens display serious information deficits and uncertainty, not least due to the 'remoteness' and minimal transparency of the political system, and are often guided by more general convictions and emotions (Reif, 1992; Niedermayer and Sinnot, 1995; Schmitt and Scheuer, 1996). Opinion leaders and the structured information they provide can play a central role in this situation.

This is the approach taken in this chapter: starting from the theoretical concept of the 'two-step flow of communication', we will look at the opinion leaders in European politics. Whom do citizens trust when they are seeking reliable information about Europe? In order to find these opinion leaders, we will present survey results identifying sources of trustworthy information on European issues. To conclude, we will discuss these empirical results in light of our theoretical observations.

## CHANNELS OF INFORMATION

Citizens generally have access to two channels of information: aside from interpersonal communication within their own social sphere, people derive information about political topics above all from the media. In modern democracies, the mass media are often assigned the role of transmitter, whose central function is providing information. Further, the media transmit messages from a variety of sources wishing to reach a public audience. In addition to their central function of providing information, however, the media also provide orientation, i.e. interpretation of facts. In this role, they function as *mediators*, above all through the editorial bias that defines the identity of individual media (e.g. in commentaries and editorials) (Schönbach, 1977). This editorial bias can overlap the structure of party competition and allows readers to process information quickly using their existing store of knowledge. Numerous empirical studies have shown that citizens prefer to draw their information from media that share their frame of reference (e.g. Page et al., 1987; Zaller, 1992): here the information source has the role of an opinion leader. Further, it was shown that these are the opinion leaders and expert opinions – also transmitted via media – that have an influence on citizens (Page et al., 1987).

The concept of opinion leaders and the 'two-step flow of communication' was first developed by Lazarsfeld et al. (1944). It is a micro-concept emphasizing the importance of the opinion of trustworthy persons in the formation of one's own opinions. These *trusted others* are often characterized as opinion leaders, since to a certain degree they determine the development of others' opinions. The central point of the model is, first, that the flow of information from the mass media to the general population is mediated through personal opinion leaders, and second, that these opinion leaders interpret the information they receive via the mass media in terms of their own social and cultural contexts.[1] Opinion leaders thus perform a sort of relay function: they receive political messages from the mass media and pass them on to opinion followers. The flow of information behaves according to a cascade model (Deutsch, 1968; Wessels, 1995). Thus mass media have much less influence and opinion leaders much more influence than originally assumed.

Further empirical research has identified a third group of 'information consumers', in addition to opinion leaders and followers: aside from those whom others ask about their opinions, and those who ask others about their opinions (with large overlaps between the two groups), Troldahl and Van Dam (1965) and Robinson (1976) have identified a third group of respondents. Over half of the respondents answered that neither were they asked about their opinions, nor did they ask others about theirs. This group derives its political information solely from the media (see also Klingemann, 1986: 391).

The occasional lack of interpersonal communication regarding political issues does not necessarily rule out the concept of opinion leader; on the contrary, due to the explosive growth of mass communication in recent decades, one may assume that today not only people in personal contact with citizens inform them and act as opinion leaders, but also people (and institutions) who are familiar to citizens only through the media. There are certainly differences between the two theoretical concepts: whereas the personal opinion leader offers the possibility of communication through personal conversation, the opinion leader in the media only 'informs', without the possibility of feedback. In addition, one can assume a difference in status between media opinion leaders and their followers which is normally not the case for personal opinion leaders. As a result, the media themselves gain influence, particularly if one assumes the existence of a hierarchy, not only for personal opinion leaders but also for the media, which guarantees a vertical influence (Merten, 1988: 630). From these observations we can derive a three-step flow of political communication, as shown in Figure 7.1.

Figure 7.1 adds the level of media opinion leaders to the two-step flow model of political communication. It does not deal with the issue of horizontal inter-relationships (*opinion-sharing*), that is, the fact that opinion leaders (personal and media opinion leaders) communicate with each other. The analysis focuses exclusively on the vertical perspective. Figure 7.1 shows two possibilities for the flow of information:

1   Information and opinions can be transferred from a media opinion leader to personal opinion leaders via the media, which takes into account the fact that each opinion leader in turn has his own opinion leader (Katz and Lazarsfeld, 1955: 319). These then convey opinions and information to citizens via personal communication.

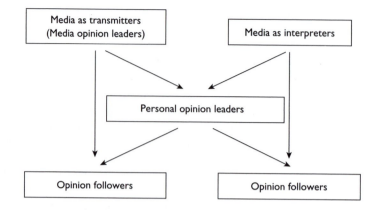

FIGURE 7.1  *Three-step flow of political communication*

2   Citizens may draw information supplied by media opinion leaders
    directly from the mass media. Bypassing personal communication in this
    way does not mean that there are no personal opinion leaders at work;
    they may also function via the media. Due to the highly specialized
    nature of expert debates on EU policy issues and the relative 'remote-
    ness' of the topic, the average citizen rarely has well-founded knowledge
    or judgements regarding these issues. Opinion leaders act as 'inter-
    preters' under precisely these conditions. One may assume that opinion
    leaders for European issues are above all media opinion leaders – in this
    way, for example, politicians (in the media) as representatives of a par-
    ticular political ideology act as an effective mechanism for reducing and
    processing complex information about Europe.
3   Often the two sources are mixed, however: citizens receive information
    via the media and from personal communication.

## IDENTIFYING OPINION LEADERS ON EUROPEAN ISSUES: OPERATIONALIZATION

Surveys are a necessary tool for identifying opinion leaders. In their original
approach, Lazarsfeld et al. (1944) attempted to identify personal opinion
leaders using two questions: (1) 'have you tried to convince anyone of your
political ideas recently?' and (2) 'has anyone asked for your advice on a
political question recently?'. Inglehart used a different approach for identifying opinion leaders: (1) 'do you regularly/occasionally/never discuss political issues with your friends?' and (2) 'do you regularly/occasionally/never
try to convince friends and acquaintances of your opinion?' (Inglehart,
1970; Inglehart and Rabier, 1979). In contrast to the operationalization of
opinion leaders originally developed by Lazarsfeld, Inglehart thus formu-
lates this theoretical concept more broadly: he is concerned not only with
the effect (i.e. others' opinions), but also with the process, i.e. participation
in political discussions. Common to both approaches is the use of survey
respondents' self-evaluation.

The approach used in this analysis attempts to identify (media) opinion leaders from the responses of others.[2] In addition to these (media) opinion leaders, who are the focus here, the analysis also identified personal opinion leaders. Here, two considerations were significant: (1) identifying the personal opinion leaders and followers indirectly makes it possible to judge the importance of mass media opinion leaders. What is the proportion of citizens who participate in political discussions and thereby come into contact with and/or function as personal opinion leaders? On the other hand, we may ask: what is the proportion of people who do not participate in political discussions and mainly rely on media opinion leaders as 'interpreters' of European issues? Further, we may try to find out whom personal opinion leaders, as compared with followers, name as trustworthy sources of information. (2) The second consideration is of a methodological nature: in order to arrive at reliable answers to the question of trustworthy sources of information on European issues, we need to identify those respondents with a general interest in such information. This group of respondents is then contrasted to a second group that cannot be assumed to have such interest (cf. the debate initiated by Philip Converse (1970) on *attitudes* and *non-attitudes*, 1970). Here, the basic assumption is that people who regularly discuss politics and political issues with their friends and acquaintances and/or would like to convince others of their opinions will have a general interest in such information. It was precisely this segment of the population that Lazarsfeld and his colleagues identified in 1940 as especially active, well-informed voters and characterized as opinion leaders.

The identification of personal opinion leaders within the framework of the Eurobarometer follows Inglehart's approach. Using the two questions regularly asked in these surveys, regarding the frequency of political discussion[3] and the ability to convince friends and acquaintances of one's own opinion,[4] respondents are to be classified according to their likelihood of acting as opinion leaders. Respondents who frequently lead political discussions and at least occasionally persuade others to share their opinion are regarded as opinion leaders; in our survey this corresponded to about 12 per cent of all respondents. On the other hand, opinion followers are defined as those who never discuss politics and seldom or never persuade others to share their opinion (on the construction of the *opinion leadership* index, see also ZEUS report, 1988). About 19 per cent of respondents were classified as opinion followers. About two-thirds of all respondents (69 per cent) could not be classified as either opinion leaders or followers. With regard to the considerations formulated at the outset, the two groups at the extremes were of special interest.

## OPINION LEADERS ON EUROPEAN ISSUES: EMPIRICAL RESULTS

The presentation and discussion of the empirical results may be divided into three steps: first, we examine the responses to the question of reliable information sources, individuals as well as institutions. Is there a trustworthy

TABLE 7.1 *Responses to the question on reliable information about European issues*

| Source mentioned | Respondents | |
|---|---|---|
| | no. | % |
| Persons and institutions | 7,881 | 48 |
| Persons, but not institutions | 3,559 | 22 |
| Institutions, but not persons | 1,720 | 11 |
| Neither persons nor institutions | 3,186 | 20 |
| Total | 16,346 | 100 |

*Source:* Eurobarometer 44.1, own calculations

TABLE 7.2 *Number of responses to the question on reliable information: persons and institutions*

| Number of mentions | Persons | | Institutions | |
|---|---|---|---|---|
| | no. | % | no. | % |
| 1 | 8,049 | 49 | 7,116 | 44 |
| 2 or more | 3,391 | 21 | 2,485 | 15 |
| Don't know/no answer | 4,906 | 30 | 6,745 | 41 |
| Total | 16,346 | 100 | 16,346 | 100 |

*Source:* Eurobarometer 44.1, own calculations

information source for European citizens? How many respondents do not know or fail to answer? And whom do they trust more, individuals or institutions (Table 7.1)? Second, we focus on the responses to the two questions: do both show similar trends, or are there significant differences (Table 7.2)? Finally, we look at the substance of the responses to see what kind of individuals and institutions are mentioned (Tables 7.4 and 7.5) and investigate possible cross-national variations.

Table 7.1 shows whether European citizens have access to trustworthy information about European politics.[5] The most important finding here is that 80 per cent of respondents know where to find reliable information.[6] About half of all respondents name both trustworthy persons and institutions as possible information sources.

Compared with institutions, individuals are mentioned somewhat more often, as shown also in Table 7.2: about 70 per cent of respondents mention persons as information sources, while 60 per cent mention institutions.[7]

From Table 7.2, we see that about half of all survey participants (49 per cent) mentioned one person in response to the question about persons as reliable information sources, while 21 per cent mentioned two or more. Nearly one-third (30 per cent) had no response or answered 'don't know'. In response to the question about associations, organizations and institutions, 44 per cent, or somewhat less than half of respondents mentioned one, while 15 per cent mentioned two or more. The number of those who answered 'don't know' or gave no response is strikingly high at 41 per cent. Around two-fifths of all respondents could not name any associations, institutions or organizations who provide reliable information – significantly

TABLE 7.3  *Number of non-responses among opinion leaders and followers (per cent)*

|  | All respondents | Personal opinion leaders | Opinion followers |
|---|---|---|---|
| 'which persons ...' | 30 | 21 | 40 |
| 'which institutions ...' | 41 | 34 | 48 |

*Source:* Eurobarometer 44.1, own calculations

more than for the question about persons.[8] How can one explain these differences and the high number of non-responses? It seems likely that many of the respondents had no opinions on the subject and thus either gave no answer or felt obligated to provide some response. In order to find more considered responses, those of the personal opinion leaders are compared with those of opinion followers. Table 7.3 compares the numbers of non-responses among personal opinion leaders and opinion followers to those of all respondents.

The differences are obvious: only 21 per cent, or one out of five personal opinion leaders, had no response to the question about persons, while two-fifths (40 per cent) of all opinion followers had none. The same tendency can be observed for institutions: 34 per cent of the personal opinion leaders (one out of three) had no response, while nearly every second opinion follower had none. The rather large variance between non-responses to the two questions is striking. The fact that more respondents respond to the question about persons hints that the concept of 'trust' – which is central to the issue of trustworthy information – is more closely associated with persons than institutions (Offe, 1996). The opinion-leader-concept is also more closely associated with persons than with institutions.

After having shown how many respondents answered the questions and the number of mentions (Tables 7.1 and 7.2), our next step is to examine the content of these responses. In order to analyse the great variety of responses to the two open-ended questions, a coding scheme was developed to summarize the answers according to content-related criteria. Data for the two questions were coded according to four dimensions: group, nation, sector, and level. For the first dimension we coded the responses according to the two main categories 'person' and 'institution'. The second dimension is nation-specific and identifies the country where the person or institution mentioned is located. The third dimension (sector) refers to various political or socio-economic sectors. The category 'politician' distinguishes between 'politician: head of government' and 'other politicians'. In the sub-category 'politician: head of government' only one person, the appropriate head of state/government (prime minister/chancellor/president) is coded in for each country. All other politicians, members of parliament, cabinet members, and local and regional politicians come under the sub-category 'other politicians'. Political parties, if mentioned by name, can be found under the corresponding category. Journalists, television and radio stations, and newspapers can be found in the 'media' category. Universities, professors, schools, libraries, etc. are combined under 'education and research'.

TABLE 7.4   *Sectors where persons with reliable information about the EU are located (multiple-response analysis, figures are per cent of cases and responses)*

| | All respondents | | Personal opinion leaders | | Opinion followers | |
|---|---|---|---|---|---|---|
| | cases | responses | cases | responses | cases | responses |
| Political parties | 2 | 1 | 1 | 1 | 2 | 1 |
| Politicians: heads of government | 38 | 25 | 32 | 19 | 40 | 30 |
| Other politicians | 92 | 66 | 100 | 72 | 85 | 62 |
| Economy | 1 | 1 | 1 | 1 | 1 | 1 |
| Media | 5 | 3 | 3 | 2 | 4 | 3 |
| Other | 5 | 3 | 8 | 5 | 3 | 2 |
| Total | 143 | 100 | 146 | 100 | 136 | 100 |
| No. of valid cases/responses | 8,834 | 13,332 | 1,274 | 2,110 | 1,315 | 1,794 |

*Source*: Eurobarometer 44.1, own calculations. Sectors are given separately only when the proportion of mentions is greater than 1%

TABLE 7.5   *Sectors where institutions with reliable information about the EU are located (multiple-response analysis, figures are per cent of cases and responses)*

| | All respondents | | Personal opinion leaders | | Opinion followers | |
|---|---|---|---|---|---|---|
| | cases | responses | cases | responses | cases | responses |
| Political parties | 14 | 9 | 17 | 11 | 13 | 10 |
| Politicians: heads of government | 2 | 2 | 4 | 2 | 2 | 1 |
| Other politicians | 58 | 38 | 64 | 41 | 50 | 36 |
| Economy | 32 | 21 | 35 | 23 | 29 | 20 |
| Media | 31 | 21 | 23 | 14 | 34 | 25 |
| Education and research | 5 | 3 | 6 | 4 | 5 | 3 |
| Other | 8 | 6 | 9 | 6 | 7 | 5 |
| Total | 151 | 100 | 157 | 100 | 140 | 100 |
| No. of valid cases/responses | 6,937 | 10,489 | 1,034 | 1,627 | 1,039 | 1,453 |

*Source*: Eurobarometer 44.1, own calculations. Sectors are given separately only when the proportion of mentions is greater than 1%

Finally, the fourth dimension is the level to which the person or institution mentioned belongs: the local, regional, national, or European level. The category 'unclassifiable/undefined' includes all responses that cannot be categorized, along with 'don't know/no answer'.

Who then are the persons and institutions who are trusted as sources of information on European political issues? Table 7.4 shows the sectors where persons mentioned as trustworthy information sources are located. As in Table 7.5, respondents are divided into three groups: the first column gives the responses of all survey participants, the second column the responses of personal opinion leaders, and the third column the responses of opinion followers.

The responses show that all participants mentioned persons from the political sector. Other sectors, such as the economy, media, or education, are hardly mentioned. The differences between the three groups are also interesting: every opinion leader mentioned a politician, and 72 per cent of their responses name politicians as trustworthy sources of information on European issues. Among the opinion followers, this sector was also the most frequently mentioned, though with 62 per cent of responses (or 85 per cent of cases) it has a less prominent position. Heads of government constitute the second most important source of information, and here too we see clear differences between the two contrasting groups: whereas only 32 per cent of opinion leaders regard heads of government as trustworthy sources of information (19 per cent of all responses), 40 per cent of opinion followers do so (30 per cent of responses). Almost all politicians mentioned are from the respondent's own country (93 per cent) and are active at the national level (87 per cent).[9] This result is true both for opinion leaders and followers. Government heads in other countries were only occasionally mentioned: 12 per cent of all respondents who mentioned heads of government named those of other countries,[10] above all Kohl, Santer, and Major.

Thus we may come to the preliminary conclusion that almost exclusively, national politicians are mentioned as a source of reliable information about European issues. Interestingly, it was not the government heads who are most visible on the national and European stage who were most often mentioned; instead, the real expertise on European issues is attributed to those who are most likely to deal with them on a daily basis, in particular cabinet members and members of parliament. Although government heads may determine the general policy on European issues, others are responsible for working out the details, coordinating and carrying it out.

Table 7.4 presents the results for institutions who are expected to provide reliable information about the European Union. All three groups of respondents (all respondents, personal opinion leaders, and opinion followers) mentioned *political* institutions, organizations and associations as the most important source of reliable information about Europe. These are predominantly (87 per cent) European-level institutions,[11] in contrast to the results for the question about trustworthy persons. In the case of institutions, it is striking that the political sector is much less dominant: looking at the column with answers from all respondents, we see that political institutions are followed by economic institutions and the media, both with 21 per cent of all responses. The picture is slightly different if one looks only at personal opinion leaders, who mentioned political institutions to a much greater extent and gave the media a noticeably smaller role: only one-fourth mention the media as a credible source of information on European issues. For opinion followers, however, the opposite is true: almost half mentioned the media as a reliable source of information; for this group, the media accounted for about 34 per cent of all responses and are the second most important source of trustworthy information. Once again, a comparison with the responses to the question about persons reveals a clear difference: respondents mentioned no persons from the economic sector, but one-third did mention economic institutions as sources of reliable information. Finally, we examined the data for cross-national differences. Are there obvious national differences with regard to the questions posed?[12] Our data show no clear national pattern. Possible country groupings we expected were 'old' EU-member states in which people might know more about EU policies and institutions and possible sources of trustworthy information than citizens in 'new' EU-member states. Another possible line of distinction between the different countries was that of cultural differences: do southern member states respond differently than northern member states? Again, no significant cross-national difference could be identified.

At this point, we may sum up our findings as follows: European political institutions are most often mentioned as trustworthy sources of information, followed by economic organizations and mass media. Comparing the responses of opinion leaders and followers reveals variations: whereas only one in five opinion leaders mentioned the mass media as a trustworthy information source, one in three opinion followers did so. This difference is not evident in the case of the question about persons, where media representatives play a minor role as information sources for both opinion leaders and followers. No significant cross-national differences could be identified.

## SUMMARY AND DISCUSSION OF THE EMPIRICAL RESULTS

In its search for the 'beacons' of Europe, i.e. persons and institutions whom citizens trust as sources of information on European issues, this analysis has provided the following results:

- 80 per cent of respondents were able to name a person and/or institution from whom they can expect to receive trustworthy information about European issues. This is the first major finding.
- Detailed analysis shows, however, that about one-third of respondents do not mention any person as a trustworthy information source, and two-fifths do not mention any institution.
- Those who do mention one or more persons as sources of information predominantly name national politicians, with those government heads most visible at the European level only in second place. The category mentioned most often ('other politicians') includes cabinet members and members of parliament, that is, precisely those politicians who are entrusted with the day-to-day tasks and are obviously regarded by citizens as the true experts. The fact that national politicians from the respondent's own country were most often mentioned, while mentions of politicians in other European countries were the exception, is not surprising given the low visibility of the European political elite.
- For the question about institutions, political institutions at the European level (Commission, Parliament) were most often mentioned, followed by a tie between economic organizations and the media. Whereas individuals from the economic sector are hardly evident, citizens are well aware of economic institutions.

The role of the media deserves special attention: they give media opinion leaders access to a broad audience. Though European policy is largely determined by collective actors, such as parties and associations, European issues are usually articulated by individual actors, such as political leaders and representatives of associations. Whereas respondents to the question about trustworthy persons did not mention media as a source of their own information, in the question about trustworthy institutions, the media play an important role, representing an important source of information for citizens, although more so for opinion followers than for opinion leaders. Here the central role of the media is evident: because the media agenda is a limited resource, the media must choose how much coverage to give to certain actors and views in their political reporting. Their decision determines the access to public attention.

But both media opinion leaders and the media stand in contrast to personal opinion leaders: after all, 80 per cent of respondents indicated that they were involved in political discussions in one form or another. Despite the significance of the media, the empirical results show that interpersonal communication and the concept of the personal opinion leader remain as important as ever.

How shall we interpret the empirical findings in light of the question, raised at the outset, of citizens' access to information about European policies as a central condition for the process of representation in the European multi-level system? This discussion has demonstrated the significance of opinion leaders – interpersonal and media – for European issues in particular. Due to large information deficits regarding European policy, European citizens depend on opinion leaders as an information shortcut and aid to interpretation. Opinion leaders whose general political preferences can be clearly identified by citizens reduce the high costs of processing information.

In conclusion, let us look critically at the empirical results with regard to governing within the European multi-level system.

For the most part, European citizens know where to find trustworthy information about European topics and issues. This certainly fulfils a necessary condition for democratic governing in the European multi-level system. However, the analysis has shown that citizens identify contact persons for their interests not at the European, but the national, level. Respondents almost exclusively mentioned national politicians and hardly mentioned actors at the European level. The European multi-level system lacks political figureheads; there is little personalization of political alternatives at the European level.

As Gabriel has described, the majority of the population imagines the political order and institutional structure as an abstract quantity, though concrete political experience is mediated as a rule via specific political actors, processes and organizations, which are also likely to influence the general relationship to the political system (Gabriel, 1994: 115). The analysis has shown that the institutions of the European multi-level system are indeed perceived as trustworthy: in response to the question about institutions, organizations or associations that provide reliable information on European issues, the European Parliament and European Commission were most often mentioned. The authority of the European Parliament has grown steadily, not least with regard to its role in the naming of the President of the European Commission. Progress in this direction could lead the way in the medium term to an increased personalization of European politics, which will probably be needed to make opinion formation and interest representation more effective at this level of governing.

## NOTES

1  We will not deal separately with the difference between the flow of information and opinion formation; see Klingemann 1986, 388–9.
2  The questions asked in the Eurobarometer survey in autumn 1995 (EB 44.1) are as follows:
    Q23 'When you need reliable information about the European Union, which persons in public life do you think of?'
    Q24 'And which associations, organizations or institutions occur to you in this context?'
3  'Would you say that when you are with friends, you often, occasionally, or never discuss political topics?'
4  'Do you ever persuade your friends, co-workers or acquaintances to share an opinion that is important to you? Does this happen often/occasionally/never?'
5  All calculations are not weighted.
6  The empirical analysis showed variations between countries, which will not be dealt with here.
7  The 20 per cent of respondents in Table 7.1 who mentioned neither persons nor institutions result from the intersection of the 30 per cent who did not respond to the question about persons and the 41 per cent who did not respond to the question about institutions as believable sources of information (see Table 7.2).
8  Given the empirical results, one cannot assume a close relationship between a mention of persons and of institutions from the same sector.
9  Table not presented here.
10  Table not presented here.
11  Table not presented here.
12  Table not presented here.

## REFERENCES

Alreck, P. and Settle, R.B. (1985) *The Survey Research Handbook*. Homewood, IL: Irwin.
Calvert, R.L. (1985) 'The value of biased information: a rational choice model of political advice', *Journal of Politics*, 4: 530–55.
Converse, P. (1964) 'The nature of belief systems in mass publics', in D.A. Apter (ed.), *Ideology and Discontent*. New York: Free Press.
Converse, P.E. (1970) 'Attitudes and non-attitudes: continuation of a dialogue', in E.R. Tufte (ed.), *The Quantitative Analysis of Social Problems*. Reading, MA: Addison-Wesley.

Deutsch, K.W. (1968) *Die Analyse internationaler Beziehungen*. Frankfurt a. M.: Europäische Verlagsanstalt.

Gabriel, O.W. (1994) 'Politische Einstellungen und politische Kultur', in O.W. Gabriel and F. Brettschneider (eds), *Die EU-Staaten im Vergleich*, 2nd revised and expanded edition. Lizenzausgabe für die Bundeszentrale für politische Bildung. Opladen: Westdeutscher Verlag.

Inglehart, R. (1970) 'Cognitive mobilization and European identity', *Comparative Politics*, 3: 45–70.

Inglehart, R. and Rabier, J.-R. (1979) 'Europe elects a parliament: cognitive mobilization, political mobilization and pro-European attitudes as influences on voter turnout', *Government and Opposition*, 14 (4): 479–507.

Katz, E. and Lazarsfeld, P. (1955) *Personal Influence. Glencoe*, Vol. 3. New York: Free Press.

Klingemann, H.-D. (1986) 'Massenkommunikation, interpersonale Kommunikation und politische Einstellungen. Zur Kritik der These vom, Zwei-Stufen Fluß' der politischen Kommunikation', in M. Kaase (ed.), *Politische Wissenschaft und Politische Ordnung*. Opladen: Westdeutscher Verlag.

Lazarsfeld, P.F., Berelson, B. and Gaudet, H. (1944) *The People's Choice. How the Voter Makes Up His Mind in a Presidential Campaign*. New York: Duell, Sloane, and Pearce.

Lepsius, R.M. (1991) 'Nationalstaat oder Nationalitätenstaat als Modell für die Weiterentwicklung der Europäischen Gemeinschaft', in R. Wildenmann (ed.), *Staatswerdung Europas?* Baden-Baden: Nomos.

Merten, K. (1988) 'Aufstieg und Fall des, Two-Step-Flow of Communication'. Kritik einer sozialwissenschaftlichen Hypothese', *Politische Vierteljahresschrift*, 4: 610–35.

Niedermayer, O. and Sinnot, R. (1995) *Public Opinion and Internationalized Governance*. Oxford: Oxford University Press.

Offe, C. (1996) 'Trust and knowledge, rules and decisions. Exploring a difficult conceptual terrain'. Draft paper prepared for the conference 'The Culture of Democracy: Democracy and Trust', Georgetown University, Washington, November 7–9, 1996.

Page, B.I., Shapiro, R.Y. and Dempsey, G.R. (1987) 'What moves public opinion?', *American Political Science Review*, 1: 23–43.

Pürer, H. and Raabe, J. (1994) *Medien in Deutschland*. München: Ölschläger.

Reif, K. (1992) 'Wahlen, Wähler und Demokratie in der EG. Die drei Dimensionen des demokratischen Defizits', *Aus Politik und Zeitgeschichte*, 19: 43–52.

Robinson, J.P. (1976) 'Interpersonal influence in election campaigns: two step-flow hypotheses', *Public Opinion Quarterly*, 40: 304–19.

Schenk, M. (1993) 'Die ego-zentrierten Netzwerke von Meinungsbildnern (Opinion-Leaders)', *Kölner Zeitschrift für Soziologie und Sozialpsychologie*, 45: 254–69.

Schenk, M. and Rössler, P. (1994) 'Das unterschätzte Publikum. Wie Themenbewußtsein und politische Meinungsbildung im Alltag von Massenmedien und interpersonaler Kommunikation beeinflußt werden', in F. Neidhardt (ed.), *Öffentlichkeit, öffentliche Meinung, soziale Bewegungen*. Opladen: Westdeutscher Verlag.

Schmitt, H. and Scheuer, A. (1996) 'Region – Nation – Europa. Drei Ebenen politischer Steuerung und Gestaltung in der Wahrnehmung der Bürger', in T. König, E. Rieger and H. Schmitt (eds), *Das Europäische Mehrebenensystem. (Mannheimer Jahrbuch für Europäische Sozialforschung Bd. 1)*. Frankfurt: Campus.

Schönbach, K. (1977) *Trennung von Nachricht und Meinung: empirische Untersuchung eines journalistischen Qualitätskriteriums*. Freiburg: Alber.

Troldahl, V. and Van Dam, R. (1965) 'Face to face communications about major topics in the news', *Public Opinion Quarterly*, 29: 626–34.

Voltmer, K. (1996) *Die Informations- und Orientierungsleistung der Medien aus demokratietheoretischer Perspektive – Eine empirische Analyse von Vielfalt, Objektivität und ideologischer Strukturierung*. FU Berlin: Inaugural-Dissertation.

Weidenfeld, W. (1991) *Wie Europa verfaßt sein soll*. Gütersloh: Bertelsmann-Stiftung.

Wessels, B. (1995) 'Support or integration: elite or mass-driven?', in O. Niedermayer and R. Sinnott (eds), *Public Opinion and Internationalized Governance*. Oxford: Oxford University Press.

Windahl, S. and Signitzer, B.H. with Olson, J.T. (1992) *Using Communication Theory: An Introduction to Planned Communication*. London: Sage.

Zaller, J.R. (1992) *The Nature and Origins of Mass Opinion*. Cambridge: Cambridge University Press.

ZEUS (1988) 'Opinion leaders: did they really become more critical about Europe and the EC?'. Report prepared on behalf of the Directorate General for Information, Communication, and Culture of the Commission of the European Communities. Mannheim.

# 8 Campaign Practices and Survey Use in the European Commission: The Eurobarometer Survey

*Christine Pütz*

This contribution deals with the campaign practices of the *Commission of the European Union*. It analyses the role survey research plays in the campaigns of the European Commission, and focuses on the use of the *Eurobarometer surveys* in the several phases of campaigning.

In more detail, this study aims at providing an idea of the internal processes concerning the use of survey research, and especially the Eurobarometer surveys, in campaign projects of the European Commission. For this purpose, the special rules of campaigning in the supranational political organization of the European Union will be discussed. Furthermore, the Eurobarometer surveys will be presented as a particular survey instrument of the European Commission. Next, we will specify the problems of survey usage that Commission campaigners face in the different phases of a campaign. A concrete example of a campaign, namely the *European Year of Safety, Hygiene and Health Protection at Work* campaign, has been chosen in order to illustrate the use of Eurobarometer surveys in all phases of a campaign. Finally, conclusions on the campaign practices and survey use by the campaigners of the European Commission will be drawn.

This contribution is essentially based on two investigations carried out in the framework of the *Campaign and Survey Project*: the *Appendix of the Campaign Handbook*[1] and *Interviews* conducted with campaigners of the European Commission.[2] The *Appendix* provides Eurobarometer data collected in the context of campaigns of the European Commission and furnishes the data of eight campaigns gathered with Eurobarometer surveys. It presents research instruments and survey results in the form of tables and trend graphs. The collection of these survey data and the accompanying information concerning the campaign strategies themselves give a general idea of the campaign practices of the European Commission. This is supported by a series of qualitative *interviews* conducted with campaign managers of the European Commission, which provide information about the practitioners' attitudes toward and use of survey research.[3]

## THE SPECIFICS OF THE EUROPEAN
## COMMISSION'S CAMPAIGNING

The European Commission, as an executive body of the European Union, has to perform its assigned task of information policy. Therefore, the process of making transparent both the functioning of the European institutions and the policy of the individual Directorates General of the European Commission is of considerable importance. Depending on their supranational level of organization and their inter- or transnational level of implementation, campaigns of the European Commission show specific characteristics.

- *Supranational organization:* the European Commission launches international campaigns that have to consider and respect the diversity of member states' systems with their own political, economic, social, and cultural traditions, and with different approaches to financing and organization.
- *Political organization:* a political organization like the EU deals with non-profit campaigns focusing on showing and making transparent its political action.

On another level, the campaigns of the European Union are governed by the general principles and postulates valid within the European Union, two of which, subsidiarity and decentralization, are especially relevant.

- *Subsidiarity:* according to this principle, EU institutions are not to intervene in any areas not defined as union policy areas when issues may be dealt with at lower (i.e. national, regional or local) levels. Only if Union activity seems the better option because of the enormous dimensions of the action should European institutions be engaged. A great majority of the campaign topics documented in the Appendix deal with areas covered by the principle of subsidiarity. Although this means that responsibility lies essentially with national authorities, a European-wide campaign will be launched if national/local authorities cannot entirely provide the necessary input to meet the challenges posed by the specific problem. In this case, the Commission's activity is limited to information and advisory policy in close co-operation with the national levels.
- *Decentralization:* the objective of the Union's policy is a greater decentralization of decision-making and political action. As a consequence, campaign organizers of the Commission have to increase the integration of national, regional and local levels, not only in terms of staff but also in terms of financial co-operation. National authorities are financially engaged and thus have a right to a say in the matter, which means that the Commission's role is limited to co-ordinating the campaign at the European level and serving as a link that provides background support and plays an advisory and facilitating role in bilateral relationships with the individual member states. Concrete activities are implemented and organized on the national level. In this context, the national Representation Offices of the European Commission have a key function

channelling the information to the respective target audiences and recruiting national and local authorities, NGOs etc. This kind of structure offers opportunities but also leads to problems. On the one hand, it creates new platforms of action and guarantees a more effective and closer implementation. Furthermore, a scale of national programmes can be established that goes far beyond what could be financed and organized by the Commission alone. On the other hand, this kind of close co-operation makes the Commission highly dependent on the national actors' good-will and commitment to co-operation. In the framework of some campaigns, national co-ordination groups are specially established to provide better resource conditions for implementing the campaign.

## EUROBAROMETER SURVEYS: A SPECIAL TOOL FOR THE EUROPEAN COMMISSION

The Eurobarometer (EB) surveys have been carried out since the early 1970s by the European Commission, namely by the *Surveys, Research, Analysis (Eurobarometer)* Unit of the Directorate General X *Audio-Visual, Information, Communication, Culture*. They are the product of a unique programme of cross-national and cross-temporal research in applied social science.

Since 1973 Eurobarometer surveys have been conducted in the form of Standard Eurobarometer surveys and carried out twice a year, in spring and autumn. In addition to obtaining regular readings of support for European integration and the perceived quality of life, each of the Eurobarometers has explored a variety of special topics. A Standard Eurobarometer consists of a basic module of trend questions asked regularly in an identical format in combination with socio-demographic variables, along with a set of variable questions on various topics. In addition to the Standard Eurobarometer, Flash surveys are conducted as needed, at irregular intervals several times a year. A Flash Eurobarometer is smaller and usually contains only one or a few topics of question fields. The variable-question part of the Eurobarometer consists of sets of questions specially ordered by EU institutions or other customers.

The Eurobarometer surveys are conducted in all member states of the European Union among people aged 15 and over. Multi-stage national probability samples and national stratified quota samples are drawn. For the Standard Eurobarometer, generally about 1,000 respondents per country are interviewed face-to-face (in Luxemburg 300, Northern Ireland 500, and in West and East Germany each 1,000 respondents). The Flash Eurobarometers are conducted via telephone with a smaller sample (generally 500 interviews per country).

Thus, three main features make the Eurobarometer data set invaluable: first, its international comparability thanks to the representative samples simultaneously carried out in all member states; second, the regular repetition of key questions establishing short- and long-term trends and thus the possibility for time series; third, the inclusion of socio-demographic variables in each Eurobarometer, allowing investigations to be carried out subsequently using focus groups matched on those variables.

With the Eurobarometer surveys, the Directorates General (DGs) have their own intra-institutional survey research at their disposal. Campaign managers of the different DGs can order questions of specific interest in forthcoming surveys or make use of the ongoing Eurobarometer survey data, although there may be budget constraints on ordering extra questions, which are not free of charge. In addition, the data material delivered by on-going surveys is often considered too general for a specific campaign topic and not really useful for planning a specific campaign (see interviews). Nevertheless, Eurobarometer surveys are a very useful instrument for the Commission's campaigners, and the following will detail how they are used.

## THE ROLE OF SURVEY RESEARCH FOR CAMPAIGN PROJECTS OF THE EUROPEAN COMMISSION: USING EUROBAROMETER DATA IN THE SEVERAL PHASES OF CAMPAIGNING

In order to examine the concrete use of survey research in the several phases of campaigning by the European Commission, the following was necessary. First of all, it was necessary to find out which campaigns had made use of Eurobarometer survey data, or better, which questions had been asked within the context of a campaign. This information was fundamental for the Appendix. Due to its decentralized structure, however, it was not possible to obtain systematic data from the Commission itself. Based on the (ZEUS) Eurobarometer question bank, however, eight campaigns could be identified that used Eurobarometer survey data in at least one phase of their campaigning. With this systematic search we mainly found 'institutionalized' campaigns of the Commission, such as the *European Year* or the *European Week* campaigns. By establishing *European Years* or *European Weeks*, the European Union has made an effort to institutionalize its campaign activities. Every year, the European Union chooses a specific topic or problem as the subject for a year-long information campaign and popularizes the chosen topic by providing information and generating publicity. In the framework of *European Week*, the same efforts are accomplished but limited to a one-week time period.

For this article, we needed to examine in more detail exactly how these survey data had been used during the various phases of the campaigns, so we asked the relevant Directorate Generals to provide the necessary information.[4]

The eight Commission campaigns do not necessarily constitute a representative selection; however, they do serve as valuable examples of campaigning by this institution. Moreover, the results of these investigations are confirmed by the interviews conducted with campaign managers of the Commission. It is true that, taking into consideration all the information gathered, we cannot really know *all* 'insider' habits, but we can surely formulate tendencies allowing systematic generalizations about the use of Eurobarometer surveys in the several phases of a campaign.

## Planning Phase

Our study reveals that the use of survey research in the context of European Commission campaigns is concentrated in the planning phase. All the campaigns in question using survey research do so in the planning phase. Apart from Eurobarometer surveys, sometimes other surveys, for example national ones, were utilized (e.g. Omnibus surveys). In addition, the interviews prove that the idea and conceptualization of a campaign are not only developed on the basis of survey data, but also on other – and at least in part non-scientific – sources of information. The point of departure for a campaign is a manifest problem in the political, economic, and/or social realm that could already have been revealed beforehand.

In this case, survey research serves as empirical and scientific proof of a general and known phenomenon. Consequently, the objective of a detailed situation analysis is not only to obtain actual knowledge about attitudes and/or behaviour, but also to justify a need for information. We could identify three reasons to draw up a situation analysis with the help of survey research:

1  to prove the existence of a problem and to justify the need for information as well as the usefulness of a campaign. This is important for approval and financing of the campaign by the Commission and the European Parliament (which controls the Commission's budget) and also with regard to the public (e.g. the practice of distributing survey results in a press folder at the beginning of the campaign);
2  to document the actual state of awareness, of attitudes and/or behaviour for the purpose of defining a campaign strategy, and ideally
3  to establish a yardstick relevant for the evaluation.

## Conceptualization

The definition of the campaign strategy relies on the results of the situation analysis. Campaigns organized by the European Commission mostly consist of both a general strategy and a more differentiated national one. The general and national strategies most often deal with the same broad goals and messages. The definition of means of communication and the concrete activities may vary considerably in the various member states (in line with the principle of decentralization). The degree of national differentiation also depends on whether the campaign topic is subject to the principle of subsidiarity; if so, organization and implementation of the campaign are then handled by the national authorities.

The criteria documented below are rarely defined already during the phase of conceptualization. Some of them emerge during the implementation phase.

- *Definition of budget and time frame:* as already mentioned, the budget has to be allocated by the European Parliament. The budget amount not only determines scope, duration and thus strategy of the campaign, but also the use of survey research. According to the interviews, the budget for survey research is a priori restricted in case of scarce resources. The share of survey research in the overall budget was estimated at an average of 5 per cent.
- *Definition of goals:* In the campaigns examined we could detect a variety of goals: informing and raising awareness, but also influencing attitudes or promoting action. A clear definition of goals in the planning phase is a prerequisite for evaluating a campaign's success after its completion.
- *Definition of messages and target groups:* although the examined campaigns often direct some of their messages towards the entire public, special target groups are always defined according to age, profession or other socio-demographic determinants. Survey research plays an important role in identifying the target audience. The message, i.e. central ideas and topics, however, does not necessarily always differ – at least not substantially – between the different target groups. In the interviews we found that the messages are sometimes tested focus groups.
- *Definition of means of communication:* The campaigns of the European Commission cover the whole range of communication channels: print media (brochures, posters, own publications); press releases, press conferences; audio-visual media (TV or radio spots, cassettes, video tapes, films); new electronic media (Internet, World Wide Web); events (lectures, discussions, open houses, exhibitions, competitions).

### Implementation Phase

During the implementation phase, survey research does not seem to play a role in the campaigns organized by the Commission; at least it was not possible to gather any clarifying information in the Appendix or through the interviews. The use of survey research during the implementation phase only makes sense in long-term campaigns and is therefore not really an option for *European Weeks* or *European Year* campaigns.

Campaign projects on a long-term basis, e.g. the *Europe against Cancer* campaign carried out since 1987, would be much more suitable, as *time series* are produced in the framework of such campaigns, which means that the Eurobarometer surveys ask the same questions about attitudes and behaviour of Europeans concerning smoking, eating and drinking habits, or regular medical examinations. Unfortunately, we do not have any information about the potential influence of these results on implementing the campaign phases that follow, i.e. we do not know whether the strategies are brought in line with the survey results.

### Evaluation Phase

Based on the results of the Appendix and the interviews, survey research does not play an important role during the evaluation phase, which means that survey techniques are rarely used for evaluating a campaign. The eight campaigns documented in the Appendix use Eurobarometer surveys only twice for the purpose of evaluation (compared with eight times in the planning phase). For the purpose of assessment, survey research is often supposed to justify or declare the campaign a success for EU institutions and the public.

### Evaluating the Campaign's Success

Assessment can measure several aspects of a campaign. After examining the different evaluation methods applied by the Commission, it is evident that survey research, when used for assessments at all, is mostly employed to measure the scope of the campaign rather than the possible change of attitude or behaviour or even the reduction of the problem identified at the beginning of the campaign. Elsewhere in this Handbook, Leon Ostergaard introduces useful terminology labelling the different aspects or *levels* of a campaign that can be evaluated. Following this terminology, evaluation in the examined campaign projects of the Commission is limited to the *campaign-knowledge level*. This result is also valid when evaluation is carried out by survey research.

*Campaign-knowledge level:* if survey techniques are used to assess the campaign level, the question is whether the campaign did in fact reach its target audience, and whether the target audience did notice the campaign and perceive the given information. This means in particular: awareness of the campaign and media-specific awareness (does R remember the kind of media?); recognition of the campaign content and recall of substantial information; response to the campaign (did R become active?); requirement of more information or increasing activities of the EU in this field.

The corresponding *sample* may be made up of both specifically selected groups, such as *opinion leaders* or the *target groups*, and a standard sample of a representative random selection. If the campaign projects use Eurobarometer surveys, they often refer to the standard samples, but special samples are also carried out in especially commissioned Flash Eurobarometers.

*Attitudes/behaviour level and problem level:* attitudes and behaviour are much more difficult to assess. For this purpose *time series*, which ask the same questions before and after the campaign at least at two points in time, are needed. Proving a causal connection between a change in attitudes/behaviour and the campaign's effects is very delicate and costly. Finding out if the initial problem has been alleviated faces the same difficulties, because most political and social problems are caused by a multitude of factors. Due to the problematic nature of causality and the multi-causality of effects, survey research is hardly used in this sector. A significant statement made in the context of the *European Drug Prevention Week (1992)* elucidates the problem.

> Considering the circumstances under which it took place and the varying backgrounds of the participating countries, it would be unrealistic to expect that an event such as the European Drug Prevention Week could produce immediate and tangible results. That was never the intention; too much should not be expected

of what was always to be a modest initiative. Only over time, and after further Weeks have been organized at sensible intervals, will significant progress be achieved. In any event, the Week alone could not be expected to produce tangible results. It should be judged only in conjunction with a range of other actions designed to reduce demand for drugs in the Community. Any other approach would lead to mistakes or disappointment, and would not reflect the reality of the situation. *Given these premises, it is not possible to prove that the Week was successful and beneficial. In the absence of objective indicators, conclusions have to be drawn on the basis of subjective assessments and statements made by individuals.*[5]

In fact, however, this statement seems to confirm the problem of defining a campaign's goals. Even the most modest campaign can be successful, if realistic and realizable goals on the respective levels of a campaign have been defined in the planning phase.

### Evaluation Methods

Whenever survey research is employed, it is used in addition to other scientific and non-scientific methods. The following list of evaluation methods is not exhaustive; it documents all instruments we found to be used more or less systematically by the campaigners of the European Commission.

- *Survey research:* when campaigners of the Commission use survey research, they most often refer to the Eurobarometer surveys.
- *Official statistics:* statistics are used in addition to surveys, e.g. sales figures or accident rates, to examine the possible reduction of the problem dealt with in the campaign. In the examined campaign projects, however, this kind of measurement is used predominantly in the planning phase because, as discussed above, an assessment of the problem level is not usual.
- *Media content analysis:* the intensity of media references to the campaign or the campaign topic is measured. We could also identify partially-selected media analyses, namely, if press releases have been distributed to selected media (e.g. women's magazines). In this case, a content analysis of only these specific media sectors was conducted. Evaluation by media analysis is limited to the assessment of the campaign's scope.
- *Co-operation with the European 'relays' in the member states:* established information networks, such as European documentation and information centres, can assess possible increases in the demand for information about the campaign's topic.
- *Discussions with colleagues, insiders, or experts:* discussion with colleagues or experts on the spot seems to be a very important evaluation method for the campaign organizers at the Commission. In this context, close co-operation and exchange with the Representation Offices in the member states plays a very important role. This kind of evaluation is mostly based on non-scientific subjective statements.

TABLE 8.1   *The use of Eurobarometer surveys in the different phases of a campaign*

| Campaigns | Use of survey research | | |
| --- | --- | --- | --- |
| | Planning phase | Implementation phase | Evaluation phase |
| European Year of the Elderly and Solidarity between the Generations (1993) | X | | |
| European Year of Safety, Hygiene and Health Protection at Work (1992) | X | | X |
| European Year for the Environment (1987) | X | | |
| European Year for Traffic Safety (1986) | X | | |
| European Drug Prevention Week (1992) | X | | |
| European Week for Business (1993) | X | | |
| Europe Against Cancer (1987–  ) | X | | X |
| Special Information Programme on German Unification (1991–92) | X | | |

- *Feedback and responses:* with reference to the *stimulus–response model*, feedback and reactions from the public should reflect the success of the campaign. Some of the campaigns explicitly encourage target groups to become active, e.g. using toll-free telephone numbers or Internet addresses. Interviews showed that this method is becoming an increasingly important evaluation tool. Quantity and quality of the reactions are evaluated as an indicator for the campaign's success. In this context, it should be mentioned that this kind of evaluation cannot substitute for survey research, as it only measures a small and non-representative part of the target groups, and its results cannot be generalized.

## SOME CONCLUSIONS: EUROBAROMETER SURVEYS IN THE SEVERAL PHASES OF A CAMPAIGN

The study of survey use in the several phases of campaigns reveals that European Commission campaigners use Eurobarometer surveys most often during the planning phase. Their aim is not only to define a campaign strategy (with goals, message, target groups and means of communication), but also to offer a scientific justification that proves the need for the campaign. Only rarely are surveys initiated to evaluate a campaign. Taking the eight campaigns documented in the Appendix as a reference, surveys were used only twice during the evaluation phase while in all cases a Eurobarometer survey was launched in the planning phase (see Table 8.1). Whenever evaluation is made with the help of survey research, it is generally reduced to campaign level in order to measure the scope of the campaign.

In the following step, we will illustrate the use of Eurobarometer surveys with a concrete example, presenting a campaign of the Commission that was accompanied by Eurobarometer surveys.

## THE EUROPEAN YEAR OF SAFETY, HYGIENE AND HEALTH PROTECTION AT WORK: AN EXAMPLE OF CAMPAIGNING BY THE EUROPEAN COMMISSION

The campaign in question, the 1992 *European Year of Safety, Hygiene and Health Protection at Work,*[6] is one of the few examples in our analysis that made use of survey research not only in the planning phase but also in the evaluation phase. In the context of this campaign two Eurobarometer surveys were launched, namely Eurobarometer 35.2 in Spring 1991 and Eurobarometer 39.2 in Spring 1993.

### Background and Framework

The topic of working conditions falls under the domain of Union policy and is part of the activities of the European Union. As European integration is supposed to take place not only on the economic and political but also on the social level, the European Union takes an active part in improving security and health standards at work and in reducing work-related accidents and illnesses. Yet, there are still important national differences with regard to legislation and safety standards, and as the free circulation within the Single European Market necessitates a harmonization of security standards, it is the declared aim of the Commission to reach a sufficiently high level of common minimum EU safety standards to facilitate the free circulation of workers. Since the activities of the EU should not be limited to legislative measures, but should also include information and advisory activities for employers as well as workers in the member states, this specific *European Year* campaign was launched. It constituted an important part of the extensive commitment of the European Union to safety and health at work in recent decades and took place in the context of a larger programme for working conditions. The European Council of Ministers decided to organize a *European Year of Safety and Hygiene at Work,* and their decision was approved by the European Parliament. The campaign was carried out by the Directorate General V for Employment, Industrial Relations, and Social Affairs and lasted from March 1992 until February 1993.

The style of organization is perfectly in line with the above-discussed principles of *decentralization* and *subsidiarity*. In order to guarantee the principle of subsidiarity as a basis of all national activities, the European Commission organized this *European Year* in close co-operation with the national contact committees created for this purpose at the national level. The national committees had the task of transmitting all relevant information to the national, regional and local levels and of organizing activities in all the member states. All activities took the diversity of the national systems of legislation and practices into account. This decentralized organization is also reflected in the *budget*: 60 per cent of the total budget of twelve million ECU were provided by the member states and were allocated for national activities.

## Planning Phase

The situation analysis of current working conditions in Europe was carried out on the basis of survey research and statistics. As described above, in this case the situation analysis functions not only as a basis or starting point for the campaign's conceptualization and strategy, but also provides justification. The collected data showed the need to improve working conditions and the need for information, and both factors justified the campaign's usefulness.

### STATISTICS[7]

Although much progress has been achieved in recent decades, statistics about working conditions in Europe show that there are still too many work accidents and work-related illnesses. At the end of the 1980s the situation even worsened and the number of accidents again increased, which shows that insecurity and risks in the work place continue to be important. In one year (1991), about 8,000 persons died due to work accidents. In the European Community[8] of 1993, with its 120 million workers, about ten million work-related accidents and illnesses were registered. In this respect, danger at work is still an important issue and has negative social consequences not only for individuals. It also affects the competitiveness of the businesses concerned as well as the economy in general, as each year a considerable amount of money is spent on compensation for work-related accidents and illnesses (e.g. about 26 billion ECU in 1991). Expert studies also revealed that most work-related accidents and illnesses must be seen in connection with poor management and could have been prevented. It seems therefore sensible that management use the available resources in the most efficient way to ensure workplace safety and workers' health while improving workers' motivation and productivity.

### SURVEY RESEARCH

Complementary to the statistics one survey was launched: Eurobarometer 35.2 of Spring 1991 asked questions especially commissioned by the campaign project in order to obtain an overview of the situation at work in Europe determining the conditions under which the *European Year* campaign should take place. The EB 35.2 is composed of a matched sample of EB 35.0 and 35.1; only the active European population was included in this sample.

### QUESTIONS

The first part asked general questions about working conditions and the respondents' workplaces. The questions dealt with shortcomings and hazards

TABLE 8.2   *Health or safety risk at work: 'Do you think your health or safety is at risk because of your work?'*

| | B | DK | D | EL | ES | F | IRL | IT | L | NL | P | UK | EC 12 |
|---|---|---|---|---|---|---|---|---|---|---|---|---|---|
| DK/NA No. of cases | 52 | 41 | 156 | 11 | 17 | 31 | 49 | 63 | 27 | 69 | 23 | 40 | 627 |
| col-% | 5.2 | 4.1 | 7.8 | 1.1 | 1.7 | 3.1 | 4.9 | 6.3 | 5.3 | 6.9 | 2.3 | 4.0 | 5.0 |
| YES | | | | | | | | | | | | | |
| No. of cases | 182 | 214 | 549 | 443 | 626 | 319 | 194 | 249 | 168 | 151 | 316 | 258 | 3767 |
| col-% | 18.2 | 21.4 | 27.4 | 44.3 | 62.6 | 31.9 | 19.4 | 24.9 | 33.6 | 15.1 | 31.6 | 25.8 | 30.1 |
| NO | | | | | | | | | | | | | |
| No. of cases | 766 | 745 | 1295 | 545 | 357 | 651 | 757 | 688 | 306 | 780 | 661 | 702 | 8106 |
| col-% | 76.6 | 74.5 | 64.8 | 54.5 | 35.7 | 65.1 | 75.7 | 68.8 | 61.1 | 78.0 | 66.1 | 70.2 | 64.8 |
| TOTAL | | | | | | | | | | | | | |
| No. of cases | 1000 | 1000 | 2000 | 1000 | 1000 | 1000 | 1000 | 1000 | 500 | 1001 | 1000 | 1000 | 12500 |
| col-% | 100 | 100 | 100 | 100 | 100 | 100 | 100 | 100 | 100 | 100 | 100 | 100 | 100 |

*Source*: Eurobarometer 35.2 (Spring 1991)

with regard to safety and health conditions, the frequency of work-related illnesses, and the number of accidents. The second part asked the interviewees how satisfied they were with the measures taken in their companies and what their opinion was about possible improvements, persons in charge, workers' participation in decision-making processes, adequacy of information, and professional training. Some of the questions focused on the need for information and the role of the European Community (EC) concerning legislation of working conditions. These questions dealt with the awareness of EC activities in this field, the need for more information and legislation at the European level.

SURVEY RESULTS

The first part of the survey about the actual working conditions proved that a danger to safety and health still exists and that was also manifest in the feeling of many Europeans: nearly one-third (30 per cent) of the active European population felt that their health and safety are at risk because of their work (see Table 8.2).[9] About 40 per cent of the respondents thought that work exposes them to the risk of accident or injury (see Table 8.3).

The second part of the survey proved that actions to improve working conditions are required, as is more information: 16 per cent of the active European population was not satisfied with the actions taken to ensure safety, hygiene and health at their current place of work (see Table 8.4). Furthermore, a significant majority of active Europeans had a positive attitude towards EC involvement to improve working conditions: 87 per cent were in favour of common EC legislation for all member states concerning safety, hygiene and health in the workplace (see Table 8.5). Further, 61 per cent of the interviewees wanted more information on EC actions to protect workers (see Table 8.6).

TABLE 8.3  Risk of accident at work: 'Do you think that your work makes you run the risk of accident or injury?'

|  | B | DK | D | EL | ES | F | IRL | IT | L | NL | P | UK | EC 12 |
|---|---|---|---|---|---|---|---|---|---|---|---|---|---|
| **DK/NA** No. of cases | 22 | 7 | 25 | 0 | 2 | 5 | 22 | 6 | 6 | 29 | 21 | 23 | 153 |
| col-% | 2.2 | 0.7 | 1.3 | 0 | 0.2 | 0.5 | 2.2 | 0.6 | 1.2 | 2.9 | 2.1 | 2.3 | 1.2 |
| **YES, VERY MUCH** | | | | | | | | | | | | | |
| No. of cases | 110 | 71 | 179 | 203 | 132 | 117 | 66 | 99 | 80 | 50 | 98 | 81 | 1241 |
| col-% | 11.0 | 7.1 | 9.0 | 20.3 | 13.2 | 11.7 | 6.6 | 9.9 | 15.9 | 5.0 | 9.8 | 8.1 | 9.9 |
| **YES, A BIT** | | | | | | | | | | | | | |
| No. of cases | 250 | 220 | 601 | 291 | 371 | 316 | 276 | 265 | 149 | 247 | 317 | 275 | 3677 |
| col-% | 25.0 | 22.0 | 30.1 | 29.2 | 37.1 | 31.6 | 27.6 | 26.5 | 29.8 | 24.7 | 31.7 | 27.5 | 29.4 |
| **NO, NOT REALLY** | | | | | | | | | | | | | |
| No. of cases | 233 | 238 | 506 | 148 | 225 | 170 | 239 | 160 | 85 | 253 | 181 | 231 | 2659 |
| col-% | 23.3 | 23.8 | 25.3 | 14.8 | 22.5 | 17.0 | 23.9 | 16.0 | 16.9 | 25.2 | 18.1 | 23.1 | 21.3 |
| **NO, NOT AT ALL** | | | | | | | | | | | | | |
| No. of cases | 385 | 465 | 688 | 358 | 269 | 392 | 397 | 470 | 181 | 421 | 383 | 390 | 4770 |
| col-% | 38.5 | 46.5 | 34.4 | 35.8 | 26.9 | 39.2 | 39.7 | 47.0 | 36.2 | 42.1 | 38.3 | 39.0 | 38.2 |
| **TOTAL** | | | | | | | | | | | | | |
| No. of cases | 1000 | 1000 | 2000 | 1000 | 1000 | 1000 | 1000 | 1000 | 500 | 1001 | 1000 | 1000 | 12500 |
| col-% | 100 | 100 | 100 | 100 | 100 | 100 | 100 | 100 | 100 | 100 | 100 | 100 | 100 |

Source: Eurobarometer 35.2 (Spring 1991)

TABLE 8.4  Satisfaction with actions for safety: 'How satisfied are you with the actions taken to ensure the safety, hygiene and health of people at your current place of work? Are you ...?'

|  | B | DK | D | EL | ES | F | IRL | IT | L | NL | P | UK | EC 12 |
|---|---|---|---|---|---|---|---|---|---|---|---|---|---|
| **DK/NA** No. of cases | 107 | 43 | 46 | 84 | 48 | 112 | 55 | 108 | 39 | 40 | 66 | 53 | 804 |
| col-% | 10.7 | 4.3 | 2.3 | 8.4 | 4.8 | 11.2 | 5.5 | 10.8 | 7.7 | 4.0 | 6.6 | 5.3 | 6.4 |
| **VERY SATISFIED** | | | | | | | | | | | | | |
| No. of cases | 277 | 441 | 651 | 131 | 195 | 215 | 508 | 222 | 189 | 391 | 123 | 424 | 3640 |
| col-% | 27.7 | 44.1 | 32.6 | 13.1 | 19.5 | 21.5 | 50.8 | 22.2 | 37.8 | 39.1 | 12.3 | 42.4 | 29.1 |
| **QUITE SATISFIED** | | | | | | | | | | | | | |
| No. of cases | 483 | 385 | 1049 | 447 | 552 | 471 | 358 | 488 | 201 | 480 | 591 | 414 | 6071 |
| col-% | 48.2 | 38.4 | 52.4 | 44.8 | 55.2 | 47.1 | 35.8 | 48.8 | 40.1 | 48.0 | 59.1 | 41.4 | 48.6 |
| **QUITE DISSATISFIED** | | | | | | | | | | | | | |
| No. of cases | 93 | 103 | 203 | 207 | 160 | 141 | 39 | 134 | 41 | 82 | 159 | 86 | 1484 |
| col-% | 9.3 | 10.3 | 10.2 | 20.7 | 16.0 | 14.1 | 3.9 | 13.4 | 8.2 | 8.2 | 15.9 | 8.6 | 11.9 |
| **VERY DISSATISFIED** | | | | | | | | | | | | | |
| No. of cases | 41 | 28 | 51 | 130 | 46 | 60 | 40 | 48 | 31 | 7 | 61 | 24 | 501 |
| col-% | 4.1 | 2.8 | 2.6 | 13.0 | 4.6 | 6.0 | 4.0 | 4.8 | 6.2 | 0.7 | 6.1 | 2.4 | 4.0 |
| **TOTAL** | | | | | | | | | | | | | |
| No. of cases | 1000 | 1000 | 2000 | 1000 | 1000 | 1000 | 1000 | 1000 | 500 | 1001 | 1000 | 1000 | 12500 |
| col-% | 100 | 100 | 100 | 100 | 100 | 100 | 100 | 100 | 100 | 100 | 100 | 100 | 100 |

Source: Eurobarometer 35.2 (Spring 1991)

TABLE 8.5   *Is R for/against common EC legislation on safety:* 'Would you be for or against the application of common legislation in all the countries of the European Community, concerning safety, hygiene or health at places of work?'

|  | B | DK | D | EL | ES | F | IRL | IT | L | NL | P | UK | EC 12 |
|---|---|---|---|---|---|---|---|---|---|---|---|---|---|
| DK/NA No. of cases | 102 | 69 | 186 | 51 | 60 | 94 | 109 | 45 | 46 | 54 | 75 | 78 | 954 |
| col-% | 10.2 | 6.9 | 9.3 | 5.1 | 6.0 | 9.4 | 10.9 | 4.5 | 9.2 | 5.4 | 7.5 | 7.8 | 7.6 |
| FOR – VERY MUCH |  |  |  |  |  |  |  |  |  |  |  |  |  |
| No. of cases | 448 | 248 | 739 | 729 | 625 | 425 | 578 | 655 | 235 | 456 | 542 | 446 | 5996 |
| col-% | 44.8 | 24.8 | 37.0 | 72.9 | 62.5 | 42.5 | 57.8 | 65.5 | 47.0 | 45.6 | 54.2 | 44.6 | 48.0 |
| FOR – TO SOME EXTENT |  |  |  |  |  |  |  |  |  |  |  |  |  |
| No. of cases | 421 | 385 | 891 | 196 | 304 | 441 | 290 | 286 | 183 | 440 | 375 | 406 | 4850 |
| col-% | 42.1 | 38.5 | 44.5 | 19.6 | 30.4 | 44.1 | 29.0 | 28.6 | 36.5 | 43.9 | 37.5 | 40.6 | 38.8 |
| AGAINST – TO SOME EXTENT |  |  |  |  |  |  |  |  |  |  |  |  |  |
| No. of cases | 25 | 131 | 166 | 19 | 8 | 25 | 15 | 12 | 24 | 38 | 8 | 54 | 543 |
| col-% | 2.5 | 13.1 | 8.3 | 1.9 | 0.8 | 2.5 | 1.5 | 1.2 | 4.8 | 3.8 | 0.8 | 5.3 | 4.3 |
| AGAINST – VERY MUCH |  |  |  |  |  |  |  |  |  |  |  |  |  |
| No. of cases | 5 | 167 | 18 | 5 | 2 | 15 | 8 | 2 | 12 | 13 | 0 | 17 | 156 |
| col-% | 0.5 | 16.7 | 0.9 | 0.5 | 0.2 | 1.5 | 0.8 | 0.2 | 2.5 | 1.3 | 0 | 1.7 | 1.2 |
| TOTAL |  |  |  |  |  |  |  |  |  |  |  |  |  |
| No. of cases | 1000 | 1000 | 2000 | 1000 | 1000 | 1000 | 1000 | 1000 | 500 | 1001 | 1000 | 1000 | 12500 |
| col-% | 100 | 100 | 100 | 100 | 100 | 100 | 100 | 100 | 100 | 100 | 100 | 100 | 100 |

Source: Eurobarometer 35.2 (Spring 1991)

TABLE 8.6   *R wants more info about EC-actions:* 'Would you like to receive more information on the actions of the European Community concerning the protection of workers in companies and institutions such as yours?'

|  | B | DK | D | EL | ES | F | IRL | IT | L | NL | P | UK | EC 12 |
|---|---|---|---|---|---|---|---|---|---|---|---|---|---|
| DK/NA No. of cases | 124 | 68 | 312 | 41 | 63 | 84 | 114 | 91 | 43 | 97 | 44 | 58 | 1198 |
| col-% | 12.4 | 6.8 | 15.6 | 4.1 | 6.3 | 8.4 | 11.4 | 9.1 | 8.7 | 9.7 | 4.4 | 5.8 | 9.6 |
| YES |  |  |  |  |  |  |  |  |  |  |  |  |  |
| No. of cases | 470 | 460 | 941 | 851 | 831 | 611 | 596 | 762 | 281 | 472 | 860 | 533 | 7578 |
| col-% | 47.0 | 46.0 | 47.1 | 85.1 | 83.1 | 61.1 | 59.6 | 76.2 | 56.1 | 47.2 | 86.0 | 53.3 | 60.6 |
| NO |  |  |  |  |  |  |  |  |  |  |  |  |  |
| No. of cases | 407 | 472 | 746 | 108 | 106 | 304 | 289 | 146 | 176 | 432 | 96 | 409 | 3724 |
| col-% | 40.7 | 47.2 | 37.3 | 10.8 | 10.6 | 30.4 | 28.9 | 14.6 | 35.2 | 43.1 | 9.6 | 40.9 | 29.8 |
| TOTAL |  |  |  |  |  |  |  |  |  |  |  |  |  |
| No. of cases | 1000 | 1000 | 2000 | 1000 | 1000 | 1000 | 1000 | 1000 | 500 | 1001 | 1000 | 1000 | 12500 |
| col-% | 100 | 100 | 100 | 100 | 100 | 100 | 100 | 100 | 100 | 100 | 100 | 100 | 100 |

Source: Eurobarometer 35.2 (Spring 1991)

## Conceptualization

### DEFINITION OF PURPOSES AND GOALS

The main purpose of this *European Year* was to solve human and economic problems created by the high number of work-related accidents and ill-nesses. There were two strategies:

1 raising awareness and encouraging actions on the part of the authorities, such as European institutions, member states, and social partners, to improve working conditions.

2 Since the Eurobarometer survey indicated that too many citizens in the active population still lacked sufficient information about EC initiatives, the second purpose of the campaign was to inform the public, especially workers, and to enhance public awareness of working conditions.

## DEFINITION OF CENTRAL TOPICS

The European Commission concentrated its campaigning activities on central topics such as air quality, improving safety standards, noise control and well-being at work.

## DEFINITION OF TARGET GROUPS AND MESSAGES

These target groups seem to have been selected mainly on the basis of statistics, though reinforced by the survey results. The campaigners chose specific target groups based on professional sectors: agriculture, construction, and the fishing industry. This selection was motivated by the fact that up to now, these three sectors have had the most dangerous workplaces with the highest rate of accidents and permanent disability. Apart from the general goals, specifically adapted objectives were defined for each target group.

- *Construction*: This sector, with about 10 million workers (1992), was chosen in order to provide more information about causes and risks, rules in force and their observance by the employers. More than half of the respondents working in this sector estimated that their work affected their health, compared with one-third of the whole active European population.
- *Agriculture*: Modernization in the agricultural sector not only brought the automation of work, but also frequently exposed workers to fertilizers and pesticides, both of which have made working in agriculture more dangerous than ever. For this reason, the European Community aimed at improving training for those who worked with heavy machinery and providing more information about the use of chemical products. Activities aimed at this special target group concentrated on the countries where agriculture is (still) an important sector, such as Greece, Portugal, Spain, and Italy.
- *Fishing*: Motorization and modernization of fishing fleets have not improved working conditions on boats, and fishing remains a high-risk enterprise with the highest accident rate. Consequently, the *European Year* set two goals: to provide the 280,000 European seamen (1992) with better information about risks on board, and to exert more effective influence on those responsible for designing and building fishing boats.

Apart from these three sectors, two further target groups were chosen.

- *Young people in professional training*: Statistics proved that young people without professional experience face a higher risk of accidents. The Eurobarometer survey showed that young people in particular would like more information about this issue. Sensitization and training activities should be part of the responsibility of schools. Although the message was the same, the individual activities on national level differed.

- *Small and medium-sized businesses*: About 13 million small and medium-sized businesses in Europe employ about three-quarters of the work force (in 1992), but have fewer resources at their disposal than larger businesses to deal with safety problems, provide information about safety rules, or make substantial investments in modernizing machines and tools. The *European Year* had a strategy of partnership between local collectivities, national authorities and social partners such as trade unions, employers and administration.

### MEANS OF COMMUNICATION

Just as the national strategies differed, so did the means of communication and activities on the spot, although the main means of communication were used in all countries. The campaign started with information activities that included widespread distribution of information brochures and technical documentation as well as broadcasts of numerous programmes on the leading national channels. Concrete actions and events followed, with altogether about 2,600 activities (conferences, film festivals, competitions) emphasizing activities on the national level. Video proved to be an important instrument of communication, and many video clips promoting the improvement of working conditions were produced. Some of them were shown at the European Film Festival of Formation and Information in the Field of Health and Safety.

## Implementation Phase

No survey research was used in the implementation phase, for reasons discussed above. Overall, the limited time frame of the *European Year* has to be mentioned. The role of the national actors in implementing the campaign is noteworthy. About 2,000 of the 2,600 activities carried out during this *European Year* were organized without the Commission's support. The 500 activities financially supported by the Commission were focused on small and medium-sized businesses and young people in professional training.

## Evaluation Phase

As mentioned, this European Year campaign is one of the few that carried out survey research for its evaluation; this was, however, reduced to the assessment at campaign level.

### SURVEY RESEARCH

In Eurobarometer 39.2 of Spring 1993 the questions measure the campaign's scope. Assessment of changing tendencies at attitude/behaviour level or problem level was not included. The sample of EB 39.2 is matched by the samples of EB 39.0 and 39.1. In contrast to the Eurobarometer survey 35.2 used in the planning phase, the present sample is not limited to the active

TABLE 8.7 *EC should check application of safety legislation more:*
*'Do you think that the European Community should do more, about the*
*same or less? Checking the application of community legislation on health,*
*safety and hygiene at work'*

| | B | DK | D | EL | ES | F | IRL | IT | L | NL | P | UK | EC 12 |
|---|---|---|---|---|---|---|---|---|---|---|---|---|---|
| **MORE** | | | | | | | | | | | | | |
| No. of cases | 574 | 610 | 1187 | 876 | 616 | 698 | 550 | 662 | 269 | 586 | 870 | 755 | 8152 |
| col-% | 60.4 | 58.8 | 56.6 | 91.4 | 77.2 | 64.4 | 65.5 | 74.3 | 55.4 | 62.4 | 84.5 | 59.3 | 65.2 |
| **ABOUT** | | | | | | | | | | | | | |
| **THE SAME** | | | | | | | | | | | | | |
| No. of cases | 198 | 253 | 565 | 19 | 60 | 252 | 139 | 86 | 98 | 159 | 81 | 249 | 2331 |
| col-% | 20.9 | 24.3 | 26.9 | 2.0 | 7.6 | 23.2 | 16.6 | 9.7 | 20.1 | 17.0 | 7.8 | 19.5 | 18.7 |
| **LESS** | | | | | | | | | | | | | |
| No. of cases | 32 | 68 | 39 | 2 | 3 | 14 | 5 | 1 | 4 | 25 | 3 | 53 | 224 |
| col-% | 3.4 | 6.5 | 1.9 | 0.2 | 0.4 | 1.3 | 0.6 | 0.1 | 0.9 | 2.6 | 0.3 | 4.2 | 1.8 |
| **DK/NA** | | | | | | | | | | | | | |
| No. of cases | 146 | 108 | 307 | 61 | 119 | 120 | 145 | 142 | 115 | 170 | 77 | 217 | 1787 |
| col-% | 15.4 | 10.4 | 14.6 | 6.4 | 14.9 | 11.1 | 17.3 | 15.9 | 23.7 | 18.1 | 7.5 | 17.0 | 14.3 |
| **TOTAL** | | | | | | | | | | | | | |
| No. of cases | 950 | 1039 | 2098 | 958 | 798 | 1084 | 840 | 891 | 486 | 940 | 1030 | 1274 | 12495 |
| col-% | 100 | 100 | 100 | 100 | 100 | 100 | 100 | 100 | 100 | 100 | 100 | 100 | 100 |

*Source:* Eurobarometer 39.2 (Spring 1993)

population of Europeans, but is composed of a matched standard sample of a representative random selection of all European citizens over age 15. This lack of identical criteria for the two samples entails that care is required when comparing answers to the same survey questions and identifying trends with a limited content.[10]

QUESTIONS
The questions aimed overall to measure respondents' awareness of EC activities, and especially of the *European Year of the Protection of Safety and Hygiene at Work*, the media-specific awareness, i.e. the recall of the information channels, and the requirement of increasing the activities of the European Community.

SURVEY RESULTS
Asking the same question in both surveys on awareness of EC activities in the field of safety, hygiene and health at work showed that such awareness increased during the *European Year*: from Spring 1991 to Spring 1993, the percentage of Europeans[11] who had heard anything about the activities of the European Community rose from 18 per cent to 23 per cent, and 19 per cent of Europeans were aware that 1992 was a *European Year of Safety, Hygiene and Health Protection at Work*. Concerning media-specific awareness, the best-remembered sources of information were the media (55 per cent) and one's own workplace (18 per cent). A significant majority of Europeans wanted more involvement by the EC: about two-thirds of citizens think that the European Community should do more about working conditions via legislation, information and research (see Tables 8.7–8.9).

TABLE 8.8   *Providing information on health, safety and hygiene at work:*
*'Do you think that the European Community should do more,*
*about the same or less?'*

|                   | B    | DK   | D    | EL   | ES   | F    | IRL  | IT   | L    | NL   | P    | UK   | EC 12 |
|-------------------|------|------|------|------|------|------|------|------|------|------|------|------|-------|
| MORE              |      |      |      |      |      |      |      |      |      |      |      |      |       |
| No. of cases      | 595  | 653  | 1185 | 881  | 656  | 749  | 600  | 722  | 275  | 634  | 895  | 862  | 8673  |
| col-%             | 62.6 | 62.8 | 56.5 | 92.0 | 82.2 | 69.1 | 71.5 | 81.0 | 56.7 | 67.4 | 86.9 | 67.6 | 69.4  |
| ABOUT THE SAME    |      |      |      |      |      |      |      |      |      |      |      |      |       |
| No. of cases      | 204  | 236  | 572  | 21   | 47   | 226  | 117  | 74   | 99   | 159  | 61   | 220  | 2187  |
| col-%             | 21.5 | 22.8 | 27.3 | 2.2  | 5.9  | 20.8 | 14.0 | 8.3  | 20.4 | 16.9 | 5.9  | 17.3 | 17.5  |
| LESS              |      |      |      |      |      |      |      |      |      |      |      |      |       |
| No. of cases      | 19   | 64   | 59   | 2    | 1    | 9    | 2    | 1    | 5    | 17   | 2    | 34   | 200   |
| col-%             | 2.0  | 6.1  | 2.8  | 0.2  | 0.2  | 0.8  | 0.3  | 0.1  | 0.9  | 1.8  | 0.2  | 2.7  | 1.6   |
| DK/NA             |      |      |      |      |      |      |      |      |      |      |      |      |       |
| No. of cases      | 132  | 86   | 282  | 54   | 93   | 100  | 120  | 94   | 107  | 131  | 72   | 158  | 1435  |
| col-%             | 13.9 | 8.3  | 13.4 | 5.6  | 11.7 | 9.3  | 14.3 | 10.6 | 22.0 | 13.9 | 6.9  | 12.4 | 11.5  |
| TOTAL             |      |      |      |      |      |      |      |      |      |      |      |      |       |
| No. of cases      | 950  | 1039 | 2098 | 958  | 798  | 1084 | 840  | 891  | 486  | 940  | 1030 | 1274 | 12495 |
| col-%             | 100  | 100  | 100  | 100  | 100  | 100  | 100  | 100  | 100  | 100  | 100  | 100  | 100   |

*Source*: Eurobarometer 39.2 (Spring 1993)

TABLE 8.9   *EC should stimulate worker–employer discussions:'Do you think*
*that the European Community should do more, about the same or less?*
*Stimulating discussions between workers organizations and employers organizations'*

|                   | B    | DK   | D    | EL   | ES   | F    | IRL  | IT   | L    | NL   | P    | UK   | EC 12 |
|-------------------|------|------|------|------|------|------|------|------|------|------|------|------|-------|
| MORE              |      |      |      |      |      |      |      |      |      |      |      |      |       |
| No. of cases      | 507  | 509  | 1045 | 847  | 620  | 708  | 536  | 671  | 239  | 573  | 872  | 790  | 7974  |
| col-%             | 53.3 | 49.1 | 49.8 | 88.4 | 77.7 | 65.3 | 63.8 | 75.3 | 49.2 | 61.0 | 84.7 | 62.0 | 63.8  |
| ABOUT THE SAME    |      |      |      |      |      |      |      |      |      |      |      |      |       |
| No. of cases      | 243  | 300  | 639  | 37   | 62   | 235  | 149  | 74   | 124  | 185  | 69   | 241  | 2418  |
| col-%             | 25.6 | 28.9 | 30.4 | 3.9  | 7.8  | 21.7 | 17.8 | 8.3  | 25.6 | 19.7 | 6.7  | 18.9 | 19.4  |
| LESS              |      |      |      |      |      |      |      |      |      |      |      |      |       |
| No. of cases      | 44   | 94   | 88   | 10   | 6    | 17   | 6    | 9    | 6    | 37   | 4    | 57   | 353   |
| col-%             | 4.6  | 9.1  | 4.2  | 1.1  | 0.7  | 1.5  | 0.7  | 1.1  | 1.3  | 3.9  | 0.4  | 4.5  | 2.8   |
| DK/NA             |      |      |      |      |      |      |      |      |      |      |      |      |       |
| No. of cases      | 156  | 135  | 326  | 64   | 110  | 124  | 149  | 137  | 116  | 145  | 85   | 186  | 1750  |
| col-%             | 16.5 | 13.0 | 15.6 | 6.7  | 13.8 | 11.4 | 17.7 | 15.3 | 24.0 | 15.5 | 8.2  | 14.6 | 14.0  |
| TOTAL             |      |      |      |      |      |      |      |      |      |      |      |      |       |
| No. of cases      | 950  | 1039 | 2098 | 958  | 798  | 1084 | 840  | 891  | 486  | 940  | 1030 | 1274 | 12495 |
| col-%             | 100  | 100  | 100  | 100  | 100  | 100  | 100  | 100  | 100  | 100  | 100  | 100  | 100   |

*Source*: Eurobarometer 39.2 (Spring 1993)

Based on the results of the Eurobarometer survey, the campaigners considered the *European Year* a success: it received considerable attention and managed to raise the awareness of workers and authorities with regard to health and safety risks at work and how to reduce them. Over 60 million citizens were reached by the numerous activities during this *European Year*. Some of the survey results have been furnished in the final report[12] in order to prove the success of the campaign.

The campaigners evaluate the campaign's success in the first place with regard to the campaign's scope measured in the Eurobarometer survey, but the positive feedback during the activities channelled by the Representation Offices was also an important indicator for a positive assessment. No other evaluation method was officially mentioned.

## CONCLUSION

Interpreting the results of both the Appendix and the interviews reveals basically the same tendencies.

- On the whole, it can be stated that survey research does not play a central role in the daily routine of European Commission campaigners. In addition, the interviews showed that the use of research differs considerably. The use of survey research is not only a question of budget, size and time frame, but also depends essentially on the campaign managers themselves, on their background, their training, and their attitudes towards survey research in general. The reason most often mentioned to explain the limited use of survey research was 'resource restrictions'.
- When survey research is used, however, the Eurobarometer surveys play an important role. Even though other surveys, e.g. national ones, are employed, campaigners most frequently refer to the Eurobarometer.
- When survey research is used, it is most often during the planning phase, not only to define the campaign strategy, but also to justify or to prove the necessity and usefulness of the campaign in question to European institutions (above all to the European Parliament that allocates the budget) and the public.
- Only rarely are surveys initiated to evaluate a campaign. Taking the eight campaigns documented in the Appendix as a reference, surveys were used only twice during the evaluation phase. Whenever evaluation is made with the help of survey research, it is generally reduced to campaign level.
- When comparing these findings with those documented elsewhere in this Handbook it becomes evident that campaigning in the European Commission, in spite of its specific circumstances, faces the same problems and frequently finds the same solutions as elsewhere.

## NOTES

1  The unpublished Appendix of the Campaign Handbook has been submitted to the European Commission, Directorate General X, Audio-Visual, Information, Communication, Culture/Surveys, Research, Analyses (Eurobarometer) Unit.
2  These interviews were carried out in Brussels in May 1997 with the responsible co-ordinators of a currently conducted campaign, namely the *Europe* Information Campaign composed of *The Euro: A Currency for Europe*, *Citizens First* and *Building Europe Together*. See for more detail Hans-Dieter Klingemann and Andrea Römmele, 'The use of survey research in information and communication campaigns. A practitioner's view.' *ZEUS-Report*, June 1997.

3    Christine Pütz (1996) Campaigns and Surveys. Appendix: Campaigns and Eurobarometer. ZEUS Report No. 155.

4    Because of the decentralized structure of and high fluctuation within the European Commission, it was very difficult to obtain information about projects that had already ended, and we were not able to receive material for all the campaigns documented in the Appendix information material.

5    Commission of the European Commission, Communication from the Commission to the Council Concerning an Assessment of the European Drug Prevention Week, Com (93) 353 Final, Brussels, 1993: 13 (author's emphasis).

6    Information about this campaign comes from the brochure 'Europe Sociale: L'Europe pour la sécurité et la santé sur le lieu de travail, 3/93', Luxembourg 1994; documentation sent on request by the Directorate General V.

7    Source of following data: 'Cadre Général pour l'action de la Commission des Communitées Européennes dans le domaine de la sécurité, de l'hygiène et de la santé au travail (1994–2000)' (COM (93) 560), quoted in 'Europe Sociale: L'Europe pour la sécurité et la santé sur le lieu de travail, 3/93', Luxembourg 1994 (see note 6).

8    We use the term 'European Community' instead of 'European Union', because it was the correct terminology at the time.

9    All tables and graphs are components of the Appendix of the Campaign Handbook (See note 1).

10   For this reason, the non-active population is excluded from the calculation basis in the tables of the Appendix to EB 39.2 for better comparability.

11   This trend has to be evaluated with the restictions discussed above. In the first survey, 'Europeans' means the active population, but in the second survey it refers to all European citizens over age 15.

12   See note 6.

# 9

# The Role of Survey Research in International Campaigns: What Can be Learnt From Case Studies?

## Michele Corrado

This chapter seeks to demonstrate how survey research can be a valuable tool in international communications campaigns. A number of case histories are given, drawing on international research conducted by MORI's Social Research Institute in London for the World Wide Fund for Nature (WWF International) and Greenpeace International. In each case, research has been conducted among the general public.

For the purposes of this chapter, the WWF International example will concentrate on international positioning research – research that informs an organization about how it is perceived or how an issue is perceived (in this case the environment) and can assist in the way it positions itself and its corporate communications strategy. The results were used to help WWF tailor its environmental advertising messages to different countries and cultures. The Greenpeace example will first discuss how international positioning research was used to provide Greenpeace with a better understanding of its potential supporters around the globe and how they may be reached through campaigning and fund-raising activity. Next, the Greenpeace work will then focus on two specific campaigns and the role played by subsequent research in them: nuclear testing in the South Pacific (commissioned by Greenpeace UK), and genetically modified food (commissioned by Greenpeace International). Each of these campaigns sought to measure awareness of and attitudes towards these issues among the public, use the results as a means of lobbying Brussels, and, in the case of genetically modified food, help shape the campaign as genetically engineered maize and stetbeans began to arrive in Europe from the United States.

By their very nature, international campaigns differ from national ones. International campaigns need to focus on a *consistent* message across the countries they are designed to influence, but *also* need to take into account each country's preoccupations and cultural nuances, to ensure the maximum uptake of messages. Often, with international campaigns, and indeed research that informs international campaigns, there are many stakeholders – the international client, national client organizations, the audience in each country, research agencies, advertising and public relations agencies – and a lot of co-ordination is required to ensure consistency and to meet timing and budgetary constraints. While positioning research can be used to inform strategic thinking and broad campaigning and communications issues, research findings for *specific* campaigns tend to be used more tactically, often with a very specific goal in mind (e.g. to lobby members of parliament on a particular issue).

## CASE HISTORY 1: WWF INTERNATIONAL

### Background and Objectives

WWF International is a leading international nature conservation and environment charity, with headquarters in Gland, Switzerland. Founded in 1961, WWF now has projects in 100 countries on five continents, offices in 70 of those countries, and comprehensive national organizations in 25 of those. WWF International's role is to co-ordinate the communications, campaigning, and international legislative advocacy activities of the 25 national organizations in the WWF family. Each WWF family member has its own Communications and Advocacy Unit and has developed in its own distinct way to reflect the needs and aspirations of its particular culture. The individual family members share their experiences with each other directly, through regular communications meetings organized by WWF International, and through frequent consultations with International's professional staff.

The objectives of the research programme – which comprised qualitative research in the form of focus groups per country, followed by a national quantitative survey – were to examine:

- the importance of the environment compared with other concerns;
- the perceived important environmental issues of the day, locally, nationally, and globally;
- people's behaviour with respect to the environment: whether they care enough to do something about it, and differences in attitude by environmental activism;[1]
- awareness of environmental groups (NGOs and others), and how this differs by country for those operating in more than one country;
- the public's image of WWF, particularly in the areas of providing information on the environment, saving the environment for future generations, educating people, and lobbying governments;
- willingness to take part in various activities linked to support for WWF and protection of the environment, and the relative popularity of each of these in different countries;
- the *nature* of each country's understanding of the environment, to provide information to help tailor environmental messages accordingly.

Qualitative research helps provide deep insight into *why* people feel the way they do, while quantitative work provides hard, statistical evidence.

TABLE 9.1  *WWF International research*

| 1991 | 1992 | 1993 | 1994 | 1995 | 1996 |
|------|------|------|------|------|------|
| Australia | Austria | Greece | Denmark | Brazil | Russia |
| Canada | New Zealand | Hong Kong | India | Japan | |
| France | Spain | Malaysia | Pakistan | | |
| (West) Germany | Switzerland | Belgium | | | |
| Great Britain | | Finland | | | |
| Italy | | Hungary | | | |
| The Netherlands | | South Africa | | | |
| Sweden | | Poland | | | |
| | | (by Pentor)[a] | | | |

[a]Parallel work in Poland was carried out for another purpose and made available for use. We are grateful to Professor Piotr Kwiatkowski of Pentor, Warsaw, Poland, for his permission to quote the Polish findings.

## The Countries Surveyed

The research programme spanned six years, from 1991 to 1996, and built on earlier work conducted by MORI for WWF International in 1988. In all countries, focus groups were conducted among a mix of environmental activists[1] and semi-activists (those carrying out three or four activities from the same list). Thus, the qualitative phase was conducted among the more environmentally active. This was in order to examine *their* level of concern for and understanding of environmental issues, and how best this could be used to communicate to the public at large the need to act in an environmentally responsible way and encourage others to do the same. The quantitative phase comprised research among representative samples of between 500 and 2,000 adults per country, using either face-to-face or telephone research, and generally Omnibus[2] methodology. The countries where research was undertaken are given in Table 9.1. There are plans to 'revisit' those in which research has already been undertaken, in order to monitor the effect of the campaigns and communications activities which WWF has developed in the interim.

## Qualitative Research: Main Findings

The environment emerged as an important issue to the general public in most countries, with some qualifications:

- In South Africa (surveyed in 1993), environmental concerns were not of prime importance (from a sample that under-represented the black townships).[3] Environmental concerns were overshadowed by the social and political unrest facing the country, as illustrated by this quote: 'The first thing on people's minds is to resolve this change of government thing. Then education – real, proper education, then you start moving into the environment'.
- Some countries felt particularly hard-hit by the world-wide economic recession, notably Great Britain, New Zealand and Austria. In these countries the environment was again lower on people's priority list.

- Discussing environmental issues at greater length with respondents generally revealed that their main concerns were for their *immediate* environment, not global environmental issues.[4] A consistent concern across countries was quality of life, in particular health (especially children's health), air pollution and noise pollution: 'Antarctica is a long way off, but the rubbish is just outside my house' (Italy).
- However, many distinct national and local concerns were also cited. For example: in Switzerland, soil erosion caused by skiing installations; in New Zealand, nuclear testing in the South Pacific, urban planning, CFCs in air conditioning units and the control of domestic animal populations; in Hong Kong, living conditions (among Chinese respondents) and resource depletion (among non-Chinese).

  This posed a particular challenge for WWF International, which faced the task of communicating a *consistent* message (though tailored to various countries) through its national organizations (NOs).

- While concern for the environment was relatively high in most countries, the degree to which environmental messages had been taken on board varied considerably by country. For example, in Spain and Greece, which have become industrialized only relatively recently, some concern was expressed about the environment but there was also general support for industrialization, with consumerism seen as having led to the advancement of individuals and society. Correspondingly, the Greeks and Spanish displayed among the lowest levels of environmental activism in the quantitative phase, though the Greeks were keen on the idea of joining an environmental organization or supporting its activities.
- Tropical rainforest destruction was the most often cited global concern, perhaps reflecting the media attention it has received as well as the very real problem it presents. Global warming (one of the main consequences of rainforest destruction) and pollution (generally air, but also water) were also mentioned in the context of global environmental problems.

### Quantitative Research: Main Findings

While the qualitative phase was used to establish levels of concern about the environment, at the quantitative stage we measured the extent to which people had carried out environmental activities, and used this to determine their likely responsiveness to any advertising which carried an environmental message. Not only was the *cause* measured – 'the environment' – but also the brand – 'WWF'. Awareness of WWF was measured both spontaneously and after prompting, as was propensity to support WWF (discussed later).

Our data show that awareness of WWF tends to be higher in countries where environmental activism is higher, with The Netherlands being the most obvious example. Virtually all Dutch people have heard of WWF, and two-thirds are environmental activists, the highest figure of all the countries measured. There are probably a number of reasons why this pattern emerges: it is easier for an environmental organization to establish itself and succeed in a country where its citizens, government and businesses are more predisposed to environmental thinking. Equally, awareness of 'green' organizations is likely to be higher in such countries purely *because of* the interest which already exists towards the environment. However, there are one or two notable exceptions. For example, in Italy, only 8 per cent of the population are environmental activists, yet 81 per cent have heard of WWF, a figure that places Italy fourth among all the countries surveyed (WWF Italy is one of the largest grassroots organizations of any kind in Italy). Thus despite the fact that Italians are less likely than average to carry out 'green' behaviours, the WWF brand is readily recognized in Italy and can therefore be used to carry the environmental message. In Spain too, we can see a similar (though less marked) pattern: Spain has an activism level of just 5 per cent, yet 47 per cent have heard of WWF or Adena, the Spanish national organization.

Countries where MORI has conducted research for WWF International since the development of the advertising yield the following figures for environmental activism and total awareness of WWF (respectively): Denmark: 17 per cent and 85 per cent; Pakistan (among the literate classes): 7 per cent and 27 per cent; India (among the literate classes): 2 per cent and 56 per cent; Brazil (among an urban sample): 2 per cent and 7 per cent; Japan: less than 0.5 per cent and 41 per cent; and Russia: 2 per cent and 9 per cent.

The information from this research programme was and is used by WWF International for several important purposes:

- In planning, to develop a global communications positioning and strategic communications plan for the organization;
- To brief WWF's advertising agency, in specifically developing an international advertising positioning and tone for what is one of the largest *pro bono* advertising accounts in the world;
- To develop national communications positionings and strategic communication plans for the WWF National Organizations in the countries covered;
- To help long-term fundraising/marketing activities in various WWF National Organization countries where research was conducted.

Specifically, two different approaches were used. For countries where environmental awareness was relatively low (e.g. Greece, Italy and Spain), five silent, 30-second animated television adverts were developed, based on cartoons by the Italian cartoonist Bozetto, using light-hearted messages to convey the need to curb consumption. One depicted an elderly lady in an armchair with her cat, doing some knitting and shivering from the cold. She then gradually turns up the thermostat in her home from 20°C to 25°C. Everyone else in the neighbourhood does the same, resulting in billows of black smoke from everyone's chimneys. 'STOP', flashes a sign on the screen, the film then runs quickly in reverse until the elderly lady is donning the thick woolly sweater she has knitted, to keep off the cold. Similar adverts were used to demonstrate the need to reduce excessive packaging on purchased goods, turn off car engines when cars are stationary at traffic lights, turn off taps when not in use, and reduce the amount of artificial lighting used at home.

By contrast, for countries where the research showed environmental awareness to be well developed and environmental activism to be already established (notably the Netherlands, New Zealand, Sweden and (West) Germany), more sophisticated adverts were used to convey an environmental message, this time the need to protect tropical rainforests. This had already emerged from the research as the most often-cited global concern, which in part led to WWF embarking on a three-year forests campaign; its easily recognizable panda logo acting as a pertinent symbol for this campaign. One advert depicted a tropical hardwood table being sold at auction:

> *Ladies and gentlemen, what am I bid for this 19th-century reproduction, a handsome table in the Regency manner? Note the rare tropical woods, the ebony, the mahogany. My friends, many gave up their lives for this classic piece* (An affluent lady waves her handkerchief to signal interest) *$5,000, may I have $5,000? Thanks, that may have held the cure for disease; people have died, all for this table. Ten species of birds – gone forever. I have $10,000 in the bank, $15,000, $20,000. Ladies and gentlemen, this table contributed to global warming. Surely that is worth something? $40,000. I have $100,000. This is the last table to come out of the rainforest. Going once, going twice, gone!*

The smart rare woods table is then shown standing on its own in a stark landscape of completely destroyed rainforest.

For countries where this advert was to be used, the research had suggested that environmental activism was high and therefore many people would not require an explanation as to *why* destruction of rainforests contributes to global warming, can limit research into cures for diseases, or reduces biodiversity (the preservation of the variety of animals, plants and micro-organisms).

Similarly, the second dramatic advert would need little explanation in countries where it was to be used. It showed trees in the rainforest falling one by one as a result of timber trade activities. As each tree fell, an illness was called out:

> *Cancer, AIDS, Malaria, Parkinson's disease, Alzheimer's. The cure for many of these diseases may be hidden in the rainforest. If there's any rainforest left.*

Once again, a destroyed rainforest is shown on the screen, this time followed by WWF's panda logo and information that reads:

> *World Wide Fund for Nature, working in over 20 countries, proves that rainforests used wisely, can be used forever* (followed by WWF's telephone number).

However, as a charity, WWF relies on donated media space and air time, and therefore does not have overall control over the countries that receive its messages, or the timing of particular messages it wants to convey in those countries. Hence, all spots it develops must appeal to senior broadcasting management, be interesting and 'entertaining', and of world class in terms of their creative and technical quality. Clearly, the benefit to broadcasters who agree to work on a *pro bono* basis is that while providing air time for WWF's ads, they are at the same time enhancing their images as good corporate citizens.

As the world's largest source of information, television was the medium that WWF International concentrated on to communicate these particular environmental messages, though it also placed ads in international upmarket publications. WWF National Organizations also adapted WWF International's material wherever appropriate. Ultimately, however, the *aim* of the adverts is to raise awareness of environmental issues and encourage people to care enough to do something to help – by giving their time, donating money, joining 'green' organizations or putting pressure on others such as politicians and companies by visiting them, writing to newspapers or demonstrating. For this reason the research was also used to establish people's *propensity to support* WWF, if asked (Table 9.2). This would give WWF International an indication of the response they would be likely to get from any advertising shown in particular countries, and could be used if necessary to convince corporations considering donating air time of the likely *value* of such advertising, in terms of the numbers of people who may support WWF. However, it should be noted that not everyone who says they would be prepared to do something will actually do it. The 'conversion factor' varies, depending on the question being asked and the prevailing circumstances.

The question on propensity to support was asked in six countries, and the category 'willingness to become a member of WWF' was asked in six additional countries (i.e. twelve in all). Table 9.2 illustrates that the propensity to support WWF on a wide range of environmental or trading initiatives was fairly high among those aware of the organization. In Great Britain, where total awareness is high at 81 per cent, as many as 62 per cent of those aware of WWF said they would be willing to buy products where some of the purchase price would be donated to the charity, and 45 per cent of those aware would be happy to order gifts from WWF's catalogue. When translated into population figures (data not shown), nearly 23 million British adults said they would buy joint-sponsor products, and over 16 million said they would be willing to order gifts from the catalogue. In Canada, the same two initiatives as in Britain are popular (61 per cent for product purchase and 33 per cent for catalogue gifts), but also one in three of those aware of WWF said they would write to a politician about the environment, if asked. Though Canada's population at 18.7 million adults is much lower than Britain's 45 million, these figures translate into over 4 million Canadians prepared to buy products with a partial donation to WWF, 2.5 million happy to buy products from WWF's catalogue, and 2.4 million prepared to write to a politician about the environment (data not shown).

Even in Greece there was considerable support among those who had heard of WWF (though this is low at 8 per cent). As many as 76 per cent of those aware (the highest figure recorded) would be prepared to buy products, 61 per cent would become involved in a WWF environmental campaign, if

TABLE 9.2   *Willingness to support WWF (per cent): 'Which, if any, of these*
*would you be willing to do on behalf of WWF if asked?'*

| | Greece | Great Britain | Canada | Hong Kong | Malaysia | Spain |
|---|---|---|---|---|---|---|
| Total (awareness) | 8 | 81 | 40 | 68 | 21 | 47 |
| Buy products where some of the purchase price would be donated to WWF | 76 | 62 | 61 | 55 | 38 | 28 |
| Become involved in a WWF environmental campaign (e.g. on tropical rainforest destruction or mining in Antarctica) | 61 | 12 | 15 | 48 | 28 | 22 |
| Order gifts from WWF's catalogue | 58 | 45 | 33 | 48 | 19 | 9 |
| Become a member | 50 | 15 | 25 | 23 | 20 | 17 |
| Write to a politician about the environment | 47 | 23 | 32 | 16 | 10 | 12 |
| Volunteer time to raise funds for WWF | 44 | 14 | 20 | 32 | 20 | 9 |
| Serve on a local WWF Committee | 36 | 5 | 12 | n/a | 18 | 8 |
| Specify WWF as a beneficiary in your will | 9 | 4 | 4 | 5 | 4 | 2 |
| Already a member | 3 | 2 | 2 | 0 | 1 | 1 |
| None of these | 7 | 15 | 12 | 0 | 32 | 23 |
| Don't know | 2 | 5 | 14 | 0 | 6 | 19 |

Base: All who have heard of WWF/National Organization.
*Source:* MORI/WWF International

asked, and 44 per cent would give time on a voluntary basis to raise funds for WWF. Our empirical studies show that half of those who had heard of WWF in Greece said they would be willing to become a member, and a further 3 per cent said they already were (Figure 9.1). When these percentages are converted into population figures (data not shown), we can see that Italy, with its high awareness of 81 per cent and high population (of 46 million adults) takes the lead, with 11.5 million adults willing to become a member (or already expressing support). Germany and Great Britain tie for second with 6.2 million adults. Clearly, there is considerable propensity to support WWF, and this information proved invaluable when WWF International and its national offices (NOs) were developing their communications activity.

## *Conclusion*

In conclusion, this programme of research for WWF International clearly assisted the organization in targeting its advertising messages to its audiences in different countries, thereby maximizing uptake of messages. Without it, there would have been a greater possibility that some messages would not have been understood or acted upon.

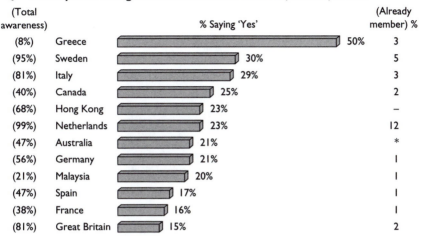

**Q   Would you be willing to become a member of WWF, if asked, or not?**

| (Total awareness) | | % Saying 'Yes' | | (Already member) % |
|---|---|---|---|---|
| (8%) | Greece | | 50% | 3 |
| (95%) | Sweden | 30% | | 5 |
| (81%) | Italy | 29% | | 3 |
| (40%) | Canada | 25% | | 2 |
| (68%) | Hong Kong | 23% | | – |
| (99%) | Netherlands | 23% | | 12 |
| (47%) | Australia | 21% | | * |
| (56%) | Germany | 21% | | 1 |
| (21%) | Malaysia | 20% | | 1 |
| (47%) | Spain | 17% | | 1 |
| (38%) | France | 16% | | 1 |
| (81%) | Great Britain | 15% | | 2 |

FIGURE 9.1   *Willingness to join WWF. Base: all who have heard of WWF/National Organization.*
(*Source*: MORI/WWF International)

## CASE HISTORY 2: GREENPEACE INTERNATIONAL

### Background and Objectives

MORI has also conducted an extensive programme of positioning research for Greenpeace International, which has helped them to establish and monitor the strategic and tactical messages that Greenpeace International is putting across. In addition, international research studies have been carried out for Greenpeace International and co-ordinated by two Greenpeace NOs to provide a 'hook' for media coverage and to lobby Brussels. One study was co-ordinated by Greenpeace UK on attitudes towards nuclear testing in the South Pacific (case history 3), and the other by Greenpeace Germany on views on genetically modified food (case history 4).

When Greenpeace International first approached Professor Robert Worcester, Chairman of MORI, for advice in 1993, they were at a crossroads. Most people knew of their activities to stop whaling and most approved of their mission, if not their tactics. But Greenpeace is more than a single-issue Save the Whale campaigning organization, and many potential supporters and donors might donate time and money if they knew more about Greenpeace's activities.

For the (positioning) research, Greenpeace International chose to concentrate not on countries where they were strong, such as Germany, Britain, the USA and The Netherlands, but where they were weaker, where the environment was not necessarily a high-profile issue.[5] By definition, the latter involved countries where Greenpeace arguably needed *more* information about how potential supporters could be reached.

TABLE 9.3  *Greenpeace International research*

| 1994/5 | | 1996 |
|---|---|---|
| Argentina[a] | Ireland | Hong Kong |
| Belgium | Italy | |
| Brazil | Japan | |
| Canada | Mexico | |
| Chile | New Zealand | |
| Czech Republic | Norway | |
| Denmark | Russia | |
| Finland | Spain | |
| France | Sweden | |
| Greece | Tunisia | |
| | Ukraine | |

[a] Fieldwork was conducted by Entrepreneur, independently of MORI

The objectives of the (positioning) research, which comprised focus groups, followed by a quantitative study per country, were to:

- identify areas of perceived strengths and weaknesses in Greenpeace's image, by comparing this with respondents' ideal environmental organization;
- quantify potential support for the organization by presenting respondents with a list of specific initiatives (including the cessation of whaling but also, for example, helping poor people to survive without damaging the environment) and asking which they would support, as well as which ones Greenpeace *is* and *should be* involved in;
- guide strategic and tactical decision-making at the international level;
- form a baseline against which progress in achieving the objectives of the organization can be measured.

### The Countries Surveyed

Most of the research took place in 1994 and commenced with two focus groups per country, among a mix of environmental activists and semi-activists. This was then followed by a quantitative survey, using face-to-face methodologies in all countries (Table 9.3). Sample sizes comprised between around 500 and 2,000 adults per country.

The research findings have been used by Greenpeace International in four main ways, namely:

1  by Greenpeace NOs (specifically by the Executive Directors and the Fundraisers) to test hypotheses about which campaigns might work with the general public in particular countries;
2  to evaluate the fund-raising potential for Greenpeace in certain countries, especially where Greenpeace is not well established as a fund-raising entity, or where Greenpeace considers that its efforts are being hampered by a particular industry (notably whaling in Norway; see below);

3  to demonstrate Greenpeace's credentials around the globe and use this to challenge trademark infringements (specifically in Hong Kong, where Greenpeace successfully challenged such an infringement);

4  to use in discussions with potential licensing partners for commercial licensing, particularly the results to the question: 'Which, if any, of the following would you be willing to do on behalf of Greenpeace, if asked: buy products where some of the purchase price would be donated to Greenpeace?' This information has been particularly useful to Greenpeace International as it has shifted from its own in-house merchandising to licensing agreements, and it is currently in the process of measuring levels of support to this question again.

Daryl Upsall of Greenpeace International comments on the use of research as a campaigning tool: 'More and more people see research as an essential tool in campaigning, rather than icing on the cake'.

Findings from two countries where Greenpeace has used the results to inform itself about its potential supporters are given below. In the Canadian case, this was before using Greenpeace's 25th anniversary to raise its profile in Canada and strengthen its image. In the Norwegian case, the results helped confirm the enormous difficulty Greenpeace Norway faces in getting a reasonable fund-raising return from the Norwegian public, particularly on anti-whaling campaigns.

In Canada, a combination of this research (commissioned by Greenpeace International) and Greenpeace Canada's own supporter research identified the need for Greenpeace Canada to invest in its own image. Greenpeace was founded in Vancouver 25 years ago; since then the timber industry has waged persistent and large-scale campaigns against it, particularly with respect to Greenpeace's campaigns against the destruction of Canadian West Coast forests. One timber, pulp and paper company, Macmillan Bloedel, ran a press campaign for some time, made up of full-page ads discrediting Greenpeace. Greenpeace felt that this campaign had reduced their support among the Canadian public. Similarly, Greenpeace felt that their campaign against the slaughter of seal pups had damaged their image in Canada, as it was seen as attacking the rights of indigenous peoples. Against this backdrop, Greenpeace Canada wished to gain an understanding of how they were perceived, beyond anecdotal evidence, and determine where they should be investing their money. Greenpeace Canada used the findings to help them understand how they were perceived in comparison to Canadians' ideal environmental organization. The findings showed, for example, that 37 per cent of Canadians perceived Greenpeace to be an active campaigning organization, a proportion similar to respondents' ideal, and one in three said Greenpeace takes members from all walks of life. While this (and many other figures) fell short of Canadians' *ideal* environmental organization, in many respects Canadians had a more positive image of Greenpeace than respondents did across the 21 countries surveyed as a whole.

The Norwegian research enabled Greenpeace to think *practically* about what might or might not work in Norway and confirms the fact that Greenpeace's international whaling campaign has had an impact on Norway and helped them identify issues (e.g. nuclear weapons/power) that *do* have a resonance with the Norwegian public. For example, just 17 per cent of Norwegians said that Greenpeace should lobby international governments to ensure that economic agreements take account of environmental issues (compared with 45 per cent of Swedes, and an average of 25 per cent across 21 countries). Similarly, just 7 per cent and 8 per cent (respectively) of Norwegians said Greenpeace should take direct action to stop whaling, or use a fleet of ships in its campaigning work, compared with Scandinavian averages of 25 per cent and 18 per cent respectively. Norwegians were also more likely to perceive Greenpeace as violent and less likely to regard them as being caring, or teaching people to live in harmony with nature, and less likely to consider it worthwhile becoming a member. However, on the nuclear issue, Norwegians were more supportive than average of Greenpeace calling for all nuclear weapons to be scrapped, or for all nuclear power to be phased out.

## CASE HISTORY 3: GREENPEACE – NUCLEAR TESTING

### Background and Objectives

In June 1995, when President Jacques Chirac announced that he would resume nuclear testing on Mururoa Atoll in the South Pacific, Greenpeace immediately launched a campaign to put pressure on the French government to reverse that decision and encourage other EU governments to do the same. This campaign was very much in the tradition of those Greenpeace had been running for the previous 24 years against French nuclear testing. No one could have anticipated the extent of public opposition and protest around the globe to the tests, which exceeded Greenpeace's wildest expectations and received considerable media coverage. By August 1995, Greenpeace realized it needed to determine the *scale* of public opposition in Europe, and use research results at the forthcoming EU Ministers' meeting in Alcudia, Mallorca on 22 and 23 September. Through MORI, Greenpeace had measured public opinion in Britain in August, prior to the first blast on 5 September, and knew from that poll that opposition in Britain was high. However, for that poll a straight 'support/oppose' question was used. This time, *strength* of feeling was sought using a scale question, asked in nine EU countries (including Great Britain again).

By 8 September, MORI was commissioned to conduct research which would

- examine the extent of public opposition in Europe to nuclear testing, but also to nuclear weapons, because Greenpeace wished to know what proportion of the public across Europe felt nuclear weapons were still necessary despite the end of the cold war;

- enable Greenpeace to publicize the results to coincide with the Mallorca meeting;
- reinforce Greenpeace's central protesting role.

It was essential therefore that the research provided nationally-representative results, valid comparison across countries, and fast turnaround, as the Ministers' meeting was fast approaching.

Research was conducted by telephone from 9–19 September 1995, among 500–1,300 adults per country in Austria, Germany, Great Britain, France, The Netherlands, Sweden, Belgium, Spain and Italy. Much care was taken with the design and translation of the questions. For example, the research associate whom MORI worked with in France (CSA) felt that French people would have difficulty understanding the word 'bomb' in the context of nuclear weapons. So instead of the word 'bomb' (*une bombe*), the phrase 'nuclear armament' (*d'une arme nucléaire*) was used. The wording used in Great Britain for this question (Q3) was as follows.

> As you may know, President Chirac of France has said that French nuclear testing is taking place in the South Pacific to provide information to develop bombs which could be made available for the defence of other European Union countries.
>
> Do you support or oppose the French proposal for a European bomb or would you say you are neutral? (IF SUPPORT OR OPPOSE) Is that strongly or tend to...?

In France, the wording was the following.

> Comme vous le savez peut-être, le Président français Jacques Chirac a déclaré que des essais nucléaires sont menés dans le Pacifique Sud pour recueillir des informations destinées au perfectionnement *de l'arme nucléaire* qui pourrait être utilisée pour la défense d'autres payes de l'Union européenne.
>
> Êtes-vous favorable ou opposé à la proposition française *d'une arme nucléaire européenne*, ou diriez-vous que vous êtes neutre? Tout à fait ou plutôt?

## Main Findings

- As many as three-quarters of Europeans disagreed that nuclear weapons are still necessary, and in all countries but France, disagreement outweighed agreement (in France, the difference was only marginal). Austrians showed the strongest opposition, with nearly everyone (92 per cent) disagreeing (see Table 9.4).
- The British figures were particularly interesting because previous polls for CND had shown less opposition than the 50 per cent recorded this time around.[6] Greenpeace thus considered 50 per cent, while lower than most European countries, an encouraging finding.
- Respondents were told that the French Government had started a series of eight nuclear tests on Mururoa Atoll in the South Pacific and asked whether they supported or opposed this (Table 9.5). Opposition was overwhelming – 81 per cent across Europe – with no majority in any country in support. In France, opposition outweighed support by 47 per cent to 30 per cent.

TABLE 9.4  Survey of attitudes to nuclear testing (per cent): (Q1), 'Do you agree or disagree with the following statement, or would you say you are neutral? "Nuclear weapons are still necessary". If you agree or disagree: Is that strongly or tend to ...?'

| | Euro-average | Austria | Germany | GB | France | Netherlands | Sweden | Belgium | Spain | Italy |
|---|---|---|---|---|---|---|---|---|---|---|
| (Base: all) | (8,289) | (501) | (1,300) | (1,006) | (1,002) | (966) | (499) | (1,010) | (1,000) | (1,005) |
| Strongly agree | 6 | 1 | 5 | 14 | 19 | 4 | 3 | 5 | 1 | 2 |
| Tend to agree | 9 | 3 | 8 | 19 | 25 | 7 | 2 | 8 | 2 | 4 |
| Neither agree nor disagree (neutral) | 9 | 4 | 6 | 17 | 14 | 5 | 9 | 13 | 5 | 4 |
| Tend to disagree | 10 | 5 | 10 | 16 | 12 | 13 | 6 | 9 | 10 | 10 |
| Strongly disagree | 64 | 87 | 68 | 34 | 27 | 69 | 78 | 63 | 73 | 76 |
| Don't know/no opinion | 3 | 1 | 1 | 1 | 3 | 2 | 1 | 2 | 9 | 4 |
| **Summary** | | | | | | | | | | |
| Agree | 15 | 4 | 14 | 32 | 44 | 11 | 5 | 13 | 3 | 6 |
| Disagree | 74 | 92 | 79 | 50 | 39 | 82 | 85 | 73 | 83 | 87 |
| Net agree | −59 | −88 | −65 | −18 | 5 | −71 | −80 | −60 | −80 | −81 |

Source: MORI/Greenpeace

TABLE 9.5  MORI/Greenpeace survey of attitudes to nuclear testing (per cent): (Q2) 'As you may know, the French Government has started a series of eight[a] nuclear tests on Mururoa Atoll in the South Pacific. Do you support or oppose this, or would you say you are neutral? If support or oppose: Is that strongly or tend to …?'

| | Euro-average | Austria | Germany | GB | France | Netherlands | Sweden | Belgium | Spain | Italy |
|---|---|---|---|---|---|---|---|---|---|---|
| (Base: all) | (8,289) | (501) | (1,300) | (1,006) | (1,002) | (966) | (499) | (1,010) | (1,000) | (1,005) |
| Strongly support | 3 | 1 | 1 | 1 | 13 | 1 | 1 | 3 | 1 | 13 |
| Tend to support | 3 | 1 | 2 | 2 | 17 | 1 | 0 | 5 | 1 | 1 |
| Neither support nor oppose (neutral) | 10 | 4 | 7 | 20 | 21 | 8 | 6 | 12 | 8 | 7 |
| Tend to oppose | 7 | 3 | 5 | 11 | 15 | 6 | 2 | 11 | 6 | 8 |
| Strongly oppose | 74 | 89 | 84 | 65 | 32 | 84 | 90 | 67 | 76 | 77 |
| Don't know/no opinion | 3 | 1 | 1 | 1 | 2 | 2 | 0 | 3 | 8 | 5 |
| **Summary** | | | | | | | | | | |
| Support | 6 | 2 | 3 | 3 | 30 | 1 | 1 | 8 | 2 | 3 |
| Oppose | 81 | 92 | 89 | 76 | 47 | 89 | 92 | 78 | 82 | 85 |
| Net support | −75 | −90 | −86 | −73 | −17 | −88 | −91 | −70 | −80 | −82 |

[a] In France 'a maximum of eight'.

All interviews conducted by telephone using national 'Omnibus' surveys (CSA in France, Sample Institut in Germany, Demoskopea in Italy, NSS in the Netherlands, DATA in Spain and IMU-Testologen in Sweden).

- President Chirac had said that French nuclear tests were taking place in the South Pacific to provide information to develop bombs which could be made available for the defence of other European countries. However, three-quarters of Europeans opposed the French proposal for a 'Eurobomb'. In France where support was much greater, still only one in three adults supported the proposal.

### Use of the Findings

How did Greenpeace use these findings during the campaign, and how did the findings contribute to its optimization? First, Desley Mather at Greenpeace International rapidly developed a press release based on the poll findings and agreed it with MORI. Then Louise Gale, Greenpeace EU Advisor, provided a comment from the EU Heads of State meeting, and Xavier Pastor, Head of Greenpeace Spain, led a peace flotilla from a Greenpeace vessel to the bay of Formentor, Alcudia, on Mallorca. Greenpeace received television coverage of its presence at the Ministers' meeting and a large front-page story in the Sunday Observer newspaper (London) on the poll findings, with the headline 'Europe Says "No" To Nuclear Tests'. All in all, the research findings served to support Greenpeace's campaign and strengthen the case for lobbying.

To maximize the use of the findings, some Greenpeace NOs wished to get a secondary release of the information. Greenpeace Germany, for example, issued a more detailed release looking at the views of Germans on nuclear testing. Greenpeace Belgium prepared an article in its newsletter for Francophone countries, and much use was made of the data by NOs to inform themselves of each country's thinking, particularly by sub-groups. Greenpeace Netherlands used the findings in a very specific way: to convince the Dutch Post Office (a private company) that the public in The Netherlands was so opposed to French nuclear testing that it would be acceptable to display Greenpeace's anti-nuclear testing posters in the windows of every single post office in the country. When Greenpeace first made the approach, they were met with the comment 'No, that would offend far too many of our customers'. However, when the research findings were quoted, that 89 per cent of the Dutch public opposes French nuclear testing in the South Pacific, 84 per cent strongly, Greenpeace was allowed to display its posters in every post office. Following their display (and other activity), Greenpeace Netherlands subsequently collected 800,000 signatures from the Dutch public against French nuclear testing, the highest number in the world.

### CASE HISTORY 4: GREENPEACE – GENETICALLY MODIFIED FOOD

### Background

Late November 1996 saw the introduction in Britain of genetically modified food – genetically changed plants and vegetables, programmed by the addition or subtraction of tiny slices of DNA to grow and behave in the way scientists want them to. For example, genetically modified soya imports from the United States had been grown to withstand heavy doses of herbicide, so that weeds around them withered while the beans themselves lived on.

Greenpeace International was running a genetically modified food (GMO) campaign throughout Europe and, through Greenpeace Germany, commissioned MORI in December 1996 to examine attitudes in six European countries towards genetically modified food. This research built on a survey already conducted in Germany. Fieldwork was conducted by telephone from 11–20 December 1996 in Denmark, France, Great Britain, Italy, The Netherlands and Sweden. Sample sizes varied from around 500–1,000 adults per country. The results were released on 9 January 1997, a week before the European Parliament vote on the Novel Food Regulation related to the development and introduction of genetically modified food.

## Main Findings

- In all six European countries, more people opposed the development and introduction of genetically modified food (59 per cent on average – see Table 9.6) than supported it (22 per cent on average). Furthermore, in all countries except Italy and The Netherlands, over half opposed it.
- Greatest overall opposition came from Sweden (76 per cent).
- Italians were relatively most enthusiastic about the development of such food, with 37 per cent actively supporting it, but even here the single largest group is those opposed to *a great extent* (32 per cent).
- In three countries – France, Italy and The Netherlands – people are even less likely to be happy about *eating* genetically modified food (see Table 9.7). In Sweden, where three-quarters are opposed to the development and introduction of genetically modified food, a similar proportion say they would not be happy about eating it, and even the lowest national figure is over half (53 per cent in Britain).
- The Danish figures were unusual in that people were a bit happier about eating such food than about its development in Denmark. One in five Danes (22 per cent) agreed they would be happy eating it (10 per cent strongly), while 16 per cent supported its development. But even in Denmark, around two-thirds are opposed both to eating genetically-modified food and to its development generally.
- Greenpeace used the findings in its campaign against the development and introduction of genetically modified food to demonstrate public opposition to genetically modified food, and urged members of the European Parliament to vote against the Novel Food Regulation. Greenpeace also called for stronger national labelling legislation by EU countries. Benedikt Haerlin of Greenpeace Germany, at a Greenpeace press conference in Brussels, said 'People who don't want to eat gene-food must have the right to know what is in their food'.

TABLE 9.6 MORI/Greenpeace survey of attitudes to genetically modified food (per cent): (Q1) 'Thinking of genetically modified food or food derived from genetic engineering, what is your opinion towards the development and introduction of such food? Would you say you ...?'

| (Number interviewed) | Denmark (580) | France (1,005) | Great Britain (1,003) | Italy (1,002) | Netherlands (750) | Sweden (500) | Average (4,840) |
|---|---|---|---|---|---|---|---|
| Support it to a great extent | 3 }16 | 4 }15 | 6 }31 | 14 }37 | 3 }19 | 3 }12 | 6 }22 |
| Support it slightly | 13 | 11 | 25 | 23 | 16 | 9 | 16 |
| Neither support nor oppose it | 14 | 18 | 16 | 14 | 22 | 8 | 15 |
| Oppose it slightly | 20 }65 | 33 }67 | 24 }50 | 11 }43 | 25 }49 | 16 }76 | 22 }59 |
| Oppose it to a great extent | 45 | 34 | 26 | 32 | 24 | 60 | 37 |
| Don't know | 6 | 2 | 2 | 6 | 11 | 4 | 5 |

Single answer only. (Order of answer categories to be rotated)
Source: MORI/Greenpeace International

TABLE 9.7 MORI/Greenpeace survey of attitudes to genetically modified food—willingness to eat (per cent): (Q2) 'To what extent do you agree or disagree with this statement:"I personally would be happy to eat genetically modified food"?'

| (Number interviewed) | Denmark (580) | France (1,005) | Great Britain (1,003) | Italy (1,002) | Netherlands (750) | Sweden (500) | Average (4,840) |
|---|---|---|---|---|---|---|---|
| Strongly agree | 10 }22 | 4 }12 | 5 }27 | 6 }19 | 1 }8 | 3 }14 | 5 }17 |
| Tend to agree | 12 | 8 | 22 | 13 | 7 | 11 | 12 |
| Neither agree nor disagree | 9 | 11 | 17 | 11 | 19 | 6 | 12 |
| Tend to disagree | 13 }63 | 24 }77 | 23 }53 | 22 }65 | 31 }65 | 12 }78 | 21 }67 |
| Strongly disagree | 50 | 53 | 30 | 43 | 34 | 66 | 46 |
| Don't know | 6 | 1 | 2 | 5 | 8 | 2 | 4 |

Single answer only. (Order of answer categories rotated)
Source: MORI/Greenpeace International

- The results of the survey continue to be quoted, including in the USA –
  home of genetically modified foods – in a newsletter entitled 'Genetically
  Modified Foods' (January 1997, Issue No. 5, published by Genetic ID,
  Iowa, USA).

TECHNICAL NOTE 1     MORI/WWF INTERNATIONAL
                     RESEARCH (CASE HISTORY 1)

|             | Research     | Sample        |               |      |       |        |
|-------------|--------------|---------------|---------------|------|-------|--------|
| Country     | Agency       | Qual          | Quant         | Size | Age   | Method |
| **1991**    |              |               |               |      |       |        |
| Germany     | Sample       | 19/20 June '91 | 5–9 Sept '91 | 500  | 14+   | Tel    |
| Australia   | MORI         | 25/26 June '91 | 6–8 Sept '91 | 1200 | 18+   | Tel    |
| Sweden      | SIFO         | Both 18 June '91 | 11–24 Sept '91 | 1057 | 16–74 | F to F |
| Italy       | Demoskopea   | 25/26 June '91 | 16–30 Sept '91 | 969 | 14–79 | F to F |
| Netherlands | Motivaction  | 17/20 June '91 | 18 Sept '91  | 508  | 15+   | Tel    |
| Great Britain | MORI       | 20/26 June '91 | 20–23 Sept '91 | 2028 | 15+  | F to F |
| France      | CSA          | 14/22 June '91 | 26–30 Sept '91 | 1000 | 15+  | F to F |
| Canada      | Environics   | 19/20 June '91 | 25 Oct – 19 Nov '91 | 2004 | 18+ | Tel    |
| **1992**    |              |               |               |      |       |        |
| Spain       | DATA         | 21/25 May '92 | 16 June – 7 July '92 | 1007 | 15+ | F to F |
| Austria     | IMAS         | 7/9 Sept '92  | 15 Sept – 9 Oct '92 | 1150 | 16+ | F to F |
| Switzerland | AES          | 27 Aug '92    | 24 Sept – 7 Oct '92 | 1000 | 15+ | F to F |
| New Zealand | CM           | 1/3 Sept '92  | 30 Sept – 14 Oct '92 | 1000 | 15+ | Tel    |
| **1993**    |              |               |               |      |       |        |
| Greece      | Focus        | 15/23 Mar '93 | 22 April – 16 May '93 | 1970 | 15–70 | Tel[a] |
| Poland      | Pentor       | –             | 20–27 February 1993 | 1000 | 15+ | F to F |
| Malaysia    | SRM          | 8/9 June '93  | 3 June – 31 Jul '93 | 1257 | 15+ | F to F |
| Hong Kong   | ACR          | 8/9 June '93  | 23–26 July '93 | 504 | 18–64 | Tel    |

continued

| | | | | | | |
|---|---|---|---|---|---|---|
| South Africa | MCA | 11/13 May '93[b] | TBC | c.2500 | 16+ | F to F |
| Belgium | Gates | 7/10 June '93 | – | – | – | – |
| Finland | Marketing Radar | 1/2 Sept '93 | – | – | – | – |
| Hungary | AMER | TBA | TBA | TBA | TBA | TBA |
| **1994** | | | | | | |
| Denmark | AIM | 1994 | 18–24 April | 1,373 | 13+ | F to F |
| Pakistan | Aftab | 20/23 Oct | 10–25 Dec | 1,112 | 15–59 | F to F |
| India | IMRB (Indian Market Research Bureau) | 31 Aug/1 Oct | 30 Nov – 15 Dec | 802 | 15+ | F to F |
| **1995** | | | | | | |
| Brazil | CBPA | 1995 | 21 Mar – 3 Apr | 1,400 | 18+ | F to F |
| Japan | Nippon | 27–28 Aug | 5–11 Oct | 1,290 | 18+ | F to F |
| **1996** | | | | | | |
| Russia | ROMIR | 13/15 Aug | 22–27 June | 1,600 | 15+ | F to F |

[a] Ad Hoc survey in Greece. All others conducted using regular 'Omnibus' surveys.
[b] Four group discussions conducted in South Africa (two in all other countries).
*Source*: MORI/WWF International

TECHNICAL NOTE 2    MORI/GREENPEACE INTERNATIONAL RESEARCH (CASE HISTORY 2)

| Country 1994/5 | Research agency | Fieldwork | Sample size | Age |
|---|---|---|---|---|
| Argentina | Entrepreneur | 7.11–19.12.94 | 1,097 | 15+ |
| Belgium | Van Nimwegen | 5–17.9.94 | 449 | 15+ |
| Brazil | CBPA/MORI | 2–25.11.94 | 1,200 | 16–65 |
| Canada | Environics | 9.6–4.7.94 | 2,026 | 18+ |
| Chile | MORI Chile | 28.12.94–24.1.95 | 1,248 | 18+ |
| Czech Republic | AISA | 10–21.8.94 | 1,113 | 14+ |
| Denmark | AIM | 6.94 | 1,407 | 13+ |
| Finland | Taloustutkimus | 7.6–10.7.94 | 944 | 15–74 |
| France | Demoscopie | 8–11.7.94 | 1,000 | 15+ |
| Greece | Focus | 22.6–14.7.94 | 2,105 | 15–70 |

continued

| Ireland | Lansdowne | 7–15.7.94 | 1,398 | 15+ |
|---|---|---|---|---|
| Italy | Demoskopea | 10–27.6.94 | 1,000 | 14–79 |
| Japan | Nippon Research | 2–8.6.94 | 1,389 | 18+ |
| Mexico | MORI de Mexico | 12–17.12.94 | 1,172 | 18+ |
| New Zealand | CM Associates | 16.7–3.8.94 | 500 (T) | 18+ |
| Norway | MMI | 7–13.6.94 | 1,006 | 15+ |
| Russia | Romir | 16.9–3.10.94 | 1,600 | 15+ |
| Spain | Data | 27.2–5.3.94 | 1,006 | 15+ |
| Sweden | Feedback | 1–14.6.94 | 1,010 | 16–74 |
| Tunisia | Amer | 24.6–23.7.94 | 1,000 | 20–59 |
| Ukraine | Romir | 16–27.9.94 | 1,200 | 15+ |
| **1996** | | | | |
| Hong Kong | ACR | 18.1–12.2.96 | 631 | 18–64 |

TECHNICAL NOTE 3

| | Fieldwork | Age range | Population represented |
|---|---|---|---|
| Denmark | 11–14 December 1996 | 13+ | 4,441,000 |
| France | 13–14 December 1996 | 15+ | 45,844,218 |
| Great Britain | 13–15 December 1996 | 15+ | 45,600,000 |
| Italy | 12–14 December 1996 | 15+ | 48,600,000 |
| Netherlands | 16–20 December 1996 | 15+ | 12,494,000 |
| Sweden | 13 December 1996 | 15+ | 7,178,000 |

All interviews conducted by telephone using national 'Omnibus' surveys (AIM in Denmark, BVA in France, DOXA in Italy, NSS in the Netherlands and IMU in Sweden).

**ACKNOWLEDGEMENTS**

Thanks to Robert SanGeorge at WWF International, and Richard Weber for their contributions. Thanks also to Daryl Upsall of Greenpeace International, Chris Rose and Pete Roche at Greenpeace UK, and Benedikt Haerlin of Greenpeace Germany. My colleagues at MORI also deserve considerable thanks: Professor Robert M. Worcester, John Leaman, Bobby Duffy, Rob Cowley, Andy Byrom, Linda Blundell and Nadia Fabbro.

**NOTES**

1  Environmental activists are defined as those who have carried out five or more activities from a list of environmentally related activities in the previous two years (list not shown).
2  An 'Omnibus' is a survey that enables different sponsors to ask their own particular question set of a shared sample of people and share common, e.g. demographic, core questions.

3  The sample was representative of urban South Africa, not all of South Africa.
4  This has been observed before, in work conducted by IBOBE in Brazil, where Brazilians were more concerned about their immediate quality of life than their wider environment (Worcester and Corrado, 1992).
5  Upsall and Worcester, 1995.
6  It should be noted that the question wording was not the same in this poll, which could have contributed to the difference.

## REFERENCES

Corrado, M. and MacDonald, A. (1997) *Awareness of Population Issues Affecting Developing Countries*. WAPOR Conference, Edinburgh.

Corrado, M. (1997) *Sustainable Trends, Sustainable Lives?* Environment Council's *habitat*.

Upsall, D. and Worcester, R. (1995) *You Can't Sink a Rainbow*. WAPOR Conference, The Hague.

Weber, R. and Corrado, M. (1993) *International Attitudes to the Environment*. WAPOR Conference, Copenhagen.

Worcester, R. (1994) 'Societal values, behaviour and attitudes in relation to the human dimensions of global environmental change: use of an environmental activist scale.' XVI IPSA World Congress, Berlin.

Worcester, R. and Corrado, M. (1992) *Attitudes to the Environment – A North/South Analysis, Environment and Development: Problems and Prospects for Sustainable Development*. Co-ordinator Abdellatif Benachenou, UNESCO.

# Part IV    ASSESSMENT OF EFFECTS

## 10    Effective Campaign Assessment: How to Learn From Your Failures

### Leon Ostergaard

The main point of this contribution will be that there are some very good reasons why campaigns are rarely professionally assessed. There are, however, even better reasons why a campaign without assessment is a waste of time and money – even if it seems to succeed. In the first part of the contribution, I shall present some of the main obstacles to effective campaign assessment. Then I shall present a simple model of campaign planning and, based on this, explain how assessment is carried out and how conclusions can be drawn from the findings.

## MAJOR OBSTACLES TO ASSESSMENT

Any modern textbook on information campaigns strongly advises that campaigns should always be properly assessed, and the same fundamental principle is taught in any university course on communications or public relations. In fact, it is hard to find a single person in the profession who will argue that assessment is not really worth the effort. It is therefore strange to note that, in practice, most campaigns are not assessed, and if they are, rarely to professional standards. The most common shortcoming is that the campaign is assessed only on the mass-media level; that is, the campaign is judged effective because it reached its target audience, who may be able to recall some of the campaign messages. In other cases, the campaign is assessed on the problem level only; that is, the problem tackled by the campaign was eliminated or reduced, and hence the campaign was judged a success. I shall return to the inadequacies of this kind of assessment later in the contribution.

## Top-Down Decisions

There are several reasons why campaigns are seldom properly assessed. The first has to do with the way many campaigns are decided. A campaign often starts with a decision-maker confronted with a problem: a politician, the head of an organization, or a business leader. The decision-maker faces a problem – social or economic – and decides that a campaign is the solution. This decision is then channelled down through the organization, to be carried out by the communications department. But as the campaign strategy (i.e. the reason for believing that mass media can have an effect on the problem) is never explicitly formulated, real assessment is impossible. This is the price paid by top-down campaign strategy. In my experience, campaigns are often used to hide the sad fact that no other effective action can – or will – be taken against the problem in question. Politicians and other decision-makers are faced with many problems that cannot be solved, or where the price of a solution in terms of money or damaged pride is too high. In order to show vigour in the face of the challenge, a campaign is an easy solution. And the public, with no knowledge of the limitations of campaigns, may easily agree. This is one of the ways in which campaigns may contain hidden agendas, though not the only one. Mass-media campaigns are often highly visible, which may be seen by the head of an organization as beneficial to himself or the organization, apart from the official objective of the campaign. But hidden agendas make it impossible to assess a campaign: it may succeed in its official objective, but it is impossible to tell whether the hidden objectives were met. It is certainly possible to assess the effect of a campaign on the image of an organization or its head – but only if this is stated explicitly in advance as one of the objectives of the campaign!

## The 'Strategic Black Hole'

Another major obstacle to professional assessment is the absence of an explicit and detailed campaign strategy. This is much more often the case than might be expected. Many public information campaigns are carried out by public bodies with little experience in communications. When they decide, maybe for the first time, to carry out a campaign, they turn to an advertising agency because they assume that this is the proper way to run a campaign. But advertising agencies usually deal with commercial marketing and have little or no experience with public information campaigns; and in commercial marketing, the business customer as a rule has a professional marketing department, which puts forward a proposal for the basic campaign strategy. In other words, the advertising agency will expect the customer to come up with the basic strategy. But the inexperienced public customer does not have a professional department to think out the communication strategy and may not even be aware that the translation of their problem into a mass-media campaign demands strategic insight. So when the public customer and the advertising agency meet at the conference table, they will often experience what one might call a 'strategic black hole' in the

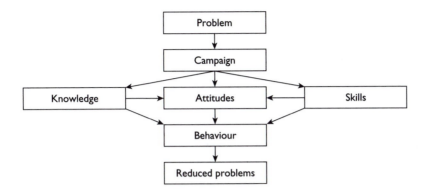

FIGURE 10.1  *A simple campaign model*

conversation: the agency expects the customer to come up with the strategy, and the customer expects the agency to take care of it. The advertising agency, of course, does not want to lose the customer, so after some confusion they undertake to formulate a campaign proposal. And in so doing, they draw on their knowledge of commercial marketing strategy. But strategies for marketing soap and cereals are certainly not able to solve a serious social problem, and without a detailed and explicit strategy, as will be shown later, no assessment is possible. Even when assessment does take place, it is often carried out by the campaign organizers themselves, and when you judge yourself it is only to be expected that the criteria for success will not be too harsh. If the organization in question does have a communications department, this department will want to secure its financing and staffing for the next year, and they do not need the millstone of a failure in the internal competition for limited budgets. They will consequently want to arouse only modest expectations for the campaign, as will the advertising agency. Many professionals will refuse to make any predictions of the outcome at all in order not to be proved wrong. Under such circumstances, any outcome could be called a success!

## A SIMPLE CAMPAIGN MODEL

Here I should like to introduce a simple model (Figure 10.1) of how public information campaigns could be planned and conceived. I want to stress that this is certainly not the only way information campaigns can be conceived, and other models may be more appropriate when we want to focus on other aspects of the process. The box at the top of the figure illustrates the fact that a campaign, as I have mentioned, always starts off with some decision-maker confronted with a problem. The decision-maker wants to get to the box at the bottom of the diagram, where the problem is reduced or (even better) solved. It might be a Minister of Transport who wants (or is under political pressure) to reduce the number of young drivers killed on the roads. Or a Minister of Health who wants to reduce the burden on the national health care system of the large numbers of people suffering from heart disease. The Minister of Transport has several ways to reduce his problem. But, for political reasons, he may not want to raise the legal driving age, and for economic reasons he may not want to upgrade driver education or reinforce police surveillance on the roads. Or he may simply not believe in these solutions. Similarly, the Minister of Health has different ways of approaching his problem. But for the sake of taxation revenues, he may not want to reduce the amount of cigarette smoking nor impose on the food industry a ban on foods with high fat content. Hence, the decision-makers may decide to go for the campaign solution, either because they have to show political 'action', or because they simply believe that a campaign is the answer. In both instances, the decision is made 'top-down': from the outset, a campaign is chosen as the correct problem-solving strategy, and the ministry staff is left with the unenviable job of making this prophecy come true. And when talking about campaigns, most decision-makers only think in terms of mass-media campaigns, leaving out efficient campaign alternatives based on strategies of networks and local intermediaries. Now, this world contains many social problems that will certainly not be solved by mass-media campaigns. Even though I am a professional campaign manager myself, I freely admit that most of the problems of this world are of this kind. Consequently, the 'top-down' decision strategy inevitably produces many campaigns with little or no detailed strategy, and with similar hopes of success. This is all very well for the campaign organizers, the advertising agencies, and the commercial mass media – but not for the reputation of the profession or for public finances. In fact, a campaign should be decided 'bottom-up', that is from the bottom of the diagram to the top.

### The First Question

The first question must always be: what are the conditions for solving or reducing the problem? What behaviour by which persons is contributing to the problem? Is it possible to point to precise behavioural changes in specific groups which are most likely to reduce the problem? When analysing the problem, we should always be aware that most social problems are caused by a multitude of factors and social agents at work simultaneously with our effort to influence the problem. When formulating our strategy we must try to anticipate as many of these factors and agents as possible in order to assess their possible effects on the problem. From time to time we encounter public information campaigns with no expressed behavioural target. The campaign makers try to express the aims of these campaigns in more general terms: 'putting it on the public agenda', 'raising public awareness'. In my opinion, this just indicates a lack of hard thinking. Public campaigns may work over very long terms, and they may work in different phases: awareness, attitudes, action. But any campaign that does not aim to make someone do something someday is a waste of public money. It is all very well to make people change their attitudes towards ethnic minorities or the physically handicapped, but an attitude that does not at some point result in some change in behaviour is effectively useless. After all, an attitude is by definition just a tendency to act in a certain way in a certain situation, hence my claim that all public information campaigns must in the end aim to change some behaviour. If the target behaviour is not explicitly stated – not necessarily to the target audience, but at least in the campaign planning phase – no assessment is possible afterwards, and the campaign will be a waste of time and money. If in the planning phases it is not possible to point to a precise behaviour which will reduce the problem, the whole project should be dropped.

Returning to the diagram, there is some encouraging news after all: the link between behaviour and problem reduction, shown here by an arrow, is one which traditionally has been covered pretty well in scientific research. As a general rule, this is the area of the natural sciences: engineering, medicine, chemistry, and so on. The Minister of Transport will find a large body of scientific evidence showing that high driving speed leads to more accidents, and that a change in speeding behaviour by young drivers will most certainly reduce the number of accidents. Our Minister of Health will similarly receive convincing evidence that the high intake of animal fats increases the risk of heart disease at a later age, and that a change in eating habits will most certainly reduce the health problem. Of course, the scientific evidence will sometimes show either that the problem in question is not liable to change as a result of behavioural change, or that it is not possible to point to the particular behaviour that may cause it to change. In both instances, campaign planners should conclude that a campaign is not worthwhile and that other solutions should be sought. Campaigns carried out without a precise description of the behaviour desired in the target group are a waste of time. After all, if not even the campaign organizers with access to all available evidence are able to describe exactly what people are supposed to do, how can we expect the innocent citizen to find out for himself?

### The Second Question

However, it is often possible to point to a particular behaviour by some target group which will reduce the problem, but then comes the second question: what are the conditions for achieving this behaviour? Or, in other words: can we work our way further up the diagram? We know that human behaviour can be controlled by power, either physical or economic, but in terms of campaigns, behavioural research has shown that human behaviour is affected by at least one or more of the three factors: knowledge, attitudes, and skills. We can then rephrase our question: is it possible to point to changes in knowledge, attitudes, or skills – or a combination of these – which with a great degree of certainty will change behaviour in the desired direction? In terms of the diagram we may ask: can we produce evidence that there is a probable cause-and-effect relationship (indicated by an arrow) between one or more of the boxes on the Knowledge–Attitudes–Skills level and the box on the Behaviour level?

Evidence of this kind must come from the behavioural sciences, in particular psychology and sociology, and here the amount of available research is far smaller than in the natural sciences. In my experience, this is the level at which most campaigns fail because they are unable to argue convincingly why a change in specific attitudes, skills, or knowledge will probably affect behaviour. When no research specific to the problem area is at hand, you have to rely on basic research experience from psychology and sociology. And the basic research shows that the presentation of new knowledge does in fact occasionally change behaviour – though as a general rule it does not. Similarly, basic research has shown that a change in attitudes will under certain circumstances be followed by a change in behaviour, though under other circumstances it will not, in which case we may speak of just a 'declared' attitude. And new skills may be acquired but never used in practice. When the available research evidence is insufficient to establish a probable cause-and-effect relationship, the only logical solution is to drop the idea of a campaign and look for other measures to combat the problem in question. Before doing so, however, it is worthwhile making an effort to find the necessary evidence. It may be possible to commission research on the problem, or, if time is short, a survey in the target group may be able to show whether the available general evidence can in fact be applied to the specific problem at hand.

### The Third Question

If, and only if, a probable cause-and-effect relationship can be established between a change in one or more of the factors of knowledge, attitudes, and skills and a change in behaviour in the desired direction, the third question follows: what are the conditions for achieving precisely this change in this piece of knowledge or in this specific attitude or skill? Can we work our way further up the diagram?

Behavioural research has shown that knowledge, attitudes, and skills can change for a multitude of reasons. Most changes happen as a result of personal interaction in small groups, with interpersonal communication and teaching the most outstanding examples. But some changes take place as a result of non-personal interaction or even mass-media communication. As campaign organizers we can then rephrase our question and ask in the terms of the diagram: can we produce evidence that there is a possible cause-and-effect relationship between the box on the Campaign level and the box(es) on the Knowledge–Attitudes–Skills level that has been shown to influence behaviour? Here again, we have to rely on research from the behavioural sciences, but the situation is somewhat better than at the former level in the diagram. Certainly, the available research is mostly of a general nature and not specific to the exact knowledge and attitudes in question. But nevertheless, more often than not it will be applicable to the problem. Of course the evidence will often show that the knowledge or attitudes or skills are not liable to change through mass-media campaigns – neither directly nor indirectly through intermediaries working in local networks. As a rule, knowledge is the one factor most likely to change as the result of exposure to mass media. But we are exposed to thousands of facts each day, and only some of them are added to our knowledge, in particular those which most easily fit into our internal 'files' and those which can be used immediately.

Much more difficult is the change of attitudes through mass-media communication. Most attitudes are formed and changed through interpersonal contact; the attitudes most likely to change through mass communication are the more superficial attitudes, those that do not require you to change your whole way of looking at life. For attitudes tend to be intertwined and support each other, and it is much easier to reinforce an attitude through mass media than to change it. As for skills, they are mostly changed through formal or informal teaching, but some simple skills may be changed by mass communication through do-it-yourself teaching.

In the diagram, we have put horizontal arrows from both the Knowledge box and the Skills box to the Attitudes box. This is to remind us that attitudes may be changed not only directly but also indirectly through a change in either knowledge or skills. When you acquire new knowledge, sometimes you have to change your attitudes at once or later, but not always: only if the acquired knowledge is in some state of conflict with your established attitudes. Similarly, when you acquire new skills, sometimes you have to change your attitudes: a clear-cut example is the teaching of advanced driving skills, which tends to make drivers more aware of the dangers of their vehicle, and hence more careful. So, if your analysis concludes that it will be necessary to change some specific attitude in order to achieve the desired change in behaviour, and the analysis further concludes that this attitude is not liable to change directly through mass communication, it may be worthwhile to investigate whether it might change indirectly through a change in knowledge or skills. And if this conclusion is positive, then investigate the possibility of changing the knowledge or skills.

### The Decision

But at the end of the day your analysis may conclude that the desired changes in knowledge, attitudes, and/or skills are not likely to come about as a result of mass communication, whether directly or indirectly. Then, the only conclusion is to recommend to your decision-maker some other solution to the problem. As already mentioned, a great many of the social problems of this world are not likely to be solved as a result of mass communication campaigns. So why waste our communication resources on such projects, when there are many other projects where they can be put to good use? Only if an unbroken line of probable cause and effect can be established through the diagram from the Campaign level through the Knowledge–Attitudes–Skills level and the Behaviour level to the Reduced Problems level should we in fact mount a campaign. Otherwise we must recommend some other line of action – or no action at all. In other words, one of the main qualifications of a communications manager is the ability to turn down a campaign suggestion and argue for the decision on the grounds of this 'bottom-up' analysis.

But if our analysis concludes that a campaign is a probable solution to the problem, we have described the exact strategy for achieving effects on the different levels of the diagram. We are now able (and this should be the next step in the planning process) to specify exactly which changes to expect in which parameters during the campaign process, and what reduction in the problem to expect as a result. In general, campaign managers do not like having to predict the likely effects of their campaigns. They point to the inherent difficulties of predicting human behaviour and audience reactions to the messages. But without such predictions, how can we judge the success or failure of the campaign? Inside every campaign manager (and decision-maker) are some criteria of success or failure; in other words, some expectations. After the campaign they compare the results with their expectations and are either satisfied or not. The whole art of prediction is to dare to put down on paper your unspoken expectations – more or less well-founded – and let them be confronted with reality. When doing this, you will realize that your predictions improve every time you take the effort to formalize and quantify them. You may still be wrong, but at least you learn something every time! In summary, the task is to put quantitative measures on every single parameter of the model which is expected to change. Only then will assessment be possible.

## ASSESSMENT ON STRATEGIC GROUNDS

If you have followed the model so far, not only is assessment possible, it is probable. In short, assessment boils down to measuring – on all levels of the diagram – whether the expected changes did in fact take place. But in real life, this is not the way things are done. Most campaign plans fail to quantify their expectations, even on the problem level, and most assessments are carried out only on one or two levels. Most common is assessment on the Campaign level alone: did the campaign get attention? Can the audience recall the slogan? How many press cuttings did we generate? Some campaigns are also assessed on the Knowledge and Attitudes level: how great a part of the audience did in fact acquire new knowledge during the campaign? Did the target group change attitude(s) in the desired direction after the campaign, compared with the situation before the campaign? Some campaigns are even assessed on the Problem level: was the problem reduced, and by how much? In a superficial analysis, this kind of assessment seems to make assessment on all other levels unnecessary. For surely it's the end effect that counts, isn't it? It certainly does, but assessment on the Problem level alone entails a great risk of false conclusions. Almost all of the social problems faced by campaigns are liable to change as a result of a multitude of different causes. Hence a reduction in the problem level during the campaign period may have been caused by many other factors than the campaign. And conversely, even if the problem was not reduced, your campaign may still have been a success, on the assumption that other factors have instead increased the problems during the campaign period. Thus, it is not possible to assess the results of a campaign on the Problem level alone. You cannot conclude that the campaign was successful or not from fluctuations in the problem level. In fact, you can never be certain that a campaign did work; you can only be sure when it fails. But we shall return to that later. Let us conclude the discussion of assessment levels in this way: there is no single level at which assessment should primarily be carried out. Professional assessment implies measuring, on all levels of the diagram, whenever possible, whether the expected changes did in fact take place. We shall have a brief look at the methods available for this.

## Campaign Level

At the Campaign level we want to answer the question: did the campaign in fact reach its target audience, and did they notice the campaign? There are several quantitative methods available to approach this problem, most of them based on survey techniques. Any newspaper can tell you the expected readership of a single issue, and commercial TV channels can even tell you the actual number of viewers in front of the screen. But normally they will not tell you whether the target audience did in fact notice your message. In order to know this, you will have to conduct your own survey research and ask the target group whether they noticed the information. The survey has to be carried out with the same questions asked both before and after the campaign, as a considerable part of any population will always be ready to claim they noticed a campaign even before it started. By subtracting the 'before' number from the 'after' number you will get an estimate of the net audience of your message.

For example, our Minister of Transport, who wanted to reduce traffic accidents among young drivers by reducing their driving speeds, will have to carry out a survey in the target group. He will then realize that the message did not get across to all young drivers, as he might have hoped, but only to maybe 15 or 20 per cent of the target group. And our Minister of Health, who wanted to reduce heart disease by making people eat less animal fat, will have to carry out survey research before and after the campaign. He will learn that the campaign reached maybe one-third of its target population, and maybe even more people outside the target group. A central problem in measuring exposure to a campaign is that information is generally presented in a mix of different mass media, and when asked after the campaign (e.g. in survey research), people in general are unable to say in which media they noticed the campaign; when asked, they will point to the medium which in their past experience has been most commonly used for information of this kind. So, in order to assess the effect of the different media in the campaign, survey research is certainly important, but it must be supplemented by exposure data for the individual media.

## Knowledge–Attitudes–Skills Level

On the Knowledge-Attitudes-Skills level, assessment is carried out by a combination of survey research and tests, with survey research the most important tool. Factual knowledge is pretty easy to assess, either by carrying out a survey in a sample of the target population, or (in the case of smaller target groups) by a simple test. Hence, you can ask a sample of young drivers in a survey what the speed limits are under different circumstances, and you can ask male adults about the fat content in different foods. But here again, you have to carry out the research and ask the same questions in the same way both before and after the campaign in order to get the net change in knowledge during the campaign period. Disappointingly, many campaign organizers discover that no change has taken place – which is to say, they have wasted their time telling people what they already knew!

Attitudinal change is slightly more difficult to assess, but with survey techniques and methods from sociology and social psychology it is certainly possible to measure attitudes in a reliable way. To get the net change during the campaign period, measurement again has to be carried out identically before and after the campaign. This naturally precludes the use of panel methods, as the exposure to attitudinal questioning in itself induces attitudinal change in the panel group. Instead, it is necessary to use separate samples before and after the campaign. On the Attitude level, our Minister of Transport might want to measure the attitudes of young drivers towards speed limits and police enforcement, or their beliefs concerning the risk of accidents at different driving speeds. Our Minister of Health might want to measure attitudes and preferences among male adults towards different kinds of food, and attitudes and intentions towards changing eating habits. Survey research will produce answers to these questions.

If the acquisition of new skills by the target group is part of the campaign strategy, you will have to measure the net change on the Skill level during the campaign period. This is most reliably done by testing in which samples of the target group have to demonstrate their skills in the subject before and after the campaign. For practical reasons, this method is sometimes impossible to use; instead, skills may be assessed indirectly, for example, by asking the target group whether they have participated in courses or other activities in order to increase their skills. But survey research should only be used when direct measurement of the skills in question is not possible or very difficult. In the case of our Minister of Transport, driving skills and speed control might be assessed on a sample of young drivers in a practical test on a test track or under traffic conditions. An indirect alternative might be to ask young drivers in a survey whether they participated in practical driving courses during the campaign period. Our Minister of Health might be interested in assessing the ability of adult housewives to prepare a meal in accordance with a recipe. This could be done directly in a test kitchen under controlled conditions, or indirectly in a survey by asking a sample of the target group whether they took part in activities to improve their cooking skills during the campaign period.

## Behaviour Level

Assessment on the Behaviour level is critical to most campaign assessments, but is nevertheless often neglected or only carried out superficially. It is true that assessment of some kinds of behaviour presents many practical problems, but it is important not to give up before every possibility has been examined. On the other hand, some kinds of behaviour are very easy to observe and assess, and others may be assessed indirectly, for example, through public statistical information or survey research.

Let us look at the driving behaviour of young male drivers, and in particular their speeding behaviour. We want to know whether drivers in a certain age group have changed their speeding and driving behaviour during the campaign period. Information on the driving speeds of all vehicles are automatically collected by the road authorities, but unfortunately the age of the driver cannot be registered automatically in the same process. It might be possible to combine the measurement of driving speeds in traffic with an observation by a trained observer of the age of the driver behind the wheel. Or a sample of drivers could be stopped, after measuring their driving speeds, and their age assessed by questioning. The number of speeding tickets to young drivers, however, will certainly not be a valid indicator of their speeding habits, as police focus on this offence is certainly liable to change as a result of the campaign. Hence, more speeding tickets might very well be expected, even when driving speeds were in fact reduced.

As the other example, let us look at the intake of animal fat by male adults. It is certainly difficult to observe what takes place in people's kitchens and dining rooms, but we can use indirect methods. It is safe to assume that most of the foods brought into a household will ultimately be eaten, hence observation of shopping habits will be a pretty good indicator of eating habits, and if you can get access to sales figures for different brands and types of food, this may be a fair substitute for actual observation. Only as a last resort should you rely on self-reported behaviour, as this is invariably biased: people want to appear sensible and responsible, so they tend to report their intention to change behaviour rather than their actual behaviour. But if no other way is possible, some information may be gained by survey research. For example, it is possible to ask a sample of the target group whether different family members have different eating habits, but the answers have to be judged with care.

## Problem Level

On the Problem level, assessment may be easy and quick or difficult and prolonged. With public information campaigns, very often the necessary data may be found in public statistics: social problems of all kinds, deaths by different causes, number of heart disease cases, and so on. Some of the information may be available only several years after the campaign: the connections between eating habits and death by heart disease, for example, take many years to establish. The connection between speeding and traffic death, on the other hand, is very direct. But here there may be a problem if the official traffic accident statistics are many months in preparation. For practical reasons, setting up a faster reporting routine during the campaign period might be considered. Assessment on the Problem level raises the issue of short- and long-term effects. It is often argued whether campaign effects should be assessed immediately after the campaign or on a longer time horizon. The argument is meaningless, however, if a detailed strategy for the campaign has been formulated with precise expectations of effect on all levels of the model. These expectations may be described both in the short term and in the long term; indeed, most campaigns will have effects both immediately and later, and professional assessment consists in measuring whether these expectations were met. No more, no less.

## HOW TO DRAW CONCLUSIONS

When assessment has been carried out on all levels of the campaign, where at all possible, we are left with the job of drawing conclusions. Let me stress that it is never possible to conclude that a campaign was a success. This may come as an unpleasant surprise to the practitioner, who would very much like to be able to prove his worth to his boss. But unfortunately, you are only able to draw positive conclusions when your strategy was proved wrong. You only really learn from your failures!

Let us assume that the assessment proved you right on all levels of the diagram: the campaign succeeded in reaching its intended audience and getting their attention. The predicted part of the target group changed their knowledge, attitude, and/or skills the expected amount in the expected direction during the campaign period. A somewhat smaller part of the target group changed their behaviour to an expected degree in the expected direction during or after the campaign period. And the problem level was reduced by the expected amount during or after the campaign period. All these successes will never prove that your campaign was effective because the changes may all have been caused by external factors beyond your control, and might have happened even if the campaign had never been carried out. All you can conclude is that your campaign was not demonstrably ineffective, and that the assumptions behind your strategy have been strengthened.

A common situation is that the expected effects are achieved on all but the Problem level. The campaign is noticed, knowledge or attitudes are changed, behaviour is changed too, but the problem is not reduced. In this case, the most sensible conclusion is that your theory was wrong and that the expected behavioural change was not able to reduce the problem. There is another possible conclusion, however: namely, that your campaign worked, but that some other external factor in the campaign period produced an increase in the problem level. In the case of the young drivers it might be a general increase in traffic mileage, or a period with bad weather conditions. Both possible conclusions should be investigated closely before making a conclusion about the effectiveness of the campaign.

Another tricky situation arises when you get effects on all but the Behaviour level: the campaign is noticed, knowledge or attitudes are changed, behaviour is not changed, but the problem is reduced nevertheless! In this case you can conclude that the problem was reduced either by some totally external factor or by a change in behaviour which may have been caused by the campaign but was not foreseen. In any case, you will gain new knowledge in the process.

In summary, then, assessment on all levels of the campaign model will either show the expected changes, in which case you will not have learned anything, but your professional confidence will grow and your boss will be happy. Or assessment will show that one or more of the levels did not get the expected change, in which case you have proved either that some outside factors were at work, or that your original assumptions were wrong. But you will have learned something and acquired new knowledge for your next campaign.

It is often argued that this kind of professional assessment is much too expensive. In my experience, a total of 5–10 per cent of a campaign budget must normally be set aside for assessment, and this will in most cases be sufficient for a fair degree of measurement on all levels of the model. If you think that 5–10 per cent is a large share of a campaign budget, just consider the risk that the campaign may fail completely. I maintain that a much larger proportion of all public information campaigns – maybe 40–50 per cent – are totally useless, but the campaign organizers never find out because they dare not assess them properly. The difference between professionally assessed campaigns and campaigns without proper assessment is not that the first kind are never failures. All campaigns may fail, as they are a skilful combination of scientific knowledge and creative thinking; but with professional assessment you learn from every failure. Without assessment, you go on repeating your failures because you never really find out where you are going wrong.

## REFERENCES

Baerns, B. (ed.) (1995) *PR-Erfolgskontrolle. Messen und Bewerten in der Öffentlichkeitsarbeit. Verfahren, Strategien, Beispiele*. Frankfurt am Main: IMK, Institut für Medienentwicklung und Kommunikation.

Blach, T. and Hojbjerg, J. (eds) (1989) *Håndbog i information og public relations*. Copenhagen: Borgens Forlag.

Grunig, J. and Hunt, T. (1984) *Managing Public Relations*. New York: Holt, Rinehart and Winston.

# 11

# Using Survey Research to Determine the Effects of a Campaign

*Klaus Schönbach*

## ESTABLISHING CAMPAIGN OBJECTIVES

Any attempt to determine the success of a campaign requires a clear notion of its long-term and short-term objectives. What is the campaign expected to accomplish? Its goals and objectives have to be clearly defined. The dimensions of such a definition are as follows.

1. Eventually, every campaign wants to influence behaviours. Still, many campaigners legitimately want to know if specific steps on the way to that goal were reached: for instance, was a campaign successful in conveying crucial information? In principle, two levels of campaign outcomes underlie the actions it is eventually supposed to incite:

- knowledge, e.g. about the functioning of an institution, the dangers of a specific behaviour, the plans of an organization;
- attitudes or opinions. These are defined as positive or negative evaluations of persons or organizations (their evaluations are often called 'images'), of goals, actions, policies, etc.

Studying the outcomes of a campaign is a good idea as long as they are not taken as a sufficient indication of the behavioural end result. Most often such an intellectual shortcut rests on a – usually unexpressed – 'rational choice' model, based on the idea of a hierarchy of effects. At its bottom we find awareness or knowledge, which campaigns are supposed to influence first. Attitudes toward and opinions about the subjects of that knowledge, then, are assumed to build on that foundation, and behaviours are supposed to be the final consequence of those attitudes. Certainly, there is evidence that behaviours may only develop after at least some knowledge about their causes and consequences has been acquired.

Unfortunately, people may know everything they were supposed to learn from a campaign; they may even like the ideas it propagates and still may not behave accordingly. Anti-smoking and AIDS campaigns are impressive examples of this lack of transfer.

2. The intention of a campaign does not necessarily have to be change. It can also be confirmation or stabilization, i.e. preventing the loss of knowledge, the weakening of attitudes, or the disappearance of behaviours already acquired.

3. The desired amount and extent of campaign effects should be estimated realistically: what are, for instance, the pieces of information everybody should have gained as a minimum? Or: how many people should display a different behaviour at which stage of the campaign? Or: how strong are specific attitudes supposed to be for what proportion of the audience?

4. Time-lag of campaign effects: expectations about how long it takes until the desired impact occurs should be clearly stated.

5. Last, but not least, the target group: who is supposed to be influenced? Everybody? Or well-defined subgroups such as people who should stop dangerous behaviours, as opposed to those who are to be kept from taking them up in the first place? Is the campaign devised to influence its final target groups directly or are 'opinion leaders' supposed to pass its information on or even convince other people?

Selecting the target group requires a precise notion not only of its structure and by which communication channels it can be reached, but also of its intellectual abilities. With children, drug abusers, or right-wing fanatics as target groups, particular efforts are required to devise the appropriate messages. Thus these characteristics already have considerable influence on selecting the instruments of the campaign itself. Accordingly, their persuasive power has to be estimated realistically.

## CAUSALITY AND IMPACT

Once it is clear what a specific campaign is supposed to accomplish – change or stabilization, knowledge or behaviours, long- or short-term effects, an impact on everybody or only on narrowly defined subgroups – the first issue in determining its actual effects is that of causality. The next, closely related to it, is the amount of impact, i.e. whether the campaign was as successful as conceived – in terms of producing the expected extent of influence.

1. The first question is simply: if the desired effects occurred, can they really be attributed to the campaign? Or would they have occurred anyway – for instance, because of information spread simultaneously by other sources and not by the campaign? Effects of a campaign may also be falsely assumed where 'natural' developments are their real cause: drunk driving may slowly decrease because of changes in the age structure of a society – the older people are, the less alcohol they may consume; price hikes may make it difficult to buy drugs; economic crises may render European unification more attractive.

2. The reverse is also possible: did the campaign really fail if the desired effects did not occur? For instance, it could have been very efficient in

silently cancelling out counter-effects, and thus could at least have stopped developments that otherwise would have been harmful to its objectives.

3. Also, campaigns may simply not accomplish much at all – neither change nor reinforce people's behaviours.

4. Finally, campaigns may even cause 'boomerang effects', or counter-productive results. This worst outcome of a campaign occurs when it makes people aware of counter-arrangements they had not been aware of before.

How can causality and the extent of effects caused by the campaign be measured? Sometimes causality may seem obvious. But consider this example: somebody having read a campaign ad is observed to act in the desired direction immediately afterwards. Even such a (rare) observation is not a final proof of causation. We cannot be completely sure whether reading the ad was really the cause, even if the respondent said so, and not any other inspiration that may have occurred at the same time.

Usually, social-scientific proof of causality is more modest and also more complicated. It calls for two prerequisites:

1 a genuine link between exposure to the campaign and indications of the expected effects in the audience. To prove the authenticity of that link means to simultaneously control for as many other factors as possible, factors that could have also led to those effects. Here is where good theories on the effects of communication and media, particularly on persuasive communication, help to reduce complexity, i.e. quite practically the number of factors that, in principle, may be controlled for.

2 Exposure and audience characteristics, once genuinely connected to each other, should be in the right temporal sequence. It must be clear that exposure to the campaign came first. This prerequisite sounds trivial but often cannot be met without complex and expensive research designs (see below).

Evaluating the extent of effects needs criteria: the number of people who know something of a specific stage of the campaign, for instance, compared with that number before the campaign started, or the strength of an attitude, measured on a scale, where later scores are higher than earlier ones.

## SURVEY RESEARCH

An appropriate tool to determine the success of campaigns – both in terms of causality and the extent of effects – is survey research. Of course, surveys have to be planned carefully.

1. Who is to be surveyed: for instance, only possible 'opinion leaders', their final target groups, or also other respondents? Interviewing respondents outside of the campaign target groups is necessary if effects are to be compared in order to estimate their relative size. Then it may be wise to have base-line information about the state of information or behaviours among those not targeted by the campaign.

In most cases, samples of the persons to be surveyed need to be drawn. Interviewing everybody would either be impossible or too costly. Sampling requires a clear definition of the target groups and, possibly, those people who are to be surveyed for comparative purposes. For a representative sample, one has to be sure that everybody from the totality has a determinable chance of being included in the sample. If that is the case, virtually only the size of the sample determines the error margins to be accepted.

Samples do not necessarily have to be representative, however. A campaign may be assessed by using somehow typical or particularly interesting persons – those who are assumed to be extremely resistant to the campaign, for instance, or highly powerful and influential people.

2. What kind of interviewing procedure is most appropriate? Face-to-face interviews have both advantages and disadvantages: on the one hand, they allow sophisticated instruments of interviewing: card decks, pictures, complicated rank orderings. They also exert a certain amount of social control over the respondent. Once an interview is agreed on, it is rarely interrupted early. On the other hand, it is often more difficult to get respondents to cooperate in the first place; refusal rates are considerable. In that respect, telephone surveys fare better. On the other hand, however, they have to be brief and simple, and, of course, they can only be considered if the persons to be surveyed actually have telephones. Mail questionnaires suffer from a low return rate, unless the respondents are both highly motivated to express themselves and trained in the use of written expression. Also, since there is virtually no control of the answering situation, only questions are appropriate that do not require spontaneity and individual responses.

3. Three groups of data necessary to assess campaign effects can be discerned:

- campaign exposure,
- effects expected, and
- control variables.

*Campaign exposure* may be direct or indirect, e.g. via other people who pass campaign messages on in conversations. If the latter is true, it is certainly useful to know: did 'opinion leaders' really talk about the campaign? If direct effects are to be gauged: is it sufficient to simply know that the members of the target group had the chance to see ads, movies, leaflets, etc. of the campaign? Often, campaign evaluations are content with simply finding out whether a respondent reads a newspaper or magazine in which ads were placed. Or should a 'copy test' of specific magazines be applied to make sure that every single piece of information of a campaign ad was really perceived? Copy tests ask respondents to specify which parts of every single page they remember having noticed or read.

*Effects.* The quality of knowledge expected at a certain stage of the campaign may mean recognition of information only ('yes, sounds familiar …') as well as unaided recall of well-defined pieces of information presented in a campaign. Is recall or recognition of information the – at least interim – aim of the campaign? Must attitudes be measured in subtle test batteries? Can reports on behaviours be trusted?

Advertising-effects research offers four different stages of knowledge about a campaign:

- 'resonance': has the campaign itself struck the audience? Do people remember it?
- 'awareness': is the target audience aware of a campaign on a given topic?
- 'media-specific awareness': what were the media in which the campaign was conveyed?
- 'campaign content': recall or recognition of substantial information.

*Control variables* are necessary for a comprehensive assessment of alternative sources of information and persuasion but also as 'mediating factors'. What else have people read or watched? The purpose of the latter is to find both obstacles to and catalysts of a campaign. Which individuals among the target groups experienced greater or smaller effects than expected? This is precious information that an ongoing or future campaign could take advantage of. Those intervening variables are:

- indicators of the individual's capability to process the information offered – education, age, prior knowledge, and experience;
- indicators of readiness to accept the messages of the campaign or to resist them – interest, prior attitudes, personal relevance.

4. The issue of causality is addressed with differing degrees of straightforwardness by different designs. In any case, however, at least two measurement points in time are needed to observe either change or stability in the target group.

- Trend surveys are repeated cross-sections of the population. Their repetition helps establish the right temporal order of causes and effects.
- Panel surveys – trend surveys with the same respondents – not only assess temporal order but also allow better control of conflicting, alternative explanations for effects in the audience. Fluctuation and its causes can be traced individually: who changed their minds and in which direction?

On the other hand, panel surveys may suffer from unwanted learning effects: respondents may change their behaviours because of being interviewed and thus made aware of something they had not noticed before. Panel decay is another problem that troubles this type of survey: respondents feel bothered and may not want to participate more than once. Counter-measures for both problems can be costly.

If possible, both trend and panel surveys should ideally be applied more than twice, not just before and after a campaign. The optimal solution would be a time series of surveys with only short time-lags between them. The reason for such a design is obvious: one can never be sure that the expected effect occurs exactly at the point when, for instance, the one post-campaign survey is in the field. There may be delays and curvilinear relationships – S-curves, parabolas, sine-curves – between exposure to the campaign and its impact. Effects may be temporarily exaggerated, although they disappear immediately after a survey. Zero-effects may be misleading if, after the survey, they turn into strong ones because the audience needed some time for the campaign's messages to sink in.

## ALTERNATIVES TO SURVEYS

Surveys are rarely the only way to make at least an educated guess about the success or failure of a campaign. There are alternatives.

1. Controlled experiments offer an 'anticipatory' assessment of effects before the campaign starts. They are able to test all the measures of a campaign with a small number of people before a lot of money is spent. They can simulate on a smaller scale what the campaign is supposed to accomplish.

2. What we often call 'traces' are indicators that are there anyway:

- The numbers of requests for information material, calls, of participants in write-in competitions may signal how many people were at least reached by a campaign and activated by it.
- Sales figures may serve as indicators of the desired behaviours: cigarettes, alcohol, condoms, cars with catalytic converters, fuel-efficient furnaces, energy-saving light bulbs.
- Official statistics may provide reliable data on blood donation, for instance, or on tourist visits, number of hotel nights, money spent on a particular item.

Systematic observations are particularly useful for gauging behavioural outcomes of campaigns. They can much more reliably assess the desired behaviour than reports by the respondents themselves. The latter may be distorted by social desirability or by inability to articulate attitudes or images properly. Observations with as many people as could be interviewed in a survey, however, are costly and have to be conducted carefully lest they bias a 'natural' situation. For some behaviours – such as intimate ones, for instance – they may not even be applicable in practice.

For sales figures, requests and official statistics, the major danger is 'ecological failure.' Because of the aggregate nature of the data, alternative explanations cannot be excluded on the individual level with final safety. Consider the famous example to be found in Emile Durkheim's 'Suicide': if areas with a high proportion of Protestants show a higher rate of suicide, then the plausible conclusion is that Protestants are more prone to this type of behaviour. However, one could also reason that it is the Catholics who tend to kill themselves in higher numbers, the smaller their minority among the Protestants. By analogy, an information campaign to increase voter turnout may seem successful if the turnout is actually higher than before. In principle, however, this increase may be due only to those who were not reached by the campaign.

# 12   Using Market Research Techniques to Determine Campaign Effects

## Rolf Pfleiderer

This contribution describes marketing research techniques used in determining the effectiveness of advertising campaigns. These techniques were not developed for political or other public information campaigns, but rather for commercial advertising for consumer goods and services, in which as a rule the only goal is to sell a product. Even 'image campaigns' – for example, those carried out by the association of private banks in Germany, the chemical industry association, etc. – are primarily concerned with increasing sales, or at least countering negative attitudes, prejudices, or possibly justified social critique in order to improve the chances of achieving particular economic goals.

Thus the ultimate goal of all research techniques developed for business advertising is to prove whether and to what extent a particular campaign has assisted in the company's commercial success: whether the campaign has 'paid off'. Banal as it may seem, this goal is extremely difficult to achieve: the factors for market success are so varied and interdependent that even the most carefully formulated research techniques are often unable to determine the exact qualitative or even quantitative effect of advertising or of a particular campaign on the success or failure of a product or service. Although advertising aims at the consumer's wallet, it does so indirectly, often via the consumers' heads and hearts in such complex associations that simplistic assumptions about their operation should be avoided.

A further complication is that simply designing a print ad or filming a TV spot is not enough; the ad must then be conveyed to the consumer via some medium, with varying effectiveness depending on the advertising goals, target groups, or situations. In order for advertising to have the intended effect, it must not only be 'good', however that may be interpreted in individual cases, it must also be presented to the consumer via an equally effective medium.

Because the effects of advertising can rarely be measured by the commercial success of a product or service (in other words, a product's success can almost never be attributed solely to advertising), market research has developed models to represent the relationships between individual parameters of advertising effectiveness and also their relationship to criteria measuring commercial success, such as sales volume, profit, etc.

It is beyond the scope of this contribution to examine these extremely varied and in some cases highly complex models in detail. Rather, I wish to point out that most of these models share three basic parameters of advertising effectiveness, which, taken individually, are relatively simple to test empirically and are not concerned with units sold, sales volume, or profits, a point relevant for measuring effectiveness in public information campaigns. These three parameters are

1 ability to attract attention;
2 ability to communicate the message;
3 ability to exploit media resources effectively.

## EMPIRICAL MEASUREMENTS OF THE THREE BASIC PARAMETERS OF ADVERTISING EFFECTIVENESS: CONDUCTING PUBLIC OPINION RESEARCH

### Attention-Getting Effectiveness

In the following, 'attention-getting effectiveness' refers to a specific aspect of the effect of a particular means of advertising, or combinations thereof, within a campaign. 'Means of advertising' refers to the individual print advertisement, advertising poster, radio or TV spot, etc.

One ordinarily assumes that the attention-getting effectiveness of an advertisement is a quality inherent in the ad itself and therefore quantifiable according to general standards, or at least comparable with other ads without great difficulty. This is unfortunately not the case, however: a print ad, poster, TV or radio spot only operates within a particular editorial context, traffic situation, TV programme, etc., at a particular time of day – among readers, passers-by, listeners, and viewers with extremely varied attitudes and levels of interest.

For example, there are certainly advertisements especially suited to 'grab attention' by virtue of their formal qualities such as strong visual or textual contrasts, but the media context and target group make-up may have a greater effect than such qualities apparently inherent in the advertisement. One need think only of the very different effects of a large colour print ad in an almost entirely black-and-white daily newspaper as opposed to a highly-coloured magazine, or of the different levels of attention given an ad promoting condom use that appears in a trendy youth magazine as opposed to a church newsletter.

The construct 'attention-getting effectiveness' is problematic in another way as well: in order to measure an ad's effectiveness at gaining attention, as a rule market research measures not the act of 'paying attention' itself, but the traces the ad leaves in the memory of those surveyed. This makes an essential difference in terms of what is actually being measured, or, in concrete terms, what is to be asked, and which means should be used to support this questioning.

To be sure, biophysical methods can be used to measure the act of perception: recording visual activity, measuring skin resistance, and so on while viewing advertisements. These methods can certainly provide interesting insights into the effects of advertising on perception, but their usefulness in measuring advertising effectiveness is limited, for one because such tests are generally possible only under laboratory conditions. Further, in advertising the act of perception is ultimately less important than the step that follows it, namely, that of being processed as information and stored in the memory. Biophysical testing is expensive and can therefore be performed on only a relatively small subject sample; because of the variety of advertising targets, this unrepresentative sample makes it impossible to draw general conclusions.

Measuring attention-getting effectiveness through questioning does not focus on perception itself, then, but on that which remains in the memory. But what exactly is that? Not the 'trace of perceiving', which is normally not remembered; for this reason, asking the test subject when he or she first or last noticed a particular advertisement does not provide meaningful results. One must ask instead about a particular detail of substance or form, a particular impression, a more or less complete picture, and so on. It should be immediately apparent that the phrasing of the question is of immense importance in measuring attention-getting effectiveness and especially in comparing the results of different advertisements. Unfortunately for devotees of rigid norms, there can be no generally applicable rules for formulating questions; rather, questions must be phrased in accordance with the particular goals of the advertisement or campaign.

### THE SIGNIFICANCE OF ATTENTION-GETTING EFFECTIVENESS
### IN PUBLIC INFORMATION CAMPAIGNS

As a rule, advertising research focuses on campaigns for particular 'brands', that is, for goods and services of particular companies that wish to publicize, explain, or portray them in a new or unusual light in order to sell them. Thus advertising research focuses on brand-name recognition, and empirical studies ask questions first about the subject's familiarity with particular brands (i.e. by asking about certain types of products, etc.) before moving on to more or less specific questions about advertising for brands of particular products.

The only responses that matter are those showing that the interviewee can reproduce a brand name from memory. Those who can spontaneously recall a particular ad without remembering the brand or company associated with it are treated the same as persons who cannot recall anything at all about the ad in question. (In face-to-face interviews, displaying the print ad or showing the TV spot on the interviewer's laptop computer can ascertain which subjects can recall the ad but not the brand name; in telephone interviews, radio spots can be played back to aid the memory.)

Considering that commercial advertising is always ultimately concerned with selling a product or service, it is entirely appropriate for research on commercial ad campaigns to limit its concept of 'ad memory' to 'brand-name memory'. For public information campaigns, however, the question of what the subject remembers is less straightforward and must be formulated for each campaign to be analysed; depending on the campaign's goals, the differences may be enormous. If one takes as one's standard spontaneous recall, without showing the ad to aid the memory, then results will differ significantly depending on whether one asks: 'Can you recall any advertising against drug abuse?', 'Can you recall any advertising in which famous sports figures speak out against drugs?', or 'Can you recall any advertising using the slogan "No Power to Drugs"?'.

The first question is formulated too broadly to ascertain the attention-getting effectiveness of a particular anti-drug campaign, because other anti-drug initiatives besides those of the relevant campaign would also appear among those remembered. The question is thus too broadly worded, and the attention-getting effectiveness of the campaign can only be determined through further questioning, such as 'What details can you recall about the advertising against drugs?'

The second question already provides one detail of the campaign to aid memory. The 'stimulus' provided by the wording is no longer the general and abstract 'against drugs' but the more concrete and easier to remember 'famous sports figures against drugs'. If the testimonials of famous sports figures against drugs are the campaign's unique feature, then one can reasonably assume that positive answers to this question actually refer to the campaign in question. On the other hand, this wording can hinder subsequent analysis of the campaign's communicative effectiveness, since it already reveals or at least hints at specific informational content. Clearly, there are no simply 'right' or 'wrong' questions; how the question is phrased has implicit influence on the subsequent analysis of campaign effectiveness.

The third example is formulated most like questions used in research on brand-name advertising: here the slogan 'No Power to Drugs!' serves as the 'brand' or 'trademark'. At the same time, this slogan expresses the goal of the campaign and its learning objective. This question is better for measuring the communicative effectiveness of the campaign; the wording is too specific for determining attention-getting effectiveness.

What can we learn from this example, which is typical for public information campaigns? For one thing, spontaneous recall of an ad or campaign as a measure of attention-getting effectiveness is highly dependent on the concrete question formulation, especially in public information campaigns. Since for pragmatic reasons and according to the communicative goals of the campaign (consider such varied goals as fighting drug abuse, showing the achievements of a particular European government agency, or publicizing an administrative measure) questions can be worded in very different ways, comparing the results of spontaneous recall of different campaigns is only possible on extremely limited terms. This does not mean, however, that testing the spontaneous recognition of a campaign is a waste of time.

Campaign recognition using campaign advertising materials is much more appropriate for comparing effectiveness, and questions must be directed at individual ads as precisely and concretely as possible: for example, 'Have you ever seen this ad in a magazine or newspaper?' while showing the ad in its original size and colour. To test aided recall of a campaign consisting of several different print ads, posters, or TV and radio spots, as many as possible of these different materials should be displayed and appropriate questions asked about them. Derived in this way, attention-getting effectiveness – that is, the recall of at least one piece of advertising used in the campaign – constitutes a value that can be used in comparing different campaigns.

While research on brand-name advertising may derive useful and often adequate measurements for the comparative analysis of attention-getting effectiveness by testing for spontaneous brand-name recall, research on public information campaigns should as a rule use ad materials with questions designed to aid recall of the campaign (also known as the 'recognition method'). This means that interviews to determine attention-getting effectiveness can usually only be carried out face-to-face or possibly on-line, but not by mail or telephone.

## MEASURING ATTENTION-GETTING EFFECTIVENESS IN PRE-TESTING

Since a campaign's success at attracting attention is without question necessary for its overall success, it is a popular target for tests attempting to provide some certainty about the presence of this crucial quality before running expensive advertisements in the media. Such tests necessarily have an experimental, 'laboratory' character, since a central aspect of advertising campaigns, namely broad public exposure, is missing. Yet the attempt must be made to ensure that test conditions are as realistic as possible in order to derive results truly predictive of the subsequent campaign outcome.

In practice, this means that certain limitations must be accepted: for example, it is normally too complicated to realistically test the synergy between ads in different media, and financial considerations mean that the effects of repeated exposure (e.g. through multiple contact with the same print, poster, or TV ad) can rarely be analysed. 'Realistic conditions' for pre-testing thus means above all that the ad is not tested in complete isolation from the environment in which it would normally appear. In this case 'environment' does not refer to the situation in which ad contact ordinarily occurs, i.e. on the interviewee's couch in front of the TV, in the recliner, or over breakfast. On the contrary, the situation is entirely unusual for the interviewee, since it involves the presence of an interviewer or a visit to a testing studio. Therefore the media environment at least must be 'realistic'. For the various forms of advertising to be pre-tested, that means that print ads should be displayed in magazines, dummy layouts or newspaper montages, etc. specially designed for the test in a form typical of the subsequent ad placement.

In practice, this is usually done by producing a 20–40-page test dummy (usually based on earlier issues of a particular publication) in which the test ad is pasted into an appropriate position or used to replace an already-existing ad. This publication is then usually given to the test subject, who is asked to look through it either at home or in the testing studio before answering some questions about the (new or in some way altered) magazine. Thus the attempt to reproduce 'realistic' conditions is made by not directing the interviewee's attention to the advertising, but by giving him or her the impression that the editorial or formal make-up of the publication is of concern, which is 'realistic' since one does not usually read a magazine for the advertising.

After a more or less extensive examination of the test magazine, the interviewee is asked about its editorial content and formal design before approaching the subject of the advertisements, especially the test ad (at first open-ended and without special aids to memory, then after showing the test ad again). In analysing the specific attention-getting effectiveness of the test ad, it is especially helpful to determine the recall values for the other ads for purposes of comparison; values from other comparable studies are also useful.

It should be noted that testing the attention-getting effectiveness of advertising in this way provides results derived in a situation with no significant lapse of time between exposure to the ad and the interview, and thus measures short-term recall of the ad. This situation is not entirely realistic, especially with regard to the 'selling effect' usually intended. Advertising can be considered effective at gaining attention when recall can still be measured after a longer period, such as one or two days. These conditions can of course be reproduced in testing, for example by asking questions about ad recall in a second interview one or two days later. Doing so is however more complicated and significantly raises testing expenses. One can generally assume that a high degree of short-term recall indicates a high degree of medium- to long-term recall, and that an ad that is forgotten a few minutes after exposure will certainly not be remembered one or two days later.

Pre-testing of poster advertising under anything like realistic conditions is practical only with the aid of test posters. The particular effect of poster advertising, and above all its ability to attract attention, lies precisely in its oversized representation of the ad content and its omnipresence, an aspect that is especially difficult to reproduce under testing conditions. It is therefore a good idea to display the test ad in different locations with differing visibility conditions and to survey passers-by. Again in this case, values from other comparable tests are of course helpful in evaluating results. The observations on short-term recall noted above apply here as well; it is not difficult to arrange with passers-by an interview appointment a day or two later in order to test the medium- and long-term recall of poster advertising.

In order to pre-test the attention-getting effectiveness of television spots realistically, it is especially important to insert such spots within a particular television programme or on a particular channel, all the more so since 'normal' TV-viewing behaviour is strongly characterized by attempts to avoid television advertising. Commercial breaks are seen as opportunities to change channels or 'go get a beer', or at least for reducing attention paid to the screen. For this reason, testing in which the test subjects are a captive audience, unable to switch channels or turn off the set, is problematic; if carried out in a movie-theatre-like setting, there can be no question of realistic conditions.

To test attention-getting effectiveness realistically, then, there remains only the relatively expensive method of including the test spot in an actual broadcast with other commercials, carrying out interviews immediately afterwards. For financial reasons it is advisable to choose a local TV station or an inexpensive broadcast slot to save on costs. Since locating persons at random who have actually seen the test spot is time-consuming and expensive, it is necessary to recruit subjects in advance for this kind of pre-testing.

As in the pre-testing of print ads, test subjects are initially not informed about the test objective; they are requested simply to watch a certain broadcast on a certain station at a certain time. Immediately following the broadcast, the interview is carried out, usually by telephone. Questions regarding the overall broadcast are asked first, then questions to ascertain recall of the test spot itself; questions about the other commercials in the broadcast should also be asked for purposes of comparison. In analysing and evaluating the results, here again it is a great advantage to be able to compare results of earlier testing.

As with print and poster ads, with this method it is also possible to conduct the interview one or two days following exposure to the ad rather than immediately after the broadcast. Because individual TV commercials tend to fade quickly from memory, waiting presents the danger that one will find little concrete recollection of the ad, or that the number of interviews will have to be increased significantly in order to provide a statistically representative base, which is expensive.

### MEASURING ATTENTION-GETTING EFFECTIVENESS IN POST-TESTING:

### ADVERTISING RESONANCE STUDIES

Analysing the resonance of advertising appearing in one or more media should reveal whether the campaign's goal was achieved. In order to learn from these results for future advertising campaigns, the resonance analysis should also show which media or which ads contributed to the resonance (and if possible, to what extent), and ideally how the ads' effectiveness developed over time and depending on the actual exposure to them. Determining attention-getting effectiveness is in this context only one of multiple elements in determining advertising resonance. As shown above, it is the precondition for the communicative effectiveness or 'learning objectives' especially important in public information campaigns.

As we have already seen, analysis of attention-getting effectiveness in public information campaigns usually cannot be limited to the spontaneous resonance or recall of the campaign in question. Instead, the most important campaign ads – even better, the complete advertising materials – must be displayed as aids to memory, with ad-recall tested separately for each. Because print advertising campaigns usually use more than one medium, and are therefore perceived in more than one medium, it is sufficient to display print ads in their original form and colour, rather than in their editorial context. To aid in recalling poster advertising, photographs of the ad on billboards, advertising columns, or light poles should be provided. TV spots should be shown on the interviewer's laptop computer, if possible; as a last resort, the interviewer may show it on videotape, although this interrupts the interview and assumes that the interviewee has a VCR. Using storyboards is appropriate for public information campaigns only in limited circumstances, because both the acoustic dimension and the dynamic image characteristic of TV advertising are missing. For radio advertising campaigns, the ad should be played back on tape or on a laptop with audio capacity. Analysis of monophonic radio campaigns may also be conducted over the telephone, as the ad may be transmitted directly via the telephone studio's central computer system.

Depending on the type of public information campaign and its goals, it may be difficult for the interviewee to distinguish whether he or she has 'learned' particular facts or behaviours from a certain campaign or rather from the media or general public opinion. The specific attention-getting effectiveness of such campaigns may be demonstrated precisely by the fact that discussion of the relevant theme gains more attention in the media. In such cases it is therefore advisable when analysing campaign resonance to take into account whether and to what degree the campaign theme enters the media or the general public debate, and how it is received. This information is often indispensable in order to distinguish between the direct and indirect effects of the campaign and if necessary screen out effects of the media representation of the issue that are not attributable to the campaign. To be able to analyse these effects more precisely, as a rule 'before' and 'after' studies are necessary, or the interview responses should be analysed at widely spaced intervals. It should be mentioned that the measurement of attention-getting effectiveness rests on clearly definable exemplary campaigns. If 'learning success', modified behaviour, etc. depending on campaign exposure are to be studied, then multiple checkpoints, at least one before and one at the end of the campaign, are essential. More will be said on this point in the following section.

## Communicative Effectiveness

In advertising research, the term 'communicative effectiveness' refers to the content, images, impulses, etc. transmitted to the advertising audience via an advertisement or campaign. In many cases this may seem banal: what could be difficult about figuring out the communicative intent of an ad showing a shapely bottle of Brand X and in large print the text, 'New! Improved cleaning power! Buy Brand X!'? Unfortunately, the world of communication has grown extraordinarily complex, and consumers can see through advertising claims. In the above example, the message that comes across is not simply the command 'buy Brand X', but something like this: the producers of

Brand X have noticed that other detergents work better, so now they want to make us believe that their detergent is new and improved. But not even the bottle has changed, proving that they haven't come up with anything new, and it's all just 'advertising'! Further, the colours used in the ad may be conventional or unusual, compatible with the previous image of Brand X or not; favourable or unfavourable reports about the maker of Brand X may have appeared in the news, and so on. Thus what an ad actually communicates is by no means predefined, which is all the more true since messages as simple as the one in the above example are the exception; public information campaigns in particular usually have a more complicated message to convey.

The study of communicative effectiveness constitutes the second major topic of advertising research, precisely because advertising campaigns usually attempt to 'package' complex messages in as brief and 'catchy' a form as possible. Since the advertising audience is subjected to rational and emotional appeals, very different methods can be used, depending on the nature of the message or its special formal elements, to find out whether the message was received as intended. Standardized interviews are often inadequate for determining communicative effectiveness, especially when the ad is intended to convey emotions or moods or create a certain brand image. In this case, psychological, associative, or biophysical testing, etc. may be considered, with the addition, if necessary, of standard tests.

As a rule, however, public information campaigns are usually concerned with conveying rational attitudes or behaviours, even if they use emotionally-affective advertisements to do so. Yet public information campaigns are primarily aimed at the rational faculties of their audiences, and the communicative effectiveness must be considered poor if the campaign message is not understood, or if the advertising audience can only remember irrelevant details or formal design qualities from the ad. For this reason, special standardized interviews of selected members of the advertising audience are the most important method of determining communicative effectiveness in public information campaigns.

### MEASURING COMMUNICATIVE EFFECTIVENESS IN PRE-TESTING

In order to determine whether an advertisement has been correctly understood, it is not absolutely necessary to display the ad in its media context. It can, however, be helpful to use pre-testing to determine whether the details and content necessary to convey the message can be comprehended within the time allowed under real conditions, since the advertising audience usually does not peruse ads for minutes at a time: studies have shown that the average time spent looking at newspaper ads, for example, is between one and two seconds – if they are noticed at all. The number of people who look at an ad for five or even fifteen seconds is minuscule.

It is of course essential to show the ad to the test subjects in pre-testing for communicative effectiveness, but one must be careful not to reveal the theme and goal of the ad in such a way as to influence the subject's attitude toward or understanding of it. In general, group discussions are not appropriate in pre-testing, since opinion leaders or 'quick studies' can prevent real conceptual weaknesses from becoming apparent.

After showing the ad, the subject should be asked open-ended questions about what he or she thought about the ad, what s/he particularly noticed, etc. Then subjects should be asked, in equally open-ended form, what they think the ad's intention is, what one is supposed to do as a result of having seen it. After that, questions about particular details (if necessary after showing the ad again), judgement of the ad, and agreement or disagreement with its statements may be asked.

In practice, pre-tests of communicative effectiveness are often used to select the best of various advertising drafts. In these cases, one must take into account that the subject's awareness of one draft may influence his or her understanding of a different one; here the interviewees must be split into different groups, with the first group viewing Ad A first, then Ad B, while the second group views Ad B first, and then Ad A. If there are many drafts and/or campaign conceptions to test, a very complicated arrangement may be required, which may also influence the decision of whether to conduct pre-testing in a studio or in the field, at the interviewee's home.

The real art of measuring communicative effectiveness in pre-testing lies less in the test arrangement and sample design than in competent analysis of the responses, especially to the open-ended questioning about the advertising materials. It is advisable to use the greatest care in encoding these responses for the subsequent tabular analysis, always keeping the communicative goal in mind. For example, it should be clear before pre-testing whether recalling a particular slogan in the short term should be counted as 'communicative effectiveness' or as 'attention-getting effectiveness' (see above).

To give an example: when attempting to acquaint the public with the new European currency by showing an ad with a picture of the euro, one should already have decided how to evaluate the response 'the ad shows a euro' in terms of communicative effectiveness; if the ad is primarily intended to overcome certain prejudices against the new currency, this can only be considered a neutral, not a positive, response. The point is that communicative effectiveness can only be measured against the intended communicative goal. Thus to pre-test communicative effectiveness, it is always essential to have clearly formulated the communicative goals of the campaign.

The limits of empirical pre-testing should also be noted: some campaigns are only fully effective after a particular length of time, in connection with a certain event, or through the combination of a series of messages over time. Pre-tests, however, are usually structured in order to show whether the concept for conveying the message is fundamentally – and therefore immediately – correct. Testing the communicative effectiveness of campaigns designed to be 'understood' only after a certain length of time is usually only possible afterwards.

Particularly in public information campaigns, it is conceivable that the 'communicative goal' involves certain changes in behaviour, such as the

HUK Association's television campaign in the early 1980s to reduce accidents in the home and during leisure activities. In pre-testing, the campaign was broadcast in a limited test area; random samples were taken – both before and after the broadcasts – in the test area and in a control area where the spots were not broadcast, to determine awareness of measures to prevent accidents in the home. Since it could not be assumed that the few TV spots would actually have an effect on behaviour, communication was to be regarded as successful if it could be shown that awareness of preventive behaviour improved in the test area as compared with the control area. Improved awareness was in fact proved in the test area, and the television campaign was subsequently carried out on a larger scale.

This brings us to a method used less in pre-testing than in determining advertising resonance.

## MEASURING COMMUNICATIVE EFFECTIVENESS IN POST-TESTING: ADVERTISING RESONANCE STUDIES

In contrast to pre-testing for communicative effectiveness, in post-testing as a rule it is unnecessary or even counterproductive to show the test subjects the campaign advertising again. Thus post-testing can usually be conducted over the telephone and at lower costs, as long as it is not intended to test the campaign's attention-getting effectiveness at the same time (see above). Open-ended questioning about recall of the campaign's content, design elements, 'primary message', etc. are again characteristic for post-testing communicative effectiveness. In addition, those who do remember the campaign can be asked about its individual details and about their evaluation of its comprehensibility, believability, originality of presentation, overall image, relevance, etc. As with pre-testing, the main difficulty lies in recording the responses to such open-ended questions precisely and accurately, encoding them with regard to the communicative goals of the campaign, and evaluating them.

Particularly in the case of public information campaigns, the nature of the campaign's objectives often requires that resonance checks be carried out not only at a particular point in time, but as a series, or even continually up to a particular end date. Examples are objectives formulated as follows: 'the majority of the population in X should be able to name the function of a particular government agency or institution', or '5 per cent of those who commute to work by car should be persuaded to switch to public transportation', etc. Testing the communicative effectiveness of such campaigns requires that the status quo be established in sampling done before the campaign, and that additional comparable sampling be carried out after the end of the campaign (at the latest). It can be especially useful to take a sample relatively early in the campaign in order to tell whether the campaign is working as planned; if needed, corrective measures or flanking manoeuvres can still be attempted before it is too late. On the other hand, if sampling shows that the goal has already been achieved ahead of schedule, funds intended for continuing the campaign may be saved.

Such tests of communicative effectiveness may provide much more differentiated analysis and lead to a much better understanding of how the campaign functions if at the same time they also seek to find out which advertisements the test subjects have actually been exposed to. This idea has led to such questions as 'And where did you see or hear advertising for ...? In the newspaper, on television, ...?' after asking about the subject's recall of the campaign. As straightforward as such questions may seem, the interviewee's responses or the conclusions drawn from them are usually false: numerous studies have proved that, for multi-media campaigns, most interviewees are unable to match their recall of an ad or details from it with the correct medium in which they were exposed to it. For this reason it is advisable to include in resonance studies a question about the subject's media use and base conclusions about the effectiveness of particular media on the correlation between media use and communicative effectiveness of the campaign.

### Media Effectiveness

The media effectiveness for a particular campaign can essentially be understood as 'effectiveness of transmission'. The media transmit advertisements to the advertising audience, and are variously appropriate according to the target group and in what form the target group is to be addressed. For example, the visual, aural, and dynamic nature of television makes it especially effective in addressing the audience's emotions, whereas complicated content and lengthy explanations are more suited to print advertisements. Such issues will not be discussed here further, but will be left to the campaign designers. In the following, I will focus instead on the transmitting qualities of various media and how to measure them.

The effectiveness of media in transmitting advertising is usually measured by studies on market coverage, carried out more or less continually, at least annually, and supplied to advertisers. As a rule, these studies are based on large sample populations and high-quality random sample data, and the interviews are also conducted to high standards. Media effectiveness is generally identified as the probability of a person (defined according to certain socio-demographic characteristics) reading or browsing through an average copy of a magazine or newspaper, or watching or listening to a particular television or radio programme at a particular time of day.

Such data can give a good idea of which media are best for reaching certain socio-demographic groups. They are typical 'planning data', normally used in designing the media use of advertising campaigns. For advertising research they are certainly of interest as reference points for checking media effectiveness as measured in advertising resonance studies, but they are not sufficient for determining media effectiveness of individual campaigns, which requires finding out each individual test subject's probability of exposure to the media used for campaign advertising during the duration of the campaign. Only by correlating the individual probability of exposure to the media actually used in the campaign with the subject's recall and evaluation of the campaign is it possible to show whether advertising was effective after limited exposure or only after repeated exposure, more effective in print media or on television, or a combination of both. Only on the basis of such information is it possible to evaluate and optimize media use.

Exposure to campaign media can be determined using essentially the same instruments as in determining market coverage, although for practical and financial reasons it is not necessary to use such a large scale or such a large number of media (and may not be possible, due to the limited patience of test subjects). One may limit one's efforts to the media actually used to transmit advertising, with the possible addition of those competing media which one must offer the test subjects to allow them to express their reading or viewing behaviour in a manner meaningful to them. In the following, some possible questioning techniques will be suggested.

### Television

Television viewing behaviour can be analysed with the greatest precision using a viewing diary: the test subject is given a diary and asked to record exactly which programmes he or she has watched over a period of one, two, or up to four weeks. Such entries provide a detailed picture of the subject's viewing habits, making it possible to determine with a fair degree of accuracy the subject's probable exposure to advertising on particular channels at particular times. The disadvantage with this method is that it is extremely time-consuming and therefore expensive. In practice it is seldom used for resonance studies on individual campaigns, but rather for more fundamental studies of how advertising functions.

Advertising resonance studies usually include a question about which television networks the test subject watches at least occasionally. Subjects are then asked about the networks associated with the campaign: for each network, how often during the week they watch at particular times. These time slots can be chosen to correspond closely with the campaign's actual broadcasts, while remaining meaningful to the test subject; time slots should never be narrower than 30 minutes, and subjects should be asked about no more than 6 to 10 time slots.

It should be apparent that probability of exposure can be calculated on the basis of such information, although probability remains only a general approximation of actual viewing behaviour and thus actual exposure to advertising. Precisely because financial considerations usually prohibit detailed surveying of advertising resonance, it is necessary to define an adequate statistical base at least for those groups to be analysed in greater detail, which means that a relatively large number of interviews must be conducted for such advertising resonance studies.

### Radio

Determining exposure probability for radio advertising is done in essentially the same way as for television. The number of radio stations to be taken into account will depend on the region tested; for example, for national radio campaigns in Germany one must figure on a minimum of 180 different stations. However, since few of these stations are broadcast nationally, samples may be divided into regional units, with smaller numbers of stations to be included in testing.

### Print Media

While most market coverage surveys for print media involve showing the interviewee the publication titles and logos to aid recall, in determining exposure probability this step is necessary only in rare cases; it is usually sufficient to inquire (over the telephone or face to face) about those publications used by the campaign, whether the interviewee reads them at least occasionally, and, if so, how many of the last 12 issues he or she has read. The last question may be asked using a verbal scale, i.e. whether the interviewee reads the publication regularly (every or nearly every issue), often, occasionally, rarely, or never. Exposure probability values may then be assigned to the publications according to the responses.

Depending on which print media are used for campaign advertising, it may also be helpful to ask whether the interviewee usually reads the entire magazine or newspaper; if not, whether he or she reads about three-quarters of the pages, half, one-quarter, or less.

If the campaign to be tested was relatively short, one need not ask about general reading habits but should ask instead about the specific time period of the campaign, i.e. 'How many issues of X Magazine have you read in the past six weeks?'. In some cases it may also help to display the covers of the relevant issues of the publications, especially for monthly magazines that readers tend to accumulate over longer intervals and pass on to others, etc.; for daily newspapers and magazines with more 'perishable' news content, exposure to older back issues with no relevant campaign advertising is not a concern.

### Outdoor Advertising

Exposure probability for outdoor advertising – i.e. on billboards, advertising columns, light poles, public transport, etc. – usually cannot be determined with any great precision. On the whole, highly mobile people who spend much of their time outside the home are especially likely to be exposed to outdoor advertising. One must decide for each campaign whether, based on the deployment of outdoor advertising, it makes sense to conduct surveys in particular locations, neighbourhoods, or streets in order to calculate the probability of exposure to the campaign.

## STRUCTURING EMPIRICAL INVESTIGATIONS TO MEASURE ADVERTISING EFFECTIVENESS

While the previous section of this contribution focused on how to construct the questions to analyse advertising effectiveness, some directions on structuring empirical investigations into advertising effectiveness will be given here which survey methods are appropriate for particular ends, and what to watch out for when taking samples. Clearly this topic exceeds the scope of this contribution, and the reader is referred to the extensive scholarly literature on the subject. Here a few practical tips will be provided.

## Pre-Testing

As we have seen, pre-testing may concentrate exclusively on the communicative effectiveness of advertisements or campaign conceptions, and may be carried out before the advertising to be used has received its final 'polish'.

Pre-testing for communicative effectiveness is usually not particularly difficult with regard to statistical construction and survey methods. The sample should of course include members of the advertising target group, determined according to their socio-demographic status, lifestyle, or class status; it is usually not a crucial issue whether the sample is a truly random selection from this target group or not. The main concern here is to find out whether the communicative effect operates as intended; thus, gaining insight into how it functions is more important than finding out which segment of the target group displays what resonance.

Financial considerations usually preclude taking broad random samples, but standardized pre-tests require a base of at least 60 interviews; more detailed descriptions by target group segments need a correspondingly larger base. The number of interviews must be great enough that trends in the responses to open-ended questioning and spontaneous associations with the tested advertisement can be recognized. This is not usually possible with only 20 or 25 cases, unless one is interested in very simple directional indicators, in which case it is doubtful that a pre-test is needed at all.

Since the sample does not usually have to be a random sample, it may be possible to use quota samples, allowing for interviews in studios, laboratories, etc. If a geographical distribution of the sample is needed for some reason, the pre-tests may be carried out in studios distributed over various regions.

The question of survey methods should be dealt with pragmatically, and above all depends on being able to present the advertisement appropriately. Mail surveys are usually not appropriate due to the lack of control over testing conditions; telephone surveys can only be considered for pre-testing radio advertisements. For television advertising, if face-to-face interviews are not conducted in a studio, then the interviewer should, if possible, be able to play the ad on the spot using a multi-media laptop computer.

If pre-testing is also intended to determine attention-getting effectiveness, then the sample must meet higher standards. For such testing, 120 interviews are normally needed, in some cases significantly more. In constructing the sample, one must be sure that the campaign target group is not only represented, but that its composition is also as 'realistic' as possible, with the appropriate age structure, education levels, etc.

As described above, the attention-getting effectiveness of particular advertisements or a campaign can only be measured under testing conditions that are as realistic as possible; above all, test subjects should have no opportunity for 'mental preparation'. This is a danger when recruiting subjects, whose first question upon being asked to participate in a survey is, understandably, what the survey is about. As soon as the interviewer answers this question truthfully, the chances of gaining a realistic measure of attention-getting effectiveness are usually small. For this reason, subjects should be chosen at random; if this is not possible, special precautions should be taken to ensure that subjects do not guess the goal of the investigation ahead of time.

As for the rest, the same methods should be used for investigating attention-getting effectiveness as for communicative effectiveness.

### Post-Testing: Advertising Resonance Studies

Advertising resonance studies are usually carried out on a larger scale than pre-tests. Studies accompanying the campaign or summing up afterwards should, as a rule, not only demonstrate that the target group as a whole was reached and influenced as intended, but also reveal any weaknesses in the campaign, such as segments of the target group displaying too little resonance. Further, studies should provide insights into how the campaign's effects were actually achieved, in order to organize and continue the campaign with even greater efficiency; often, studies are used to reveal any effects of 'campaign fatigue', i.e. information about those exposed for long periods and/or with high frequency to the campaign. In order to gain such information, significantly larger samples are required than for pre-tests.

In particular, if changes in attitudes or behaviours as a result of public information campaigns are to be measured, sufficiently large random samples are required, usually of several hundred, but possibly well over 1,000 cases (in some cases per survey 'sweep'). The reason for this is clear when one considers how long it takes for attitudes and behaviours to change, and how small the measurable differences between 'before' and 'after' may be, even for very successful campaigns. In order to be sure that such small differences are actually statistically significant, large numbers of cases are essential when comparing independent random samples.

As in the pre-testing of attention-getting effectiveness, revealing the subject of the advertising resonance study, for example when recruiting the test subjects, may seriously undermine the study's goals. Thus in general, random samples are also quota samples, which the interviewer must recruit according to certain characteristics relevant for the study goals; this is of special importance for studies in which several relatively closely-spaced sweeps are taken using the same or similar question formats: by the third sweep at the latest (particularly with hard-to-locate target groups), it is nearly impossible for the interviewer to find test subjects who have not already been asked to participate in the relevant survey. Controlling such unwanted 'feedback' is extremely difficult and never totally attainable.

Studies constructed with repeated questioning of the same test subjects may only be used in special situations and with extensive restrictions on initial questioning, due to pre-conditioning and subsequent bias in the second interview. There must be no opportunity for the test subjects to discover the study goal in the first interview round; thus no 'leading' questions about the object of the campaign under investigation can be asked in the first interview – with absurd results in many cases. Where this is possible, however, it is interesting for statistical reasons alone: since the same persons are involved in the first and second interviews, there are no statistical variations between independent samples to be accounted for in the analysis, thus significantly fewer cases are required in such 'panel' studies.

Regarding survey methods for advertising resonance studies, the same conditions as for pre-testing apply: mail surveys are usually not appropriate, since they cannot properly convey the necessary spontaneity; telephone surveys may be considered wherever it is not necessary to show test subjects examples of campaign advertising materials. For the reasons outlined earlier, face-to-face interviews (if possible with computer support as needed to show TV advertising) are generally the best choice.

Marketing research institutes offer a whole series of standard surveys on advertising resonance, which may also be used for public information campaigns. One advantage of such standard instruments is that they provide extensive experience and comparison values for the central parameters of advertising effectiveness, which may considerably aid in interpreting the results of one's own campaign. On the other hand, procedures and values developed for consumer goods and services may not always be applicable to public information campaigns. The strength of standard instruments lies precisely in the wealth of data gathered on parameters such as spontaneous and aided brand familiarity, and spontaneous and aided brand preference – parameters that may not be relevant or may even obscure results of true significance for public information campaigns.

CRITERIA FOR CHOOSING A MARKETING RESEARCH INSTITUTE

In choosing a marketing research institute to carry out an advertising resonance study for a public information campaign, it is not recommended to base one's selection on the institute's experience with commercial marketing campaigns or the number of standard instruments it has to offer. Particularly for public information campaigns, special emphasis should be given to technical and 'instrumental' competence (e.g. enough interviewers, equipped if necessary with the appropriate laptops), as well as the expertise and commitment of the project leaders.

For example, in testing the resonance of the 'No Power to Drugs' campaign, the institute's experience with surveying young people on controversial topics will likely be decisive, as young people often will not give truthful responses to 'typical adult' interviewers; the same would probably apply to a campaign against AIDS. If one can find an institute with the relevant experience and necessary resources, as well as experience in other areas of advertising research, then expense should not be the only consideration.

One consideration that may be of special importance particularly for public information campaigns is that advertising research projects may be carried out not only on the national, but on the European level (or may focus on certain core EU countries). If it is not possible for the commissioning agency to combine such projects and assume the overall co-ordination, due to lack of time, resources, and/or proper authority, choosing an institute with experience in carrying out Europe-wide studies is strongly recommended, or at least a consultant with such experience to supervise and co-ordinate various institutes working at the national level. Europe still has a long way to go in standardizing its culture of marketing research, and since research results should not be achieved 'democratically', but on the basis of the greatest experience and best research methods, centralization is to be preferred over regional diversity.

# CONCLUSION

## 13

### Using Survey Research in Campaigns: A Summary and Checklist for the Student and Campaign Practitioner

*Hans-Dieter Klingemann and*
*Andrea Römmele*

The contributions in this handbook all demonstrate the important role survey research plays in the different phases of a campaign. Since it is the aim of the handbook to address scholars, students and practitioners, we summarize the main findings as a checklist. This list brings together all the major findings of the book and proceeds through the various stages of a campaign, indicating where survey research can be used. We have also posed questions the campaign manager may ask him/herself in order to make a successful campaign more likely.

### AIM OF THE CAMPAIGN

The aim of the campaign has to be clear:

- What is the campaign aiming at?
- Does the campaign aim at changes on the knowledge, attitude, or behavioural level?

This step is of primary importance, since the declared goal of a campaign will be the yardstick with which all steps of the campaign will be compared. Therefore, the exact point of departure has to be pinned down. What is the level of knowledge about, the behaviour towards, the awareness of the specific topic of your campaign among the target audience?

*A survey among the target group regarding their attitude towards, knowledge about, and/or awareness of the specific theme you build your campaign on answers these questions and serves as a yardstick for all your following actions.*

## PLANNING AND IMPLEMENTING THE CAMPAIGN

In a second step, organizational, conceptual, and financial considerations need to be taken into account.

### *Organizational Considerations*

For the overall campaign strategy, responsibilities have to be clearly assigned. Who is responsible for the overall campaign strategy: the advertising agency or the campaign manager him/herself? More often than not one party assumes that the responsibility lies with the other. A second organizational problem often arising in international campaigns is that of decentralization. For example, a campaign launched by the European Commission is conceptualized and managed in Brussels, but then implemented by the representation offices in the different member states. This decentralization may cause problems the campaign manager should be aware of from the very beginning. Though the campaign is the campaign manager's top priority, it may not be at the top of the to-do lists of the respective representation offices in the member states. This might be time-consuming and should be taken into account from the beginning of a campaign plan and time schedule.

### *Conceptual Considerations*

The next step focuses on the communication plan and the message to be transmitted.

The composition of the target audience depends on the problem the campaign deals with. A campaign may want to inform the general public or specific subgroups. This book has discussed two possibilities of contacting an audience: through the mass media or via opinion leaders. In the opinion-leader concept, research has shown that interpersonal communication plays a key role: people discuss political and other issues with their friends, families and neighbours. Interpersonal sources are very important in the process of evaluation: in everyday life, individuals often use mutual co-orientation to evaluate messages originally received from the media. Others, especially opinion leaders, are sought out for additional information. Co-orientation and exchange of opinions in the interpersonal environment determine the real meaning of information and messages from the mass media. Contacting opinion leaders or so-called multipliers can spread the word of the campaign. It is a very effective and inexpensive method of communication. The task of the campaign manager then is to identify these opinion leaders.

*Opinion leaders can be identified via survey research. Whom do people trust when it comes to providing credible information or an opinion on the campaign subject?*

General statistics provide valuable information on media use among the population, including details on which segment of the population prefers which newspaper, news channel, etc. According to the financial budget available, a campaign manager will make the decision on these grounds. Whether or not the campaign is directed through the proper channels and finds its way to the target audience can be found out through a survey conducted with a sample of the target audience.

*Did the campaign get the attention needed? Survey research with the simple question of whether somebody has heard about the campaign or not will make sure that the campaign is on the right track.*

Qualitative research is a very powerful tool when it comes to audience understanding. Which message works best?

*The message should be tested via focus groups and then pre-tested in a small area.*

One of the examples in the book has shown the importance of framing a message: in the 'fire alarm' campaign, a message with heightened emotions and rather shocking TV ads (children dying in a fire, the idea of dying in one's sleep) seemed to work best. In the case of an international campaign, the campaign manager should be aware of the fact that some frames might work well in one country, but not in others.

*In an international campaign, the message should be tested with national focus groups.*

The message should be simple and easy for the audience to 'process'. Citizens are exposed to thousands of facts each day, and only some of them add to their knowledge, in particular those which most easily fit into their internal 'files' and those which can be used immediately.

### Financial Considerations

*As a general rule, the use of survey research is not a matter of money (all campaigns are short of money) but a matter of priorities.*

### ASSESSING EFFECTS

Results of campaign assessment are of use both to public officials who commission and have to pay for campaigns, and to those agencies that design and organize them. While public officials consider effectiveness and costs in the first place, agencies that design and implement campaigns are more interested in learning how to improve their product.

There are many potential users of evaluation results, and they place varying emphasis on evaluation questions. On the one hand, issues of effectiveness, impact, or cost-benefit are often of interest to federal officials, for their mandate is to see whether or not a programme is achieving its intended goals. On the other hand, the designers and deliverers of services like to assume that what they do is effective, and they usually want to learn how to improve their practices so as to reach more of the target audience and implement activities more smoothly.

The campaign can be assessed on different levels. In general it is advisable to distinguish between assessment of the campaign's effectiveness and impacts, of costs, and, probably the most difficult task, of the causal processes.

### Effectiveness and Impacts

Questions of effectiveness are a major concern of any campaign assessment. Have the goals been reached? Has public knowledge about the relevant issues improved? Has there been the desired change in behaviour? All these and related questions can be answered at least in part by the survey method. Another type of question tries to assess the impact of a campaign on groups and organizations rather than individuals. Campaigns that aim at interaction within families, neighbourhoods, interest groups, parties, etc. may want to know whether the intended effect on these social and political systems has been achieved. Surveys using a network approach are appropriate in this instance.

*Have the goals set out at the beginning of a campaign been achieved?*

### Causal Processes

It is useful to know what effects a certain campaign has had. It is even more interesting to find out why specific effects did or did not occur. Knowledge of this nature is needed to improve campaign performance. Causal analysis addressing such questions can be based on survey data, too.

### Costs

Campaign assessment must also consider cost questions such as the relative cost-effectiveness of different methods of achieving the same goal or the cost-benefit ratio of the campaign as a whole.

# Index

## DATE DUE

| | 2007 | | |
|---|---|---|---|
| | | | |
| | | | |
| | | | |
| | | | |
| | | | |
| | | | |
| | | | |
| | | | |
| | | | |
| | | | |
| | | | |
| | | | |
| | | | |
| | | | |
| | | | Demco |

609
NOR

# STRATEGIC COLLABORATION IN PUBLIC AND NONPROFIT ADMINISTRATION

A Practice-Based Approach to
Solving Shared Problems

# American Society for Public Administration
Book Series on Public Administration & Public Policy

## Editor-in-Chief
## Evan M. Berman, Ph.D.
*National Chengchi University, Taiwan*
*evanmberman@gmail.com*

**Mission:** Throughout its history, ASPA has sought to be true to its founding principles of promoting scholarship and professionalism within the public service. The ASPA Book Series on Public Administration and Public Policy publishes books that increase national and international interest for public administration and which discuss practical or cutting edge topics in engaging ways of interest to practitioners, policy-makers, and those concerned with bringing scholarship to the practice of public administration.